THE DEALMAKERS

THE DEALMAKERS

Inside the World of Investment Banking

Paul Hoffman

Library Congress Cataloging in Publication Data

Hoffman, Paul, 1934–
   The dealmakers: inside the world of investment banking.
   Includes index.
   1. Investment banking—United States. I. Title.
HG4930.5.H63   1984   332.6'6'0973   83-20711
ISBN 0-385-18287-2

DOUBLEDAY & COMPANY, INC.
GARDEN CITY, NEW YORK
1984

Library of Congress Cataloging in Publication Data
Hoffman, Paul, 1934–
Dealmakers inside the world of investment banking.
Includes index.
1. Investment banking—United States. I. Title.
HG4930.5.H63   1984   332.6'6'0973   82–46034
ISBN 0-385-18287-2

To

Allison
Barbara
Diane
Edna
Elena
Jeff
Judith
Lois
Red

and other dear friends
who helped in my
time of trial.

CONTENTS

CONTENTS

Introduction

THE CATALYSTS OF CAPITALISM

Soon after I started the research for this book, a friend who espouses an eclectic sort of socialism asked what my next project was.

"To do the same thing for investment bankers that I did for Wall Street lawyers [in *Lions of the Eighties*]," I said.

"Aha!" he exclaimed. "The Rockefellers!"

"Wrong."

"Chase Manhattan?"

"Wrong."

"Chase Manhattan's not an investment bank?"

"If Chase Manhattan put one dollar of its depositors' money into investment banking, they'd be in violation of federal law."

"How long has that been going on?"

"For fifty years," I said. "Since 1933."*

"I guess I haven't been following recent developments."

"Red," I said, using a nickname derived from the color of his hair not his politics, "how can you pretend to be a socialist if you don't know the first thing about capitalism?"

Yet many who profess to be capitalists—entrepreneurs of every sort, managers with the power to hire and fire, even investors who turn to the stock market tables the first thing every morning and

---

* Actually, I was a year off. The Glass-Steagall Act, passed in 1933, did not go into effect until the following year.

who monitor the ticker on cable television—don't know what investment banks are or what investment bankers do. As New York Senator Alphonse D'Amato said of himself, they don't know "the difference between Glass-Steagall and Steuben Glass."

To them, names like Morgan Stanley & Co., First Boston Corporation, Lehman Brothers Kuhn Loeb are just that—names, names that they sometimes notice adorning the "tombstone" ads in the *Wall Street Journal* and the business pages of the New York *Times*. They certainly are not everyday names like Citibank and Chase Manhattan, Macy's and Gimbel's, Ford and Du Pont, Exxon and Mobil. The average American doesn't pick up the telephone and call an investment bank as routinely as he dials his doctor, his grocer, or even his broker at E. F. Hutton. In fact, except for a relative handful of corporate executives, government officials, and high-powered lawyers, most Americans go through their entire lives without dealing with an investment bank.

So Morgan Stanley? First Boston? Lehman Brothers? "They're bankers . . . or brokers . . . or something. . . . Something financial, down on Wall Street." In short, they're not exactly sure of what they are or what they do.

If the investment banks are unknown, the investment bankers are even more so. Bankers, by nature, tend to be anonymous men. Not since the days of the legendary John Pierpont Morgan has a banker loomed larger than life on the American scene and commanded instant name recognition.* Investment bankers are no exception. Felix Rohatyn may grab a few headlines—but for his unpaid services to New York City and State, not his merger brokering for Lazard Frères. But Robert H. B. Baldwin? John H. Gutfreund? John C. Whitehead? George L. Shinn? Robert E. Linton? For all even the well-informed average citizen knows, they could be the crew of the Columbia space shuttle or the starting team of the Seattle SuperSonics.

That is the purpose of *The Dealmakers*—to tell who the investment banks and bankers are and what they do.

* David Rockefeller might be considered an exception, but he became known not so much for being chairman of Chase Manhattan, as for being his grandfather's grandson and his brother's brother. How many can name his successor as chairman of the Chase?

Investment banks—"I-banks," in Harvard Business School slang —are the catalysts of capitalism. By themselves, they can do little— except perhaps speculate, which some do spectacularly. They manufacture no products and offer little in the way of their own financing. Indeed, by comparison with commercial banks and *Fortune* 500 corporations, they are impoverished institutions. Until recent years only a handful had as much as $100 million in capital; today only Merrill Lynch—whose horizons extend far beyond investment banking—exceeds $1 billion.

But if investment bankers neither sow nor spin, they certainly reap. The annual draws of partners—or managing directors, as they're called in this era of incorporation—are the envy of commercial bankers and corporation executives. Indeed, the disproportionate compensation created grave problems for management when investment banks were conglomerated into other enterprises. The fees commanded by investment bankers dwarf those paid to other professionals retained by business. Superstar Wall Street and Park Avenue lawyers may bill at $250 to $350 an hour; during recent takeover battles, First Boston asked for—and got—the equivalent of $1,500 an hour for partners' time.

A Wall Street lawyer and an investment banker recently flew to Vienna for the closing of an international acquisition. "All through the flight," the lawyer recalled, "we debated which of us was the bigger whore—lawyers or investment bankers. We finally decided that the bankers were. Lawyers may be whores, but compared to investment bankers, we're street-corner hustlers."

Like chemical catalysts, investment banks create reactions—financial reactions that could not occur without them. They are the reagents that enable corporations, state and local governments, even foreign nations to tap the world's money markets and raise the capital required to launch, maintain, and expand their enterprises. They serve as brokers in "friendly" mergers and as financial advisers—a tombstone euphemism for "hired gun"—in "hostile" takeover battles.

Their actions ultimately affect almost every aspect of our daily lives. If this sounds like an exaggeration, consider the first few minutes of an average day. You wake up in the morning and flick on the light—Warburg Paribas Becker raised $350 million that financed Pennsylvania Power & Light's nuclear power projects. You turn on the radio—Lehman Brothers Kuhn Loeb serves as financial adviser to RCA. You pick up the telephone to get the time or weather—Morgan Stanley sold $16 billion worth of AT&T stock in 1982 and 1983. You fix breakfast—Salomon Brothers handled transactions for United Brands and Norton Simon, Inc., whose products range the gamut from the bananas on your cornflakes to the catsup on your scrambled eggs. You pick up the paper—Lazard Frères brokered the acquisitions that built Rupert Murdoch's American publishing empire. You drive to work—Goldman Sachs took Ford Motor Company "public," First Boston counseled Marathon Oil and Cities Service in takeover battles, and Dillon Read underwrote the bonds that built the roads, bridges, and tunnels of the Port Authority of New York & New Jersey and the Triborough Bridge & Tunnel Authority. . . .

The list could be extended for more pages than this book contains.

Investment banks even enter into the most intimate aspects of our private lives. After all, Allen & Co. bankrolled Syntex, producer of the Pill.

And yet . . .

Perhaps no industry on earth is being buffeted by so many turbulent winds of change as investment banking. Indeed, it is undergoing a second revolution. The first came with the banking and securities legislation of the New Deal. Although the Roosevelt Administration changed the ground rules of investment banking—adding designated hitters, player drafts, and protective helmets—it didn't change the way sluggers swung the bat or fielders caught the ball.

The bankers of that era would not recognize the industry today—no more than the sandlot player could fathom the Astrodome. Not only have skyscraper offices superseded cozy suites, Videcs, Xeroxes, and IBM computers replaced handwritten ledgers and rolltop desks, and globe-girdling conglomerates succeeded a handful of men in a Wall Street boardroom—what was once a gentlemen's club has become a fiercely competitive jungle, pummeled by powerful, and often contradictory, forces both within and without.

The first law of the jungle is this: Only the strong survive. This holds true both for institutions and for individuals. The past fifteen years have seen a shakeout in investment banking unmatched even in the depths of the depression, with securities houses merging for mutual survival or being conglomerated into "financial supermarkets." The era also has seen the transformation of an industry as rigidly hierarchical as the army, the Catholic Church, or the Soviet Presidium—in which men made a slow, steady progression to the peak, rarely reaching it before their twilight years—into one where aggressive go-getters may scramble to the pinnacle before the age of thirty—and burn out before fifty.

The era has seen the erosion of the half-century-old barrier dividing commercial banking from underwriting, resulting in a wildcat scramble for investors' dollars. And, for the first time since World War I erupted, there has been a massive infusion of foreign capital into American securities markets, which could have worldwide consequences. Finally, there are controversial—and still experimental —regulations that could alter drastically the basic underpinnings of American finance, shaking up the entire system of who shall sell securities and who shall buy.

"This business is changing so dramatically and there are so many crosscurrents to it," said Thomas A. Saunders III of Morgan Stanley & Co. "It becomes almost impossible to take a slice of it and say this is what the industry looks like and how it's going to come out."

Indeed, some have suggested that this book would be out of date even before it was written . . . much less published. A cut-off date had to be drawn somewhere, arbitrarily—it turned out to be Labor Day 1983—or the work, endlessly rewritten and updated, never would have seen print. But the investment banking industry continued to change as rapidly and radically throughout the tedious process that transforms a typewritten text into a bound book as it had throughout the long months of research and writing, outdating the manuscript, if not before it was written, at least before it could be published. Rather than continuously revise the text and reset the type, I have inserted late-breaking developments in footnotes.

Finally, a word about what this book is *not*. It is not a how-to book. It will not tell you how to invest, what stocks to buy or sell, or recommend whether or not to plunge into some exotic commodity—gold, silver, or farina futures.

1. That was not my purpose.

2. This is not my competence; I am a reporter, not an economist, securities analyst, or seer with a crystal ball.

3. If I had any such expertise, I would be exercising it to make my own fortune, not peddling it at $14.95 a copy to readers who would glut the market and cut my own corner.

In short, you will not become a millionaire by reading this book. But perhaps—and this is the author's hope—you will achieve a better understanding of investment banks—the institutions and individuals that play so vital a role in the nation's and the world's economy.

I

INVESTMENT BANKING
FROM A TO A$_1$

Banking—the lending of money at interest—is almost as old as civilization itself. Sidney Homer, a partner of Salomon Brothers, traced the compilation of interest rates back to Babylon in 1750 B.C. As an institution, banking developed in ancient Greece and flourished in classical Rome. According to the Gospels, the money changers were well established in Jerusalem by the first century A.D. Although Christianity carried strictures against usury—using money to make money—banking was a necessity for medieval merchants, so the outlawed profession became the province of Jews and other practitioners of heathen religions—hence Shylock and his pound of flesh in Shakespeare's *A Merchant of Venice.* *

By the Renaissance the Fuggers had established their banking network throughout Europe. The eighteenth century saw the rise of the Rothschilds, Barings, and Hambros. They were merchant bankers, men who lent their own money—sometimes for collateral; sometimes on speculation, in exchange for a share of the borrowing enterprise. When merchant banks started accepting deposits—to spread the risk, increase their capital, and broaden their scope—commercial banking developed.

Investment banking, however, is a peculiarly American institu-

---

* Contrary to popular opinion, the "merchant" of the title was the borrower Antonio, not the lender Shylock.

tion that did not arise until the nineteenth century. Financial historians differ as to which was the first investment bank. Some say Prime, Ward & King, founded by Nathaniel Prime on Wall Street in 1826. Some say Alex. Brown & Sons, which survives today, founded in Baltimore in 1830; others, Vermilye & Co.—percursor of the modern Dillon, Read & Co.—established the same year. Some trace the institution to Jay Cooke, who opened for business in Philadelphia in 1861—and went broke in the panic of 1873. Still others argue that the first true investment bank was not established until 1882, when N. W. Harris & Co. was organized in Chicago. And there are dozens of other contenders for the title.

Such confusion is understandable, for investment banking did not arise fully developed, like Athena from the head of Zeus. It evolved over the years. The financial institutions of that era did not have today's sharp demarcation of functions. One house could combine the roles of private, or merchant, banker, commercial banker, and investment banker, sometimes in a single transaction. The very term "investment banking" did not come into currency until the 1880s. But all the elements of modern investment banking were in place by then.

Let's take a closer look at this arcane industry. It won't be an exhaustive survey—not "Investment Banking from A to Z." Nor even "Investment Banking from A to B." Let's say, "Investment Banking from A to A_1."

The last third of the nineteenth century was the era of the "Robber Barons," of America's greatest economic expansion. Railroads were spanning the continent, steel mills being built to manufacture the track, and factories springing up to supply the rolling stock. It was a time of unbridled capitalism, of boom and panic and market corners, "The Gilded Age" when a Mark Twain character could boast: "Beautiful credit! The foundation of modern society . . . I wasn't worth a cent two years ago, and now I owe two millions of dollars."

Vast amounts of capital were required for the nation's new enterprises, far beyond the capacity of American finance. So America's industrialists turned to Europe—and American bankers became the middlemen in this process. As Judge Harold R. Medina, who presided over the most thorough and searching inquiry into investment banking, noted some seventy-five years later:

> Prior to World War I, the United States was a debtor and not a creditor nation. Investment banking firms in this country turned to Europe to find wealthy individuals and other investment bankers who would be willing to share the risk and underwrite the security issues of business enterprises in the United States. European banking firms also sold to investors in Europe the securities of American business enterprises.

The classic example came in 1879 when J. P. Morgan bought 250,000 shares of New York Central from William Vanderbilt for $120 each and resold them to a London syndicate for $130.

Every major American investment bank had its European connection: J. P. Morgan & Co. with George Peabody & Co. in London, where Morgan's father Junius had been a partner before the Civil War; Kidder, Peabody & Co. in Boston* with London's Baring Brothers; Kuhn, Loeb & Co. with the Rothschilds in London and, later, the Warburgs in Hamburg.

European investors were unable to evaluate enterprises across the ocean, so the task was entrusted to their American correspondents. Morgan, Drexel, and Schiff were known by European bankers; Stanford, Huntington, and Hill, not to mention lesser lights, were not. Investments of millions of dollars were based solely on one banker's evaluation of another—a development described in a classic colloquy during the so-called Money Trust investigation of 1912 when Samuel Untermyer, the committee counsel, cross-examined John Pierpont Morgan:

Q. Is not commercial credit based primarily upon money or property?
A. No, sir; the first thing is character.
Q. Before money or property?
A. Before money or anything else. Money cannot buy it.

To safeguard their investments, bankers often demanded seats on the boards of borrowing enterprises, where they could oversee operations and ensure that dividends were paid. "This was especially important in connection with foreign investors," Judge Medina noted. Conversely, borrowers often invited bankers onto their

* Not related to the London Peabody.

boards in hope that their presence would insure investment in the securities. Thus, there sprang up the system of "interlocking directorates" that has been the whipping boy of conspiracy-theory economists ever since.

During this period there developed two basic elements that separate investment banking from other forms of banking—underwriting and syndication.

Railroads and later steel mills and still later utility companies required massive capital investments. Putting millions of shares on sale at one time might glut the market and so depress the price that companies could not realize the capital they required. So investment bankers *underwrote* the issues, guaranteeing a set price and reselling the shares. If the shares failed to meet the price, the bank was out the difference. It is believed that the first underwriting was handled by Jay Cooke, who had made his fortune selling government bonds during the Civil War, and a syndicate of seven other houses in 1869—a $2 million issue for the Pennsylvania Railroad.

Underwriting required bankers to be astute evaluators not only of the markets in which they traded, but of the enterprises whose stock they sold. This, in turn, led to a degree of specialization by investment-banking houses: Morgan and Kuhn Loeb in railroads and later steel; Halsey, Stuart & Co. and Blyth, Witter & Co. in utilities; and Lehman Brothers and Goldman, Sachs & Co. in retailing.

If underwritten stocks started slipping in price, investment banks often would try to "make a market" for them—buying shares on the open market at or above the underwritten price in hope that other investors would follow suit. When it worked, the investment bank could unload its unsold shares at a profit; when it didn't, the bank got stung for the difference—and partners often had to cough up out of their own pockets. Thus, it became imperative for investment bankers to foretell what price the market would bear.

Since the value of a single underwriting often was far greater than its investment bank's total capitalization, *syndication* was introduced—spreading the risk among two or more houses. There was a second necessity behind syndication. Few underwriters had networks to distribute their shares—indeed, until World War I there were only some 250 securities dealers in the United States, concentrated along the Baltimore-to-Boston corridor—so other hands had to be called in to find customers.*

This led to a multilevel syndication system that varied from issue to issue. At the apex was the "originating broker" or "house of issue"—now called a manager—that did the spadework of investigating the enterprise, determining how and how much capital would be raised, setting the price and volume of the issue, and finally, and often most importantly, deciding when the shares would be put on the market. The originating banker usually took the largest block of shares. In later years it was also paid a fee for its services.

Behind the originating banker—or bankers—was a larger group called the purchase syndicate whose members took lesser volumes of shares at a slight step-up in price, usually 1/2 of 1 percent or 1 percent. Behind the purchase syndicate might be an even broader "banking syndicate," whose members took even fewer shares, again at a second step-up in price. Later, as the number and dollar volume of stock issues increased, fourth and fifth tiers—the "selling syndicate" and "selling group"—were added. The selling group merely sold the shares, without agreeing to accept a set amount. Unlike the investment bankers, who underwrote issues at guaranteed prices for their corporate clients, they were merely brokers, buying and selling on commission on behalf of their customers.

Such elaborate mechanisms also became necessary because many companies sought broad distribution of their shares, rather than ownership concentrated in a few hands, while others—especially utilities—wanted their stock owned by customers in their local areas. Investment banks, ensconced along the Eastern Seaboard, had no way of selling stock in Kokomo or Kankakee.

As Judge Medina noted:

> This evolution of the syndicate system was in no sense a plan or scheme formulated by anyone. Its form and development were due entirely to the economic conditions in the midst of which investment bankers function. No single underwriter could have borne alone the underwriting risk involved in the purchase and sale of a large security issue. No single underwriter could have effected a successful public distribution of the issue. . . . Unless investment bankers combined

* An investment bank's "client" is the issuer of the stock; its "customer" is the buyer.

and formed such groups there would have been no underwriting and no distribution of new security issues.

Naturally, there was a reciprocity in syndications. Those that gave got: If firm A included firm B on issue X, firm B would include firm A on issue Y. And firms that performed well on one issue would be invited back to handle another.

Though there have been changes and variations over the years, the syndicate system remains intact today. It can be seen in this recent "tombstone" ad—for the largest stock offering in history:

The "tombstone" starts with the standard disclaimer in fine print, followed by the Bell logo, the number of shares, and the name of the company. Next the price. Then the houses offering the shares—in rigid hierarchy.

Morgan Stanley, as lead manager, heads the list, followed by—in alphabetical order—Goldman Sachs, E. F. Hutton, Merrill Lynch, and Salomon Brothers. Each was allotted 1,055,200 shares.

The second tier starts with First Boston, then runs—again in alphabetical order—from Atlantic Capital through Dean Witter Reynolds. Each house was allotted 300,000 shares.

The third tier starts with Sanford C. Bernstein & Co. and runs alphabetically through Tucker, Anthony & R. L. Day, each with 90,000 shares. A fourth starts with Allen & Co. and runs through Yamaichi International (America), each with 60,000 shares. A sixth, from American Securities through Pittsfield, Mackay & Co., each with 20,000 shares. A seventh, from Craigie Incorporated through Richardson Greenfield Securities, each with 12,000 shares.

The eighth runs from Adams, Harkness & Hill through Scott & Stringfellow, each with 8,000 shares. A ninth, from Branch, Cabell & Co. through Edward A. Viner & Co., each with 4,000 shares. And a tenth, from Allen & Co. ("of Florida, Incorporated," in the subscript) through Sterling, Grace & Co., each with 2,000 shares.

At the bottom are a dozen foreign banks, each allotted 60,000 shares.*

Investment bankers have been known to bicker—like movie stars over their billing—about their place on the tombstone and the size of type in which their names will appear. Wall Street still chuckles

---

* And even more. Only 135 houses are named in the ad, but the prospectus lists 246.

16,000,000 Shares

American Telephone and Telegraph Company

Common Shares

Price $66¼ a Share

Copies of the Prospectus may be obtained in any State from only such of the undersigned as may legally offer these Securities in compliance with the securities laws of such State.

MORGAN STANLEY & CO.

GOLDMAN, SACHS & CO.

E. F. HUTTON & COMPANY INC.

MERRILL LYNCH WHITE WELD CAPITAL MARKETS GROUP
Merrill Lynch, Pierce, Fenner & Smith Incorporated

SALOMON BROTHERS INC

THE FIRST BOSTON CORPORATION	ATLANTIC CAPITAL	BASLE SECURITIES CORPORATION	BEAR, STEARNS & CO.
BLYTH EASTMAN PAINE WEBBER	DILLON, READ & CO. INC.	DONALDSON, LUFKIN & JENRETTE	DREXEL BURNHAM LAMBERT
KIDDER, PEABODY & CO.	LAZARD FRERES & CO.	LEHMAN BROTHERS KUHN LOEB	PRUDENTIAL-BACHE
L. F. ROTHSCHILD, UNTERBERG, TOWBIN	SHEARSON/AMERICAN EXPRESS INC.	SMITH BARNEY, HARRIS UPHAM & CO.
UBS SECURITIES INC.	WARBURG PARIBAS BECKER	WERTHEIM & CO., INC.	DEAN WITTER REYNOLDS INC.
SANFORD C. BERNSTEIN & CO., INC.	ALEX. BROWN & SONS	A. G. EDWARDS & SONS, INC.
MOSELEY, HALLGARTEN, ESTABROOK & WEEDEN INC.	OPPENHEIMER & CO., INC.
THOMSON McKINNON SECURITIES INC.	TUCKER, ANTHONY & R. L. DAY, INC.

ALLEN & COMPANY   ARNHOLD AND S. BLEICHROEDER, INC.   CAZENOVE INC.   DAIWA SECURITIES AMERICA INC.

F. EBERSTADT & CO., INC.   EUROPARTNERS SECURITIES CORPORATION   ROBERT FLEMING   HUDSON SECURITIES, INC.

KLEINWORT, BENSON   THE NIKKO SECURITIES CO.   NOMURA SECURITIES INTERNATIONAL, INC.

ROBINSON HUMPHREY/AMERICAN EXPRESS INC   ROTHSCHILD INC.   WHEAT, FIRST SECURITIES, INC.

YAMAICHI INTERNATIONAL (AMERICA), INC.   DOFT & CO., INC.   DOMINION SECURITIES AMES INC.   FAHNESTOCK & CO.

FOLGER NOLAN FLEMING DOUGLAS   INTERSTATE SECURITIES CORPORATION   JANNEY MONTGOMERY SCOTT INC.

JOHNSTON, LEMON & CO.   LADENBURG, THALMANN & CO. INC.   CYRUS J. LAWRENCE   LEGG MASON WOOD WALKER

WOOD GUNDY INCORPORATED   AMERICAN SECURITIES CORPORATION   BUTCHER & SINGER INC.   COWEN & CO.

GRUNTAL & CO.   HERZFELD & STERN   JOSEPHTHAL & CO.   McLEOD YOUNG WEIR INCORPORATED

MOORE & SCHLEY CAPITAL CORPORATION   NEUBERGER & BERMAN   PITFIELD, MACKAY & CO., INC.   CRAIGIE INCORPORATED

FERRIS & COMPANY   INVESTMENT CORPORATION OF VIRGINIA   JOHNSON, LANE, SPACE, SMITH & CO., INC.

KEEFE, BRUYETTE & WOODS, INC.   REINHOLDER NORDBERG INC.   RICHARDSON GREENSHIELDS SECURITIES INC.

ADAMS, HARKNESS & HILL, INC.   ANDERSON & STRUDWICK   BAKER, WATTS & CO.   BURGESS & LEITH

BURNS FRY AND TIMMINS INC.   DAVENPORT & CO. OF VIRGINIA, INC.   DOMINICK & DOMINCK,   FIRST ALBANY CORPORATION

FIRST EQUITY CORPORATION   FIRST MANHATTAN CO.   FURMAN SELZ MAGER DIETS & BIRNEY

JESUP & LAMONT SECURITIES CO., INC.   LAIDLAW ADAMS & PECK INC.   LEPERCQ, DE NEUFLIZE SECURITIES INC.

NESBITT THOMSON SECURITIES, INC.   W. H. NEWBOLD'S SON & CO., INC.   RAYMOND, JAMES & ASSOCIATES, INC.

SCOTT & STRINGFELLOW, INC.   BRANCH, CABELL & CO.   BREAN MURRAY, FOSTER SECURITIES, INC.

CRALIN & CO., INC.   DANIELS & BELL, INC.   EVANS & CO.   FIRST HARLEM SECURITIES CORPORATION

FIRST INVESTORS CORPORATION   HAMERSHLAG, KEMPNER & CO.   NEW JAPAN SECURITIES INTERNATIONAL INC.

NIPPON KANGYO KAKUMARU INTERNATIONAL, INC.   PRINTON, KANE & CO.   SANYO SECURITIES AMERICA, INC.

STERNE, AGEE & LEACH, INC.   ULTRAFIN INTERNATIONAL CORPORATION   EDWARD A. VINER & CO., INC.

ALLEN & COMPANY   BRUAN, GORDON & CO.
of Florida, Inc.

ALAN BUSH BROKERAGE COMPANY   CAROLINA SECURITIES CORPORATION   CARROLL McENTEE & McGINLEY

CECIL, WALLER & STERLING, INC.   C. C. COLLINGS AND COMPANY, INC.   FREEMAN SECURITIES COMPANY, INC.

FRANK HENJES & COMPANY, INC.   KORMENDI, BYRD BROTHERS, INC.   MABON, NUGENT & CO.

MULLER AND COMPANY, INC.   EDGAR M. NORRIS & CO., INC.   STERLING, GRACE & CO., INC.

ALGEMENE BANK NEDERLAND N.V.   AMRO INTERNATIONAL   BANQUE NATIONALE DE PARIS

BANQUE DE NEUFLIZE, SCHLUMBERGER, MALLET   BARING BROTHERS & CO.,   COUNTY BANK
Limited

CREDIT AGRICOLE (C.N.C.A.)   CREDIT COMMERCIAL DE FRANCE   BILL SAMUEL & CO.
Limited

MORGAN GRENFELL & CO.   SAL. OPPENHEIM JR. & CIE.   J. HENRY SCHRODER WAGG & CO.

March 11, 1983

about the "Great Alphabet War" of 1976, touched off when Halsey Stuart, then Bache's underwriting subsidiary, added the parent's name to its own—purportedly to procure a more prominent place in the alphabetical listings on the tombstone.

Judge Medina called it a preoccupation with "inflating their ego," which only proves that investment bankers are human, after all—and even interested in things other than money.

The men who dominated investment banking in the fifty years between the Civil War and World War I were either Yankees or German Jews. The former were in the Yankee trader tradition, while many of the latter actually had started as peddlers, though a few members of the second generation—most notably, Jacob Schiff and the Warburg brothers—had been engaged in banking in the old country. Their firms were small—four to a dozen partners, with perhaps three times as many salaried employees. Many were family fiefdoms, all but closed to outsiders.

J. P. Morgan & Co. (Drexel, Morgan & Co. until 1895) stood preeminent among American banks, just as the stocky, walrus mustached figure of John Pierpont Morgan himself dominated American bankers in that era of the "Robber Barons." Perhaps more powerful than any President of the period, he was able to sell American bonds abroad when the Treasury could not. More than any other man, he financed the construction and consolidation of the railroad lines that linked the continent. He assembled General Electric and the nation's first billion-dollar corporation—United States Steel—but his effort to create a shipping trust—International Merchant Marine—was unsuccessful.

The only banker of the era who could rival Morgan was Kuhn Loeb's Jacob Schiff. According to his official biographer, Schiff "rarely made a mistake in business judgment." In 1896, after Morgan passed up the chance—"the great banker's chief tactical error," according to one observer—Schiff teamed with E. H. Harriman to raise more than $100 million to acquire and reorganize the bankrupt Union Pacific. Within five years the line was in the black, John W. "Bet-A-Million" Gates was calling it "the most magnificent railroad property in the world," and Union Pacific had acquired the Southern Pacific, as well as 40 percent of the stock of the Northern Pacific.

The last led directly to the Panic of 1901, the result of a titanic power struggle between Schiff and Harriman, on one side, and Morgan and James J. Hill, on the other, for control of the Northern Pacific. Within five days the line's shares soared from 110 points to 1000 on the New York Stock Exchange.* Speculators who had sold short in hopes of reaping huge profits were ruined, forced to unload millions of dollars worth of other securities to cover their losses. Except for Northern Pacific, stock prices plunged, and many men were wiped out.

The Rockefeller interests finally refused further financial support to Schiff and Harriman, so Morgan and Hill won control of the line, though Schiff and Harriman were given seats on the board. After the dust settled, a reporter asked Morgan if "some statement were not due the public." The great banker replied (in words that rank with William H. Vanderbilt's "The public be damned"), "I owe the public nothing."

Until the 1890s almost all the investment banks' financing was for railroads—a steady business since the lines were constantly building, going bankrupt, being reorganized, and getting merged. Morgan reaped a fee of $500,000—a then staggering sum—for his reorganization of the Erie. For a long time, industrial stocks were considered too speculative for houses like Morgan and Kuhn Loeb. When they finally plunged into industrials, they almost always overcapitalized the issues. "Much of the water represented the fees and charges of the promoters, brokers and bankers . . . ," one historian noted. Utilities—until the 1920s and the advent of the holding company—remained beyond the pale, the province of outsiders like Halsey Stuart in Chicago and Blyth Witter in San Francisco. So was retailing, which was relegated to newcomers like Lehman and Goldman Sachs. After the turn of the century, however, all the major houses turned heavily to foreign financing.

If Morgan helped create the Panic of 1901, he single-handedly stopped the Panic of 1907—a "one-man Federal Reserve Bank," in the words of Frederick Lewis Allen. The power and imperiousness of men like Morgan inspired the muckrakers, impelled President

* Known on Wall Street as the Big Board, just as the American Stock Exchange is called the Curb Exchange from its origins in actual trading on the sidewalks of Broad Street. Over-the-counter stocks are bought or sold directly from brokers, without going through an exchange.

Theodore Roosevelt to inveigh against "malefactors of great wealth," and spurred several inquiries into Wall Street's speculations and peculations. There was the Armstrong insurance investigation of 1905, the Hughes investigation of 1909, and above all the Pujo—after Rep. Arsène P. Pujo of Louisiana, chairman of the House Banking and Currency Committee—or Money Trust investigation of 1912, which focused on the activities of six banks: Morgan, Kuhn Loeb, First National of New York, National City, and two Boston houses, Kidder Peabody, and Lee, Higginson & Co.

One result of the Money Trust investigation was the enactment by many states of blue-sky laws—so-called because unscrupulous promoters reportedly unloaded "building lots in the blue sky." In reaction, the banks organized the Investment Bankers Association of America, which has remained the industry's lobby ever since. At the outset, it had 347 members, most of them commercial banks that only occasionally engaged in underwriting. Another result was the establishment, in 1913, of the Federal Reserve System, which was intended to restrain the influence of the great banking houses on the nation's economy.

But the bankers co-opted the reform—both in its drafting and in its execution. Although the legislation creating the Federal Reserve was introduced by Senator Carter Glass of Virginia, the scheme actually had been devised at a secret meeting at Sea Island, Georgia, by Paul Warburg, a Kuhn Loeb partner and scion of the Hamburg banking family, and Rhode Island Senator Nelson Aldrich, father-in-law of John D. Rockefeller Jr. Warburg became the first vice chairman of the Federal Reserve Board, while the first president of the Federal Reserve Bank of New York, linchpin of the system, was Benjamin Strong, son-in-law of J. P. Morgan.

The reforms of the New Freedom had been framed to end the reign of the "Robber Barons." The reign did end—best symbolized by the death of J. P. Morgan in 1913—but unbeknownst to the Wilsonians in Washington, Wall Street was about to embark on a dramatic expansion—in a different direction.

The outbreak of World War I reversed the pattern of international banking, dramatically strengthening the power and influence of the Wall Street houses. "The United States had become a creditor nation," Judge Medina observed, "and, for the first time, foreign governments, foreign municipalities and foreign corporations turned to this country to raise capital from private American industry."

The House of Morgan led the way in selling more than $2 billion in bonds for the Allies, more than half of them for Britain—as opposed to only $35 million raised in America for the Central Powers—while American industry worked overtime producing matériel for the European war effort. After the United States entered the hostilities, investment banks enlisted their efforts in the Liberty and Victory bond drives, many of them developing for the first time nationwide selling networks—systems that remained in place for distributing corporate securities when the speculative frenzy started in the 1920s.

During the decade after the Armistice, both the number and dollar volume of stock issues increased, as investment banks underwrote new issues for high-flying enterprises in radio, autos, and aviation, bonds of foreign governments and corporations, as well as shares for tier on tier of jerry-built utility holding companies. Before World War I an issue of $1 million was considered large; in the Roaring Twenties issues of $20 million and $25 million became commonplace. The syndicate system swelled, as dealers rushed to unload their allotted shares and scurry on to the next issue. Many more houses than previously were signed up, and the syndicates' duration was trimmed from up to a year to a few months. Investment banking boomed, luring the giant commercial banks more deeply into the field.

The banks already were up to their ears in the speculative frenzy. More than one million Americans played the market on margin—money borrowed from the banks. By 1929 loans to brokers and their customers totaled more than $8 billion. Yet the demand for credit so far exceeded the supply that interest rates for margin were pushed to a then astronomical 9 percent.

The big banks speculated with depositors' money—and encouraged others to do likewise. "Charlie Mitchell's salesmen from the National City Company in New York are selling South American bonds to the little crossroads bank, and Anaconda Copper stock to the bank's president," Frederick Lewis Allen observed. Investment trusts—a 1920s version of the modern mutual fund—became the rage, further enabling the banks to speculate with other people's money. By 1929, $500 million worth of shares in investment trusts had been sold.

Finally, with their vast accumulations of capital, the commercial banks plunged boldly into underwriting itself. Every major commercial bank had an underwriting subsidiary, each with capital that dwarfed those of the more traditional investment-banking houses. By 1929 National City Company, underwriting subsidiary of National City Bank, had capital of $110 million; its counterpart at the Rockefeller's Chase, Chase Securities Corporation, had $101 million. "These great banking institutions and their affiliates," Judge Medina noted, "were doing a huge investment banking business and they were using the money of their depositors to underwrite one security issue after another."

Millions of hardworking, prudently saving Americans who never considered taking a flyer on "Radio" or "Big Steel" unwittingly contributed to the speculative frenzy of the 1920s. These millions, who thought their funds were safe and secure, soon learned otherwise.

The stock market reached its crest on September 3, 1929, then slipped a little. On October 14 it staggered—only to be revived and righted by a bankers' combine led by Thomas W. Lamont of the House of Morgan. It was an echo of 1907, but the rally lasted only five days. On October 29 the bottom fell out—and this time no amount of intervention by bankers, brokers, or anyone else could stem the tide. By November 12, $30 billion—on paper—had disappeared. The big bull market was dead.

The nation could have survived the stock market crash. After all, only a few bankers, brokers, and speculators were affected. The average American still had his job, his home, his car. The railroads still chugged away, steel forges still blazed, and assembly lines continued to grind out Model As and Chevrolets. But the nation could not survive the credit crunch that the crash created. As prices plummeted, stocks bought on margin automatically were put on the block, glutting the market and further fueling the plunge into economic oblivion. Margin, originally designed to enable the average American to become a capitalist, became "a beautifully contrived system of wrecking the price structure."

For investment banks, the crash had varied impact. Traditional houses were not immediately affected. In 1930 Halsey Stuart even sold $200 million worth of bonds and other securities of Samuel Insull's utilities empire. Some firms—most notably, Merrill Lynch and Blyth—merely closed down the brokerage side of the business and continued with underwriting. But Goldman Sachs, which had picked the wrong moment to float an investment trust, nearly went under. Boston's two major houses—Kidder Peabody and Lee Higginson—which had extensive private banking investments, were hard hit. Kidder Peabody's name and assets were sold to a new partnership, while Lee Higginson, which had lent $250 million to Ivar Kreuger, the Swedish "Match King," had to be liquidated and reorganized. It never again was a major force in investment banking.

When margin accounts dried up, the credit crunch spread to the banks, crossed the ocean to Europe, and came back again, stronger than ever. In September 1931, 305 American banks failed, in October, 522. As the supply of money dried up, factory fires were banked and stores boarded up. Assembly lines gave way to bread lines. The depression had reached its depths by March 4, 1933, when Franklin D. Roosevelt was inaugurated. Fifteen million Americans were unemployed, and the governors of Illinois, Michigan, and New York had closed their states' banks to prevent panic.

By then, investment banking was moribund. Both new and secondary issues were all but nonexistent. Few people had the money to buy stocks; even fewer were foolish enough to plunge into a market that kept going down . . . down . . . down.

If the depression wasn't enough to blacken the public's perception of the titans of Wall Street, the financial community was soon subjected to a double dose of degradation. During the lame duck session of 1932–33 Duncan U. Fletcher of Florida, chairman of the Senate Banking and Currency Committee, launched an inquiry into Wall Street wheeling and dealing—a probe known to history as the Pecora Investigation, after the committee's chief counsel, Ferdinand Pecora, formerly chief assistant district attorney of New York County.

The Pecora Investigation perhaps is best remembered today for a picture—a photograph snapped when a wily press agent posed Lya Graf, a circus midget, on the lap of the imperious John Pierpont Morgan Jr. But at the time Pecora's revelations were far weightier.

The $250-a-month lawyer mercilessly grilled the millionaire bank-
ers—and humiliated them. According to one account, he "brought
out so many unethical practices by Insull's principal bankers, Halsey, Stuart & Co., that Harold L. Stuart himself recommended enactment of a full-disclosure law to protect future investors."

The investigation revealed that Charles E. Mitchell, chairman of
National City Bank and its underwriting subsidiary, National City
Company, had received $3 million in bonuses in 1927, 1928, and
1929, but because of paper sales of stock to relatives had paid no
income tax at all in 1929. Mitchell and other high bank officials
who had been buying National City stock in installments were pro-
tected by the bank when the crash came, but lower-level employees
were forced to pay in full—at precrash prices. Mitchell was forced
to resign both posts and eventually had to cough up $1 million in
back taxes.

Egged on by F.D.R. to explore "all the ramifications of bad banking," Fletcher continued the inquiry into the new Congress, with
Pecora setting his sights on the great House of Morgan. He
brought out that the twenty partners of J. P. Morgan & Co. had
paid a total of only $48,000 in income taxes in 1930 and nothing
whatsoever in 1931 and 1932. Morgan had given five hundred
insiders preferential prices in buying three new issues: United Corporation, a utility holding company; Allegheny Corporation, the
Van Sweringen brothers' railroad combine; and Standard Brands.
The list of insiders read like a Who's Who of the wealthy and well
connected: former President Calvin Coolidge; Supreme Court Justice Owen J. Roberts; Treasury Secretary William H. Woodin; former Treasury Secretary William Gibbs McAdoo, son-in-law of
Woodrow Wilson and then a Senator from California; former Sec-
retary of War Newton D. Baker; General John J. Pershing; Charles
Lindbergh, son-in-law of Morgan partner Dwight Morrow; and
John W. Davis, the Morgan lawyer who had been the Democratic
Party's hapless Presidential candidate in 1924.

"For month after month, the country was treated to a series of
amazing revelations which involved practically all the important
names in the financial community in practices which, to say the
least, were highly unethical," said Joseph P. Kennedy, perhaps the
most spectacular of the speculators. "The belief that those in control of the corporate life in America were motivated by honesty and

ideals of honorable conduct was completely shattered." Operating on the admitted principle "Set a thief to catch a thief," F.D.R. named Kennedy as the first chairman of the Securities and Exchange Commission, charged with cleaning up the market.

If nothing else, the Pecora Investigation spurred the demand for banking reform and stock exchange regulation. It was swift in coming, some of it during the New Deal's First Hundred Days.

The Banking Act of 1933—or Glass-Steagall Act, as it is commonly called, after its cosponsors, Senator Carter Glass and Representative Henry Steagall of Alabama—divorced investment banking from commercial banking. Within a year of its signing on June 16, 1933, the banks had to opt for one or the other.* The giant commercial banks—Morgan included—dissolved, sold, or spun off their investment-banking subsidiaries, and no longer underwrote corporate stocks. The investment banks—which included new firms like Morgan Stanley & Co. and First Boston Corporation, arisen from the ashes of the old—could underwrite stocks only with their own money, not borrowed funds or customers' deposits.

To some, Glass-Steagall was "a classic example of firing a bullet into a corpse." Investment banking, only slowly starting to revive in 1934, remained quiescent throughout the decade. During the New Deal years, if industry needed money, it turned not to Wall Street but to Washington. The nation's most powerful banker was not Morgan or Winthrop Aldrich, chairman of the Chase, but Jesse Jones, the colorful Texan who headed the Reconstruction Finance Corporation. To others, Glass-Steagall was a sham that actually altered nothing. "The adjustments were those of firm names, not of individuals," one critic commented. "The old men did the same business under new letterheads."

If the players remained the same, the ground rules did not. The Securities Act of 1933 and the Securities Exchange Act of 1934 required full disclosure of stock issues in prospectuses and their review by the Securities and Exchange Commission. Investment bankers and their lawyers spent many long hours assembling the data and writing the prospectuses, and then waited many more anx-

---

* A last-minute rider to the bill, sought by neither its sponsors nor the administration, created the Federal Deposit Insurance Corporation, which insured bank deposits. According to historian Arthur M. Schlesinger Jr., it proved to be "one of the most brilliant and successful accomplishments of the One Hundred Days."

ious hours for the SEC's "letter of comment"—or "deficiency letter," as Wall Street termed it. Then they—usually—spent many more long hours rewriting, before the prospectus could be printed, the "tombstones" placed in the papers, and the stock put on the market. "Insider" dealings had to be disclosed and regular reports submitted, disclosing any significant change in a company's financial condition.

The Revenue Act of 1932 increased the tax on stock sales and imposed one on bonds, so the old practice of stepped-up pricing to successive tiers of the syndicate had to be abandoned. In addition, the Securities Exchange Act of 1934 imposed on underwriters liability for any misstatements or omissions in the prospectus equal to the "total price" of the securities sold to the public, while SEC rules limited an underwriter's total commitments to 1,500 percent of capital. Since a single issue could run twenty to thirty times capital —as late as 1949 only seven of the major houses had capital of $5 million or more—purchase of the issue was spread throughout the syndicate. The size of the syndicates swelled, especially after the 1937 failure of two major issues—$48 million for Bethlehem Steel and $44 million for Pure Oil.

The next major change in investment banking was touched off by a 1938 power struggle for control of the Chesapeake & Ohio Railroad—in some ways, a throwback to the battles of the Robber Barons. On one side were the holdover directors of the Van Sweringen brothers' regime, backed by Morgan Stanley and Kuhn Loeb, on the other, those maverick financiers Robert Young and Cyrus Eaton, backed by Halsey Stuart and Eaton's Otis & Co. At issue was refinancing a $30 million bond issue. Eaton and Halsey Stuart underbid Morgan and Kuhn Loeb by $3.5 million, but the directors voted to stick with their old bankers. One explained that Eaton was "in poor repute."

At this point, Young himself took up the cudgels. As the C & O's largest stockholder, he threatened to sue the other directors if they rejected the low bid. As he finished, he marched about the boardroom shouting, "Morgan will not get this business! Morgan will not get this business!" The directors recessed, consulted with legal counsel—then returned and accepted Eaton's bid.

"This was the start of competitive bidding in railroad finance," one observer noted. During the next two years Eaton and Halsey

Stuart won two more major rail issues from the Morgan Stanley-Kuhn Loeb combination because of Young's intervention. "The old railroad bankers were losing a lot of 'gravy' and it hurt."

Within a few years the practice was institutionalized. In 1941 the SEC ruled that underwriting for all companies covered by the Public Utility Holding Company Act of 1935—which limited holding companies to two tiers, thus doing away with crazy quilt empires like Samuel Insull's—had to be let through sealed public bidding. Banks could be retained to structure the issues, but they were precluded from bidding for them. Three years later the Interstate Commerce Commission adopted the same rule for the railroads—unaware that railroads were chugging into oblivion.

Investment banks, which had played such a vital role in financing World War I, virtually sat out World War II. Investment banking revived in the postwar years, with business slowly returning to the level of the 1920s, but by then the industry faced a new threat.

On October 30, 1947, the Truman administration, in an apparent attempt to revive the New Deal's crusade against the "money changers," filed an antitrust action against seventeen major investment banks. The fifty-six-page complaint charged them with attempting to monopolize the industry and to restrain competition.

The defendants included some of the major houses: Morgan Stanley; Kuhn Loeb; Smith, Barney & Co.; Lehman Brothers; Glore, Forgan & Co.; Kidder Peabody; Goldman Sachs; White, Weld & Co.; Eastman, Dillon & Co.; Drexel & Co.; First Boston; Dillon, Read & Co.; Blyth; Harriman, Ripley & Co.; Stone & Webster Securities; Harris, Hall & Co. and Union Securities Corp.

But there were some significant omissions—among them, Lazard Frères, Merrill Lynch, and Salomon Brothers, long something of an outsider among investment-banking houses. Otis and Halsey Stuart obviously were not included because they were on the other side. Eaton had played a large part in instigating the suit—"The bulk of the government's case had been drawn from Otis & Co.," the Cleveland *Plain Dealer* reported—while Harold L. Stuart testified as a government witness.

The banks formed a five-man steering committee to coordinate their defense—headed by John Hancock, the first nonfamily partner of Lehman Brothers. While each bank retained its own counsel, the legal defense was led by three of Wall Street's most distinguished attorneys: William Dwight Whitney of Cravath, Swaine & Moore; Arthur H. Dean of Sullivan & Cromwell, and Ralph Carson of what is now Davis Polk & Wardwell.

Initially, the Investment Bankers Association and a score of individual bankers also were named as defendants, but the charges against them were dropped or dismissed. The government's case echoed some of the old Populist conspiracy theories about Wall Street. It contended that sometime about 1915 the investment banks conspired to divide the nation's underwritings and exclude outsiders—an interesting theory, considering that some of the defendant firms had not even been in existence in 1915! But it forced Judge Harold R. Medina to delve into more than thirty-five years of the history of investment banking.

"Just lead me along like a child and show me how it works," he told the array of more than thirty lawyers who gathered in his courtroom for the trial's opening on November 28, 1950.

From the outset it was clear that the government was in for a tough time. When the prosecutor complained that the same banks got the same clients year after year, the judge cut in: "What's wrong? Don't many people see the same doctor because he's a good doctor?"

Judge Medina had just concluded the grueling Smith Act trial of the Communist Party leadership. *U.S.* v. *Morgan,* as the action against the investment banks was titled, was to prove equally grueling, if less emotionally charged. The trial ran through May 19, 1953, consuming 309 courtroom days. The transcripts, exhibits, and briefs filled more than 100,000 pages. In that age before computerized data banks, Judge Medina commissioned a specially constructed cabinet so that he could keep track of the evidence.

On October 14, 1953, he handed down a 212-page decision. He noted incredulously that the alleged conspiracy

is said to have gone on for almost forty years, in the midst of a plethora of congressional investigations, through two wars of great magnitude and under the very noses of the Securities and Exchange Commission and the Interstate Commerce Commission, without leaving any direct documentary or testimonial proof of the formation and continuance of the combination and conspiracy.

Judge Medina concluded:

> The seventeen defendant firms have all done business in much the same way, as occurs in any industry. But each has followed its own course, formulated its own policies, and competed for business in the manner deemed by it to be most effective, in view of its history and background, its standing in the industry, its capital, relatively large or small, its own peculiar business affiliations and contacts, and the capacities of its own officers or partners and its own personnel as individual human beings, and its own facilities for the distribution of securities. . . .
>
> These seventeen defendant banking firms went their own several and separate ways. If they had in fact acted in combination or as a unit to divide the business among themselves, and to form a monopoly vis-à-vis the other firms in the industry, as alleged, the pattern of such combination, no matter how cleverly disguised or concealed, must surely have emerged, after such prolonged and continuous scrutiny as has gone on in this case for almost three years. But it did not. . . .
>
> I have come to the settled conviction and accordingly find that no such combination, conspiracy and agreement as is alleged in the complaint, nor any part thereof, was ever made, entered into, conceived, constructed, continued or participated in by these defendants, or any of them.

The judge dismissed the suit "with prejudice"—meaning that the government could not bring another action covering the same set of circumstances.

U.S. v. *Morgan* was to be the last gasp of governmental populism against Wall Street. By the time Judge Medina's decision was handed down, Dwight Eisenhower was in the White House, the money changers were back in the temple, and investment banking was heading in new directions.

In the 1950s the bull market revived, surpassing the levels of the Roaring Twenties and cresting only in 1969. Giant corporations went to the well for new financings. In 1955 General Motors floated what was then the largest stock issue in American history—$325 million—an amount that was doubled the following year when Ford went public. Airlines borrowed to buy jet planes, while the railroads went the way of the stagecoach. Suburban shopping centers proliferated, and retail chains expanded. State and local governments, spurred by the baby boom and the surge in auto use, went on a building—and borrowing—binge, constructing new roads and schools. All this meant boom times for the investment banks.

The most spectacular action, however, was not in blue chips, but in microchips, new issues of high-technology electronics companies. It seemed that every company whose name ended with "onics" found a ready market for its issues, as buyers plunged in, hoping to ride the gravy train of another Texas Instruments. 1968–69 saw 1,300 new issues worth $3.5 billion. "The go-go years," financial writer John Brooks called them. "The great garbage market," said broker Richard Jenrette of Donaldson, Lufkin & Jenrette.

During the days of the garbage market, stocks would open, soar spectacularly for a few weeks or months—and, all too often, come crashing like a V2 rocket. The insiders cleaned up; the ordinary investor took a bath. In ten years H. Ross Perot's Electronic Data Systems, a software firm dealing primarily in medicare and medicaid payment plans, went from 16 1/2 to 160. It nose-dived in 1970, and Perot, whom *Ramparts* had described as "America's first welfare billionaire," suffered a paper loss of $450 million. National Student Marketing, which started as a small concern catering to the growing collegiate population, then went on an orgy of conglomeration, opened at $6 a share in April 1968 and reached a peak of $144 in December 1969. By February 1972 the stock had been bounced from the Big Board and was down to $2.25 bid on the over-the-counter market. By 1974 it was selling for 25 cents—and finding few takers.

The dealers who handled this surge of new issues were not established houses like Morgan Stanley and Goldman Sachs, but small banker-brokers, most of them new to Wall Street. Perhaps the most spectacular was Charles Plohn & Co. Plohn, dubbed Two-a-Week Charlie because of his volume of new issues, boasted: "I give people the kind of merchandise they want. I sell stock cheap. I bring out risky deals most firms wouldn't touch." Like most of the houses that specialized in new issues, Plohn's did not survive the shakeout of the 1970s.

If the old-line houses failed to cash in on the boom in new issues, they rode the crest of another business trend—conglomeration. Time was, a company merely made steel or autos, glass or rubber. In the 1950s and '60s, however, companies like ITT, Gulf & Western, Litton Industries, Rapid America, and LTV (for Ling-Temco-Vought, itself a conglomeration) embarked on madcap diversifications, gobbling up widely disparate concerns. The key word was "synergy," as if, somehow, the sum of the parts amounted to more than the whole. Soon old established companies got into the act—evinced by the widespread dropping of products from corporate names: Radio Corporation of America became simply RCA; Pittsburgh Plate Glass became PPG Industries; Universal Tire became Uniroyal; United Fruit became United Brands; and even Standard Oil of New Jersey became Exxon. In 1968 alone there were 4,500 corporate mergers and twenty-six *Fortune* 500 companies disappeared into even larger conglomerates.

Investment houses were the middlemen in this orgy of conglomeration, the bankers who brokered the deals—men like Felix Rohatyn of Lazard Frères, who guided ITT's acquisition of such diverse concerns as Avis Rent A Car, Hartford Fire Insurance, Bobbs-Merrill publishers, Sheraton hotels, William Levitt & Co., builders of Levittown, and even Continental Baking, makers of Wonder Bread. For men like Rohatyn it was wonder banking, deal making of the order practiced by Morgan and Schiff nearly a century before.

The story is apocryphal but worth retelling. A bevy of bankers and lawyers labored far into the night at a downtown office building to complete the paperwork for closing the sale of a hotel chain. They finally finished in the wee hours of the morning and gathered around a conference table to sign the documents.

"Wait a minute!" someone shouted. "If we sign here, we'll have to pay the stock-transfer tax."

"I know an all-night diner in Jersey," someone else suggested.

(From the mid-1960s to '70s New York City imposed a tax on stock transfers, both market trades and stock swaps. As a result, several brokerages moved to Jersey City, and closings of multimillion-dollar deals often were conducted west of the Hudson—or under it. On simple deals, the two principals would hop a PATH train—informally, the Hudson Tubes—wait until they had crossed the state line, then sign the papers. At Exchange Place they'd hop out, cross the platform, and catch the next train back to Manhattan. Total cost to save thousands of dollars: ten minutes and thirty cents.)

So the bankers and lawyers piled into the elevators, squeezed into waiting limousines, and sped through the Holland Tunnel. But when they reached the diner, they found that it had been taken over by a motorcycle gang. Lòath to enter and uncertain where else to go, they decided to complete the closing in the parking lot.

Meanwhile, the cyclists, looking out and seeing some thirty middle-aged men in pin-striped suits hovering with flashlights around the hoods of Cadillacs and Continentals, jumped to a conclusion natural to New Jersey natives: It was a conclave of Mafia dons. So they hopped onto their cycles and sped off into the night.

At first, the mergers were "friendly," but by the mid-1970s "hostile" tender offers became the rage, as the conglomerators began to gobble up companies that didn't want to be gobbled up. For years Wall Street had scorned hostile tender offers as ungentlemanly, but the lure of the big bucks was too great. By the end of the decade, practically every major house was actively engaged in the takeover wars.

The bull market collapsed at the end of 1969 and, despite periodic fits and starts, stayed slumped for more than a decade, with disastrous consequences for many banks and brokerages. Even at the peak of the go-go years there was trouble, caused by the boom itself. The market and its members had yet to enter the computer age. As small investors plunged into the action, and trading volume soared past the level of 1929's Black Monday—16 million shares— houses were inundated by a flood of paperwork and fell far, far behind. Many transactions never were completed, simply because the documents disappeared. Hayden, Stone & Co. had to hire moonlighting Coast Guardsmen to handle the load, and even Lehman Brothers was warned by the SEC to clean up its act.*

Several brokerages went under in 1969 and more during the early months of 1970. Bache & Co. reported a loss of $8.7 million in 1969—the largest stock brokerage loss in history—only to be topped by Hayden Stone's $11 million. The Big Board's Special Trust Fund, used to bail out shortchanged customers, ran dry and had to be replenished with $30 million from the Exchange's build-

* By contrast, the computerized market of 1982 was able to cope with four successive days when the Big Board volume exceeded 100 million shares.

ing fund. More firms folded, and, despite an infusion of another $5 million, the fund ran dry again.

The Exchange created a crisis committee headed by Lazard Frères' Rohatyn to matchmake—this time, not for client corporations, but for its own beleaguered members. Faltering firms were mated with stronger ones. Goodbody & Co., the nation's fifth-largest brokerage, disappeared into the "thundering herd" of Merrill Lynch, Pierce, Fenner & Smith. Francis I. du Pont & Co. was merged with Glore, Forgan & Staats and Hirsch & Co., but it, too, soon went under. Hayden Stone merged with Cogan, Berlind, Weill & Levitt, then with Shearson, Hammill & Co. Next Shearson Hayden Stone merged with Loeb Rhoades, Hornblower & Co., itself the product of a major merger only a year before. Many historic names disappeared entirely when Shearson Loeb Rhoades was conglomerated by American Express to become Shearson/American Express.

The shakeout was accelerated after May Day 1975, when fixed commissions became a thing of the past. Henceforth, institutional investors could negotiate the fees they paid to buy or sell, while retail customers could turn to discount brokers who undercut the rates of established houses.

"The broker-dealer function is much less lucrative since the advent of negotiated commissions," said one Wall Street veteran. "It's dragged the whole industry into the twentieth century, kicking and screaming."

Investment banks were not immune. Old-line houses, which had been content to underwrite stocks and bonds, sell a few to institutional investors, and spread the rest among a syndicate of banks and brokerages, found that they had to expand into full-service firms—opening retail operations, trading for their own accounts, investing venture capital, and enlarging international markets—all of which required size and capital. Hence, Lehman Brothers' merger with Kuhn Loeb.

Other firms found themselves conglomerated into "financial supermarkets," which offered not only investment banking and brokerage, but retail outlets operating in cooperation with insurance companies and in competition with commercial banks. Hence, Dean Witter Reynolds' purchase by Sears and Shearson's by American Express. Even Halsey Stuart, long a leader among utilities' underwriters, wound up as part of Bache Group, which, in turn, was conglomerated by Prudential Life Insurance.

By the end of the decade only four of the seventeen firms that had been defendants in the government's antitrust action thirty years before survived substantially intact, without a major merger —Morgan Stanley, Goldman Sachs, First Boston, and Kidder Peabody—while a fifth, Dillon Read, was sold to, then bought back from, Bechtel Group. Some disappeared entirely, while others had to turn to foreign financing for the capital to computerize operations and expand into full-service banks.

By the end of the decade the nature of the game and its players had changed in other ways.

The first was demographic. Investment banking held little attraction for men who came of age during the depression and World War II. Thus, when the Harold Stanleys, Sidney Weinbergs, and Robert Lehmans passed from the scene, those who succeeded them were not men of the Kennedy generation—to whom "the torch has been passed"—but of the generation that came of age after World War II—and even their children, members of the postwar baby boom. Investment banking suddenly became a young man's game —despite "liberation," there are still very few women in the industry, except as secretaries and clerks—and the young men played hard ball, fast and aggressively.

This was illustrated by a colloquy between a Kidder Peabody banker and one from Bear, Stearns & Co. During work on a takeover fight, the name of their opposite number at a rival firm came up in conversation.

"He's a friend of mine," the Kidder man said.

"People in our industry don't have friends," the Bear Stearns banker replied.

The young bankers had to be aggressive because the generations-old bonds that locked in a corporate client to its investment bank were dissolving. Just as in-house corporate counsel became what one Park Avenue lawyer called "sophisticated purchasers of legal talent," corporate finance officers turned into smart shoppers, skilled at hunting bargains and haggling with vendors. Unlike their predecessors, who often had come from the ranks of sales or production, they were college and business-school trained. On deal after deal, they started shopping for the best price—and the best advice.

Martin Lipton, a lawyer who specializes in corporate-takeover battles, saw this as a trend in dealings between corporations and professionals of all categories: "In earlier generations the investment banking business was all based on relationships. A company had its traditional investment banker who would sit on its board. Companies were known as a 'Morgan company' or a 'Kidder company.' But today corporations are increasingly willing to entertain a good idea from any investment bank who presents it. We are going from a 'relationship generation' to a 'transactional generation' and that will be intensified. . . ."

In the past, investment bankers sat back and waited for business to come to them. Now they had to hustle—not only to win new clients but to keep old ones. Some of the old-line houses could not make the adjustment. "Some people in this industry are probably in a rather melancholy state right now," said Peter G. Peterson, then chairman of Lehman Brothers Kuhn Loeb, "because they're waiting for the phone to ring. And the phone doesn't ring much anymore. More and more, business today must be conceptualized and initiated, not simply processed."

"This is a tough profession," agreed Sanford I. Weill, chairman of Shearson/American Express. "Business is so active. What you lose today, you won't get tomorrow."

During the 1950s and '60s several houses dissolved their partnerships and incorporated. Except for signing their letters as "managing director," rather than "partner," it didn't change the way the bankers operated.* In 1969, however, Donaldson, Lufkin & Jen-

---

* A note on nomenclature: The hierarchy of investment banks runs like this: associate, vice president, managing director (previously partner), member of the executive (or management) committee, president, chairman. Associates are recruited from the top percentile of M.B.A.s graduated from "national" business schools like Harvard, Pennsylvania's Wharton, Chicago, and Stanford. They generally serve an apprenticeship of about six years and leave if they are not promoted to a vice presidency. Partners, presidents, and chairmen may be recruited by lateral entry from law, business, or government. Raiding rival firms—ungentlemanly and unheard of a decade ago—is not uncommon. Partners share the profits; vice presidents and associates are salaried, but they—as well as the clerical and research staffs—may receive profit-sharing bonuses. In houses with brokerage operations, salesmen—"customers' men," in Wall Street jargon—are paid commissions. Few progress beyond the rank of vice president, but some may earn more than the chairman.

rette, in an effort to raise $24 million, took the next step—it went public, selling 800,000 shares at $30 each. Other major houses—most notably, Merrill Lynch, First Boston, Hayden Stone, and Bache—followed suit.

Going public could have far-reaching consequences. It has been said that commercial bankers speculate with depositors' money, while investment bankers speculate with their own. For years investment bankers had only themselves to answer to if things went wrong. Then the securities legislation of the New Deal brought them under the purview of the SEC and mandated certain responsibilities to the investing public. Going public gives them further responsibilities to their own shareholders—people with whose money they're speculating. It also gives shareholders a say in running operations. It hasn't happened yet, but the day could come when there's a stockholder derivative action against Merrill Lynch —or even a tender-offer war for control of the company.

For investment bankers, long used to operating in secrecy along their mahogany-paneled corridors of power, it means life in a fishbowl. In subsequent chapters we'll peer into that fishbowl as investment banking enters the 1980s, its era of most dynamic change.

II

THE TOP TEN

There are several ways to measure investment banks. By total capitalization Merrill Lynch is the clear leader with $1.164 billion, three times that of Salomon Brothers, its closest rival in the securities business. But the figures are misleading, for Merrill Lynch has become a financial supermarket, with less than a tenth of its revenue derived from investment banking. By total number of offices and employees, once again Merrill Lynch leads. And once again the figures are misleading, since most of those offices and employees have next to nothing to do with investment banking. Using such standards is like trying to compare apples and oranges, using a poultry thermometer!

Perhaps the best measure is of the basic function of investment banks—underwriting stock and bond issues. The table below lists the ten largest investment banks, arranged in order of the dollar volume of the underwritings they managed in 1981:*

* Because the advent of shelf registration in mid-1982 (see Chapter 5) discombobulated the traditional pattern of underwriting, 1981 figures were used for the ranking. The houses that pushed Dillon Read off the list in 1982 were Dean Witter Reynolds, $1.83 billion (10), Warburg Paribas Becker, $1.36 billion (11), Shearson/American Express, $1.10 billion (12), and Smith Barney, Harris Upham & Co., $1.08 billion (13).

RANK	FIRM	1981 AMOUNT	1982 AMT. & RATING
1	Morgan Stanley & Co.	$11.76 billion	$10.65 billion (1)
2	Salomon Brothers Inc	10.32 "	9.45 " (3)
3	Merrill Lynch Capital Markets	7.76 "	9.85 " (2)
4	Goldman, Sachs & Co.	5.76 "	7.85 " (4)
5	First Boston Corporation	5.21 "	5.76 " (5)
6	Lehman Brothers Kuhn Loeb	4.23 "	4.05 " (6)
7	Kidder, Peabody & Co.	2.68 "	2.01 " (9)
8	Blyth Eastman Paine Webber	2.27 "	3.11 " (7)
9	Drexel Burnham Lambert	2.13 "	2.16 " (8)
10	Dillon, Read & Co.	1.19 "	.96 " (14)

Finally, there are the subtle distinctions of history and of corporate personality. No two houses are alike, no matter how much their partners may dress, look, and act the same. Some remain bastions of the WASP establishment. Others had to be rejuvenated by infusions of fresh blood. Some are staid Our Crowd houses founded by German Jews more than a century ago. Others are pushy upstarts. Some are growing and expanding. And some are on the wane. These distinctions cannot be measured by statistics, but they can be described.

Let's look at the leaders. In disc jockey lingo, here are the top ten on the investment-banking charts:

Morgan Stanley & Co. is the Rolls-Royce of investment banks. It is the spiritual heir of the investment-banking arm of the great House of Morgan. In fact, it inherited more than spirit—a name, a few genes, and three partners. But none of the cash—and not necessarily the clients.

With passage of the Glass-Steagall Act, John Pierpont Morgan Jr. opted for the commercial side of J. P. Morgan & Co.'s business. The result is today's Morgan Guaranty Trust Company—or, as it styles itself, The Morgan Bank—still one of the industry's giants. But the House of Morgan no longer was involved in investment banking.

More than a year after J. P. Morgan & Co. withdrew from underwriting, three Morgan partners (Harold Stanley, William Ewing, and Henry Sturgis Morgan, son of J.P. Jr.), two Morgan staff men (John M. Young and Allen N. Jones), and two partners of Morgan's Philadelphia affiliate, Drexel & Co. (Perry Hall and Edward H. York Jr.) resigned from their firms to take up investment banking. The result was Morgan Stanley & Co.

The partners originally considered adding the Drexel name to their shingle, but there were difficulties with the family heirs. It was to be resurrected for another investment-banking house.

On September 16, 1935, Morgan Stanley opened for business at 2 Wall Street, a block from the famed Greek temple of the House of Morgan, its masonry still pockmarked by an anarchist's bomb that shattered the financial district in 1920, killing thirty and injuring hundreds. According to the firm history, Morgan Stanley and J. P. Morgan & Co. have "no relationship, other than one, we trust, of mutual respect and confidence."* But there remained enough of an emotional attachment that the Morgan Stanley founders started their firm with rolltop desks that were exact replicas of the ones they had used at J. P. Morgan & Co.

Of course, there was also the Morgan name, though young Harry Morgan, as he was called, was far better known in yachting basins than in banking pools. Though his name came second on the shingle, Harold Stanley clearly was the dominant partner. In his thirties he had served as president of the Guaranty Company, underwriting subsidiary of Guaranty Trust. In 1928 he became a partner of J. P. Morgan & Co., succeeding Dwight Morrow, America's new ambassador to Mexico—at forty-two, one of the youngest partners in Morgan history. An expert in utility financing, he headed

* In 1982, however, Morgan Stanley joined Morgan Guaranty in launching the Pierpont Fund—a name linked to a common progenitor—open to anyone with an account at either institution. Morgan Stanley served as manager of the fund, Morgan Guaranty as its investment adviser.

Morgan Stanley until his death in 1963 at the age of seventy-seven. Harry Morgan died in 1982 at the age of eighty-one.

Within a month of its founding the new firm handled three major underwritings—a $19 million issue for Consumers Power, $20 million for Dayton Power & Light, and $43 million for AT&T. Indeed, Morgan Stanley soon "had more business than they could handle," a circumstance that Judge Medina later attributed to "the experience, the very numerous personal relations with issuers, the technical skill in matters of finance, and especially the absolute integrity of Harold Stanley. . . ."

From the outset Morgan Stanley attracted blue-chip corporations with their eight- and nine-figure offerings. Its roster of clients came to include nearly half the nation's fifty largest corporations—in addition to AT&T, Exxon, General Motors, IBM, Du Pont, and General Electric. Almost every year Morgan Stanley was the leader among investment banks, if not in total number of issues, in their dollar volume.

Morgan Stanley men were bankers, not traders or brokers. The firm did not acquire a seat on the Big Board until 1942, and it still lacks a retail network to market the issues it underwrites. For years it refused to participate in a stock syndication unless it was the sole manager and its name headed the tombstone. In 1979, however, its refusal to act as comanager of a $1 billion IBM debt offering caused it to lose a major client to Merrill Lynch and Salomon Brothers. It subsequently comanaged underwritings for General Electric Credit Corp. and Du Pont and even participated in syndications on other issues. In 1982 Morgan Stanley and Salomon were selected by AT&T as joint advisers on the divestiture of its twenty-two operating companies.

More than any other investment house, Morgan Stanley was "white shoe," projecting a WASP, Ivy League image. It did not take in a Jewish partner until 1973, and "even the Jews are WASPs," as one Wall Street lawyer quipped.

Morgan Stanley's chairman, Robert H. B. (for Hayes Burns) Baldwin, a "Morgan Stanley type" who automatically appends the words "Republican" and "Presbyterian" to his *Who's Who* biography, resents such implications.

"I get wild when they talk about that white-shoe thing," he said. "Why are we number one? Because we are nice people? Because we play golf? I stand on our record. It wasn't because of these so-called school ties. These people are in a tough business. Do you think these people can't compete? If we are getting the cream of the best business schools, they can't be robots."

Morgan Stanley also is one of the most inbred houses, bringing partners up through the ranks—the path Baldwin followed. Baldwin was also one of the few to leave the firm—even briefly—to seek greater glory in government service. In 1965, with the Vietnam War heating up, L.B.J. tabbed him to be Undersecretary of the Navy. Unlike such predecessors as Theodore Roosevelt, F.D.R., Adlai Stevenson, and John Connolly, Baldwin did not use the post as a political springboard. His actions rarely rated a headline, and his name appears in none of the histories and memoirs of that turbulent era—not even *The Pentagon Papers.*

Baldwin returned to Morgan Stanley in 1967 with the idea that the sedate old firm had to move into the modern era—only to find himself stymied by his seniors, who insisted on running the firm the way it always had been run. Frustrated, he announced his resignation in 1968 to become president of Hartford Fire Insurance. But before he could clean out his desk, Hartford was conglomerated by ITT. So Baldwin remained at Morgan Stanley.

In 1971 Morgan Stanley took in six younger partners, and Baldwin finally found a majority for the changes he sought—symbolized by the firm's 1972 move from lower Broadway to the new Exxon Building in Rockefeller Center, the first major investment house to desert the financial district for midtown Manhattan.

Under Baldwin's leadership—he was elected president in 1973 —Morgan Stanley created a research department, now considered one of the best in the business. It cultivated a "retail" business—not on every street corner like Merrill Lynch, but with institutional investors, which put it in a preeminent position when shelf registration took effect. The firm also created a foreign branch—Morgan Stanley International—headed by Alfred Hayes, former president of the Federal Reserve Bank of New York. In one area, however, Morgan Stanley became the pacesetter—corporate takeovers. Under Robert F. Greenhill, its mergers-and-acquisitions department became the acknowledged leader in investment banking.

Within the decade Morgan Stanley's payroll grew from some two hundred to 2,300. Baldwin moved up to the long vacant chairmanship in 1982 and instituted even more changes—especially an interest-rate business, trading in commercial paper, an area the firm traditionally scorned as beneath its dignity. Just as he had raided other houses to build Morgan Stanley's research and trading departments, Baldwin plucked John D. Paulus from Goldman Sachs to be the firm's chief economist—surprisingly, a new post at Morgan Stanley.

The firm even abandoned its traditional reliance on blue chips to plunge into new issues, taking public companies like Activision—concerns that a decade before it wouldn't have touched with a 10K microchip.

Baldwin's credentials may be old school, but his manner is of the new—all business. "I can't imagine him engaging in idle chatter, ever," said one associate. "I've never seen him just sit down and relax." Indeed, one of the few frivolous things in his existence is a needlepoint sampler pillow on his office sofa. It says: "The harder I work, the luckier I get."

S. Parker Gilbert, Baldwin's successor as president, has a dual Morgan heritage. His father, Undersecretary of the Treasury under Woodrow Wilson, later became a partner of J. P. Morgan & Co.* After the elder Gilbert's death in 1938, his widow married Harold Stanley.

Two decades ago a listing of the ten largest underwriters would not have included **Salomon Brothers.** The firm probably would not have made the top two dozen. Founded in 1910 with a $5,000 investment by Herbert, Arthur, and Percy Salomon, sons of a Wall Street money trader named Ferd Salomon, for more than a half century it remained primarily a dealer and trader in government bonds, growing to be one of the biggest. Even though it managed the first major issue under SEC regulations—$45 million in bonds for Swift & Co.—it was not noted for underwriting or investment banking. It certainly wasn't significant enough to be included in the government's antitrust action, but then Salomon always was a bit beyond the pale.

In 1963 Percy's son William seized control of what was then

---

* The Pecora investigation disclosed that by making Gilbert a partner on January 2, 1931, rather than the customary December 31, 1930, the House of Morgan was able to claim a $21 million capital loss for the year.

Salomon Brothers & Hutzler in what was described as a "palace revolution" and embarked the firm—which soon reverted to its original name—on a spectacular expansion, transforming it into the nation's second-largest underwriter and largest privately held brokerage. At the time, Salomon's trading rooms—soon moved to even larger quarters at 1 New York Plaza—constituted the world's largest privately held securities market. The annual dollar volume of the securities traded there exceeded that of the New York Stock Exchange by $17 billion. But the firm was so little known that its change in management did not merit a mention in the New York *Times.* Nor is the firm mentioned in Vincent Carosso's standard history of the industry, *Investment Banking in America,* published in 1970.

Under "Billy" Salomon the firm behaved like a pushy arriviste who had elbowed his way into an exclusive club. Salomon traders quickly developed reputations for being "unusual opportunists." "We'll bid for almost anything, and we take many baths," boasted Billy Salomon. Others echoed his view. "There never has been a firm as willing to speculate as Salomon Brothers," said the head of a rival house. Another observed that Salomon "lived and breathed to try to outtrade the markets."

Among other things, Salomon joined with Merrill Lynch, Lehman Brothers, and Blyth & Co. to form the "fearsome foursome" that consistently outbid rival syndicates for utility company issues in the 1960s. During the 1970s it stood by Big MAC—New York's Municipal Assistance Corporation—when other houses jumped ship, and it rode out the storm. It helped reorganize GEICO—the Government Employees Insurance Company—and served as financial guardian for the beleaguered Chrysler Corporation.

As it expanded into investment banking and other areas, Salomon became an astute raider of talent from other houses. It also acquired an impressive array of "public partners," including former FCC Chairman Newton Minow, former Commerce Secretary Philip Klutznick, and as a limited partner, former Labor Secretary, former Supreme Court Justice, and former U.N. Ambassador Arthur Goldberg.

William Simon, who had built a reputation as a ruthless, hard-driving bond trader—"the Vince Lombardi of the financial world" —came out of the firm to serve as energy czar in the Nixon administration and Treasury Secretary under Gerald Ford. Simon sought to return to the firm on terms that would have permitted him time off to campaign for the 1980 Republican Presidential nomination, but "Billy told him he'd have to work like everybody else," one partner noted. "He said, 'No, thanks,' and he didn't even manage to say it politely."

But perhaps Salomon's best known personality was its chief economist, Henry Kaufman, Wall Street's "Doctor Gloom," who possessed an uncanny ability to predict interest rates. For months his gloomy prognostications sent stock prices into a tailspin. But in August 1982, after Kaufman predicted that rates would fall, investors responded with what was termed a "buying panic," the biggest rally in history that sent the Dow Jones industrial average soaring 81.25 points in four trading days, while Big Board volume twice topped the 100 million mark.

Billy Salomon retired in 1978, a year before his sixty-fifth birthday, because of a brain tumor. By then he had become a respected member of the club, a man who "built an outstanding firm which has had a remarkable growth record," according to John C. Whitehead, senior partner of Goldman Sachs & Co.

Salomon's successor was John H. Gutfreund (spelled in the German, but pronounced in English "good friend"), who had studied literature at Oberlin and served with the Army in Korea. On his return he lunched with Billy Salomon, a family friend, and the next day started as a $45-a-week trainee at Salomon Brothers. At the age of thirty-four he became the first nonfamily partner.

In 1978 Salomon helped Engelhard Minerals & Chemicals spin off its Philipp Brothers subsidiary. Philipp, a commodities trading firm founded in 1914 by two German-Jewish brothers, Oscar and Julius Philipp, had outgrown its parent company. It was said of Phibro—as the new company was renamed—that it owned more oil than Qatar, more copper than Kennecott, and more grain than grew in all of South Dakota.

Two years later Phibro and Salomon stunned the financial world by announcing that Phibro had purchased the investment-banking house for $483 million. The decision to sell had been thrashed out among Salomon's partners during a stormy, weekend-long, locked-door meeting at the Tarrytown Conference Center in Westchester County, north of New York City.

"I view it not as a merger but as a marriage," Gutfreund, who remained as head of the new subsidiary, said at the joint announcement. "We are going to operate autonomously."

"I don't think anybody on Wall Street thought that Salomon Brothers wanted to do this," said I. W. "Tubby" Burnham II, then chairman of Drexel Burnham Lambert. "It's been a private firm for all of its history, but this offers the opportunity for the partners to take their capital out, and it must have been very tempting."

Indeed, it was. Gutfreund's share was $13.6 million. J. Ira Harris —the Chicago-based partner who had orchestrated Marvin Davis' acquisition of Twentieth Century-Fox—Kaufman, and two other partners got $10.2 million each. But the takeover left many younger employees bitter. They no longer had a path upward to partnership; they would remain salaried employees. Once, a partnership at Salomon meant becoming an "instant millionaire." "Being a partner in that firm is the closest thing to being a partner in the U.S. Treasury," as one observer put it. After the merger, profits that once went to partners would go to Phibro.

Even before the takeover there had been a heavy turnover at Salomon—it was so volatile—and several departing partners sued the firm for their cut on deals that they'd consummated. After the takeover the stampede started. In 1982 four partners departed. Among them was forty-year-old Richard Rosenthal, who, with Harris, had negotiated Salomon's sale. Rosenthal, a high school dropout, said he didn't want to spend the rest of his life just making money.

For Phibro, however, the acquisition was a godsend, for the company was hard hit by the oil glut and the Reagan recession, which slowed the demands for metals and grain. Phibro's fourth-quarter statement for 1981—the first in which figures for the investment bank were included—showed that of the company's $81.7 million profit, Salomon accounted for $77.7 million. A few months later Phibro recognized reality and changed its name to Phibro-Salomon Inc. The subsidiary remained Salomon Brothers Inc (the name written without a period).

However, the merger posed a major problem for Salomon. Because of their Jewish ownership and support of Israel, both Philipp and Engelhard had been placed on the boycott list maintained by twenty-one Arab nations and the Palestine Liberation Organization.

Salomon was added to the list in May 1983—a move that threatened to cost the firm a lot of business. One of its biggest clients was the Kuwaiti Investment Office, which had $5.6 billion invested in the United States, largely through Salomon. What action the Kuwaitis might take remained to be seen.

Merrill Lynch Capital Markets is the investment-banking arm of Merrill Lynch & Co., which also is the parent of Merrill Lynch, Pierce, Fenner & Smith, Inc., the nation's biggest brokerage house. Though hardly a newcomer to investment banking, Merrill Lynch in recent years roared onto the scene like the "thundering herd," one of the company's long-standing nicknames.

Charles E. Merrill remains a legendary figure in the brokerage business. The son of a Florida country doctor, he dropped out of Amherst to play semipro baseball, then in 1910 founded his own securities firm, teaming soon afterward with Edmund C. Lynch. Although it handled a major underwriting in the 1920s—the issue that launched Safeway stores—Merrill Lynch concentrated on its brokerage activities.

Merrill was one of the few on Wall Street to foresee the Great Depression, and he advised his customers to get out of the market. He followed his own advice, turning over his brokerage accounts to E. A. Pierce & Co. For a decade Merrill Lynch concentrated on underwritings, primarily of retail stores—including the issues that launched First National, McCrory, S. S. Kresge, and Western Auto Supply.

Not until 1940 did Merrill Lynch return to the brokerage business, teaming with Pierce and Cassatt & Co. to form Merrill Lynch, E. A. Pierce & Cassatt. The following year it merged again, this time with the firms of Charles Erasmus Fenner and Alpheus Crosby Beane. At its founding, Merrill Lynch, Pierce, Fenner & Beane (the name was always written without a comma between "Merrill" and "Lynch") was the nation's biggest brokerage house. With offices across the country, it went after the individual investor, rather than the institutional account, becoming, in effect, the five-and-dime of the securities industry. By the 1950s Merrill Lynch accounted for 12 percent of all sales on the New York Stock Exchange and 20 percent of the odd-lot transactions.

In 1958, two years after Merrill's death, Beane left the firm, and the name of Winthrop H. Smith, Merrill Lynch's chief executive officer, replaced his on the shingle. ("We have Beane," trumpeted the ads for his new firm, Williston & Beane.) Merrill Lynch became the first major brokerage to incorporate, one of the first to go public, and the first to be traded on the New York Stock Exchange—under the symbol MER. Although it had called for further study of shelf registration, in 1982 Merrill Lynch also became the first securities firm to file its own shares under the SEC's controversial Rule 415—$300 million worth.

Because of its vast sales network, Merrill Lynch always was heavily involved in stock syndications, and as the years passed, it took the lead in more and more underwritings. It served as investment banker for the "bashful billionaire," Howard Hughes, who disdained dealing with more traditional Wall Street types. By the 1970s it passed Chase Manhattan as the nation's largest underwriter of municipal bonds.

Under the leadership of Donald Regan—now President Ronald Reagan's Treasury Secretary—Merrill Lynch embarked on a dramatic diversification in the 1970s, going into real estate, mortgage financing, insurance, precious metals, money market funds, and more. "The company," *Time* noted, "seeks a piece of virtually every financial transaction a client makes." The five-and-dime of the brokerage business had become a financial supermarket. By 1980 Merrill Lynch was making twice as much—$1.4 billion a year—on its other financial business as from stock sales. Investment banking accounted for only 8.6 percent of the total—enough, however, to put Merrill Lynch in third place in underwritings.

Much of this growth was due to its $50 million acquisition in 1978 of White, Weld & Co. The house had started as the partnership of Moffat & White and changed its name to White, Weld & Co. in 1910. Under the leadership of Harold R. White Sr. and Francis M. Weld it was heavily involved in "position" trading, putting approximately half its capital into businesses it was interested in building "from the ground up," holding the securities for the long haul. Still, White Weld was involved enough in conventional underwritings to rank, year after year, among the top dozen firms, both in the number of issues and in their dollar volume. Unlike Merrill Lynch, it had been a defendant in the government's antitrust case.

Merrill Lynch White Weld Capital Markets Group, as the merged entity was called until 1983, quickly plunged into the hot business of corporate takeovers. Within two years Carl Fehrenbach built the mergers-and-acquisitions section from virtually zilch to the second largest on Wall Street—behind Morgan Stanley—handling more than $5 billion worth of mergers a year. Not all his efforts were successful; among other things, Merrill Lynch counseled Mobil on its ill-fated bids for Conoco and Marathon Oil.

In 1982 Merrill Lynch promoted two men to the cochairmanship of its investment-banking subsidiary—President Edmond N. Moriarty Jr. and Executive Vice President Charles H. Ross Jr. Both men had spent their entire business careers at Merrill Lynch.

As it diversified in the 1970s and 1980s, Merrill Lynch, like many other investment houses, launched a major drive for overseas markets. In 1982, through a stock swap, it acquired a 25 percent interest in Hong Kong's Sun Hung Kai Securities and a 15 percent interest in Sun Hung Kai Bank. The deal made Fung King Hey, Sun Hung Kai's principal shareholder and Hong Kong's biggest broker, the largest shareholder in Merrill Lynch—with 4 percent, valued at $1.92 million. And the *Wall Street Journal* speculated, "Merrill Lynch, Pierce, Fenner & Fung?"*

Like several of its rivals, **Goldman, Sachs & Co.** had unpretentious beginnings far removed from the world of high finance. Marcus Goldman was a German Jew who emigrated to the United States in 1848 and opened a clothing store in Philadelphia. After the Civil War he moved to New York, rented a basement office on Pine Street adjacent to a coal chute, and hung out a shingle, "Marcus Goldman, Banker & Broker."

His specialty was commercial paper—the promissory notes merchants and manufacturers exacted from their customers. Goldman bought them at discount and resold them at fractionally higher

---

* Far from it. Fung's bank suffered heavy withdrawals, losses on loans and slumping real estate values, all fueled by fears that Hong Kong would revert to Communist China. To shore up their oriental outpost, Merrill Lynch and Paribas, the French bank that also had acquired control of the American investment house A. G. Becker Paribas (see Chapter 9), increased their Hong Kong holdings first to 20 percent each, then to a total of 51 percent. Michel Barrett, a Paribas vice president, was installed as Sun Hung Kai's chief executive; Fung remained as figurehead chairman.

prices to the banks. He literally worked "out of his hat," for that was where he stored the notes as he made his rounds.

In 1882 Goldman invited his son-in-law Samuel Sachs into his business, advancing the $15,000 for Sachs's share, and the firm of Goldman, Sachs & Co. was born. It developed an early reputation for probity. August Belmont wrote to his Rothschild sponsors in Europe that it was "one firm about which nobody can say anything against."

Goldman's son Henry was eager to get into investment banking. He and Philip Lehman, another member of the second generation who had just joined Lehman Brothers, discussed the prospect of starting their own house, but decided upon joint ventures using their two family firms. The younger Goldman was related by marriage to Julius Rosenwald, and one of the first issues (in 1906) handled jointly by Goldman Sachs and Lehman Brothers was of Rosenwald's Sears, Roebuck & Co. Over the next fifteen years Goldman Sachs and Lehman Brothers handled approximately one hundred issues, mostly of new companies in retailing or manufacture of consumer goods.

In the years before America entered World War I Henry Goldman was openly pro-German, and the loyalty to his father's fatherland persisted even after Congress declared war. When British banks threatened to blacklist Goldman Sachs, the other partners forced Henry Goldman out of the firm his father had founded. Henry Goldman's loyalty to Germany continued even after Hitler came to power. He tried to retire to the Third Reich, but he was arrested by the Nazis and subjected to many humiliations. He died soon after, a broken and bitter man.

Although several Sachses filled the firm, leadership of Goldman Sachs passed to an outsider—Waddill Catchings, a native of South Carolina, who soon severed the firm's long link with Lehman Brothers. Philip Lehman thought that Catchings "lacked balance," and perhaps he was right, for Catchings soon brought Goldman Sachs to the brink of disaster.

The firm entered the investment-trust field, forming Goldman Sachs Trading Co., capitalized at $100 million—90 percent from the public, 10 percent from Goldman Sachs, which managed the accounts. The Trading Company was merged with Financial and Industrial Corporation, which, in turn, controlled Manufacturers

Trust Company—a tangle that, after passage of the Glass-Steagall Act, took nearly a decade to unravel. At first, the Trading Company's stock soared—from its opening of $104 to $226, splitting two for one—but as the depression deepened, it fell to $1.75. Eight Goldman Sachs partners lost a total of $12 million, and many individual investors were wiped out.

Among them was the comedian Eddie Cantor, who made Goldman Sachs the butt of many of his jokes. In one routine a stooge would walk on stage squeezing a dried-up lemon.

"Who are you?" Cantor would ask.

"The margin clerk at Goldman Sachs," the stooge replied.

During the stock market crash Goldman Sachs was forced to buy up many of its issues at the underwritten price, while their traded value plummeted. Its "reputation as an investment banker was dealt a blow from which it took years to recover," Judge Medina noted. From 1930 to 1935 the firm did not manage a single underwriting. As for Catchings, he left Goldman Sachs, went to California, and became a radio producer.

The man who pulled Goldman Sachs out of the depths was Sidney J. Weinberg. The son of impoverished immigrants, he grew up in the slums of Brooklyn and was forced to leave school after the eighth grade and wend his way in the world. He went armed with a "To whom it may concern" letter from his teacher at P.S. 13:

> It gives me great pleasure to testify to the business ability of the bearer, Sidney Weinberg.
> He is happy when he is busy, and is always ready and willing to oblige. We believe he will give satisfaction to anyone who may need his services.

Weinberg took the letter and went to the top of the tallest building on Wall Street—at that time, 43 Exchange Place—and started knocking on doors. The long day was nearly over when he reached the second floor and the office of Goldman Sachs, which hired him —as assistant to the janitor. Weinberg found a "rabbi" in Paul Sachs, who sent the lad to business college, and by 1922 Weinberg was promoted to the post of trader in the bond department. Three years later—on his own!—he bought a seat on the New York Stock Exchange. He became a Goldman Sachs partner in 1927, and within three years his percentage of the firm's profits soared from 1 percent to 33⅓.

He became known as "Mr. Wall Street," and at one time sat on the boards of thirty-one different corporations. F.D.R. offered him the assignment as America's first ambassador to the Soviet Union, but Weinberg turned it down—"because I don't speak Russian," he jokingly told friends. His crowning achievement came in 1956 when, after a full year's labor, he put together the complex deal under which the Ford Motor Co. went public. At the time, the $650 million stock offering was the largest corporate underwriting in history. The Jewish banker from Brooklyn went onto Ford's board—which must have made Henry Ford I, who hated Jews and Wall Street bankers in equal proportions, turn somersaults in his grave.

Weinberg, who died in 1969, was succeeded by Gustave L. Levy, who had made his reputation as an astute arbitrageur and trader. Levy served as chairman of the New York Stock Exchange and headed a special committee that reformed American Stock Exchange procedures in the 1950s. Under his leadership, however, Goldman Sachs suffered another major setback, this time trading in commercial paper of the Penn-Central. Levy himself served as trustee for Walter Annenberg, Nixon's ambassador to the Court of St. James's, and lost $9 million of the newspaper magnate's money on investments in the soon to be bankrupt railroad. Three customers won $4 million ($3 million in damages and $1 million interest) from Goldman Sachs, while the house settled some forty-five other Penn-Central suits for about 20 cents on the dollar.

In a twist of fate, in 1983 Goldman Sachs was selected to seek a private buyer for Conrail, the government-owned combine of the bankrupt Penn-Central and five other failed Eastern railroads. The firm apparently did not approach Ambassador Annenberg, reposing in retirement in Palm Springs, California.

In 1981 Goldman Sachs acquired the metals, coffee, and currency-trading concern, J. Aron & Co.—a new field for the firm. In 1983 Aron was chosen by the Treasury to market its gold medallions, a task previously entrusted to the Postal Service. But there's a feeling among many on Wall Street that the house, now ensconced in moden headquarters at 85 Broad Street, has slipped slightly since Levy's death in 1976. Under the leadership of John C. Whitehead and Sidney Weinberg's son John—Sidney Jr. also is a partner—it remains the epitome of an old-line house. In an era when the hot shops are the mergers-and-acquisitions departments, Goldman Sachs has been curiously unaggressive. Almost alone among major investment banks, it will not represent a raider on a "hostile" tender offer.

Goldman Sachs also was slow getting into foreign markets, which accounted for less than 10 percent of its business. In 1982, however, it bought the London branch of First National Bank of Dallas —promptly renamed Goldman Sachs Ltd.—and Whitehead announced that the firm's objective was to become "a truly international investment bank."*

If Morgan Stanley & Co. is a stepchild of the Glass-Steagall Act, the **First Boston Corporation** is its legitimate offspring. A spin-off of the investment-banking arm of the First National Bank of Boston, as heir to the Chase National Bank's underwriting subsidiary, it also can lay claim to being the nation's oldest investment-banking house. Despite its name, First Boston is New York based, although its parent holding company, First Boston Inc., created in 1976, is headquartered in Philadelphia.

First Boston came into being the day Glass-Steagall took effect— June 15, 1934—under the presidency of Allan M. Pope and three other former officers of the First National Bank of Boston. The following day the new investment house made its first investment, acquiring "the name . . . and the goodwill" of Harris Forbes from Chase. With the name and goodwill came seven officers and eleven employees, including Harris Forbes's New York president, Harry Addinsell, who brought in the underwriting business of Phillips Petroleum.

Harris Forbes traced its history to 1882, when N. W. Harris & Co., which some consider the nation's first true investment bank, was founded in Chicago. Specializing in utility company issues, within a decade it spawned branches in New York and Boston. The Chicago office was absorbed by what is now Harris Bankcorp in

* The following day Whitehead announced an investment of his own: He joined Houston Astros owner John McMullen and former New Jersey Governor Brendan Byrne to buy the Colorado Rockies hockey team and bring it—renamed the New Jersey Devils—to the Brendan Byrne Arena in the Meadowlands.

1907, but the Boston and New York branches continued under the name Harris Forbes Companies.

In 1930 Harris Forbes was acquired by Chase Securities Corp., investment-banking arm of the Chase bank, which thereafter conducted its securities business under the name Chase Harris Forbes Corp. Even before enactment of Glass-Steagall, Chase decided to get out of underwriting—Chase Chairman Winthrop Aldrich was one of the few bankers who backed the bill—and before its acquisition by First Boston had been liquidating Chase Harris Forbes. Indeed, by the time First Boston moved, there was little left except "the name . . . and the goodwill."

Capitalized with $9 million, First Boston from the outset was a major force in investment banking, specializing in the utilities issues it inherited from Chase. Its position was enhanced by its 1946 acquisition of Mellon Securities, which brought in such blue-chip clients as Alcoa, Republic Steel, and Boeing.

First Boston served as adviser to the Eisenhower administration on financing the ill-fated $100 million electric plant to be operated by Mississippi Valley Generating Company—the so-called Dixon-Yates contract. It also can boast—if that's the proper word—of being a prime mover in the nation's biggest bankruptcy. In 1970, on advice of counsel, it refused to participate in a $120 million loan to the Penn-Central, forcing the line to seek a government guaranteed loan. When that fell through, the railroad filed for bankruptcy.

From 1971 through 1974 First Boston was run by a troika of Paul Miller, Emil Pattberg Jr., and Ralph S. Saul. By 1975, however, the firm was moldering in the doldrums—old-line, WASP, and white shoe; smug, complacent, unwilling to hustle for business. In that year, following a yearlong search after Pattberg's retirement and Saul's departure to become chairman of INA, the Philadelphia-based insurance company, it chose a new chairman—fifty-two-year-old George L. Shinn, president and number two man at Merrill Lynch.

Shinn, who relaxes by playing the bagpipes and piloting his own plane, soon shook up staid First Boston. According to the *Wall Street Journal,* he turned "the firm from a clubby aristocracy into a meritocracy." At Shinn's arrival there was only one Jewish partner; there are now too many to count. Among them is Albert

Wojnilower, the firm's chief economist, who is always teamed with Salomon's Henry Kaufman as Doctor Gloom and Doctor Doom.

Late in 1981 Shinn uprooted First Boston from the financial district and planted it into eleven floors—complete with private elevator bank—of the plush Park Avenue Plaza in midtown Manhattan. Included is a sixth-floor trading room—twice the size of First Boston's old one at 20 Exchange Place—which it claims is "the largest securities trading facility of any investment bank in America."

In 1983, after "three record years in a row," Shinn shocked the financial world by announcing his retirement at the age of sixty. "I have a lot of other personal interests that I'd like to spend more time on after thirty-five years in business," he explained. His colleagues, however, were not surprised. "He wanted to go out on top," one noted.

Peter T. Buchanan, a lifelong First Boston employee, was named to succeed Shinn as chief executive officer, while Alvin V. Shoemaker, who had left First Boston in 1978 for a three-year stint as president of Blyth Eastman Dillon & Co., took over Shinn's duties as chairman.

Under Shinn's leadership, First Boston became one of the most aggressive players in the hard-hitting game of corporate takeovers. Its mergers-and-acquisitions department is headed by Wall Street's —or more precisely, Park Avenue's—"Odd Couple," the Mutt-and-Jeff combination of Joseph Perella and Bruce Wasserstein. In five years they brought First Boston from a point where it was "no factor at all" in takeovers to helping barter some of the biggest mergers in American history.

First Boston's matchmaking even extended to its rivals. It brokered the sale of Bache Group to Prudential and advised Charles Schwab & Co., the California-based discount broker, on its acquisition by BankAmerica, thus helping to create two financial supermarkets offering across-the-board expertise.

There was even speculation that First Boston itself could become a takeover target. But then it already was partially conglomerated. In 1978 it joined Crédit Suisse in an international venture— Financiere Crédit Suisse First Boston. With a $24 million investment, First Boston owns slightly more than half of Financiere, which, in turn, owns 38 percent of First Boston.

Sometimes the two partners get their signals crossed. While First

Boston was advising Cities Service, Crédit Suisse was among the institutions financing Mesa Petroleum's "hostile" bid for the oil company.

Lehman Brothers Kuhn Loeb is the epitome of an Our Crowd investment house—or, more precisely, two Our Crowd investment houses.

The first half traces its origins to Henry, Emanuel, and Mayer Lehman, three German-Jewish brothers who emigrated to the United States in the 1840s and opened a cotton brokerage in Montgomery, Alabama. The infant firm soon built branches in New Orleans and New York. Henry Lehman died of yellow fever in New Orleans in 1856, but the other brothers carried on—Emanuel in New York, Mayer in Montgomery.

After the Civil War, which virtually put the firm out of business, Mayer joined Emanuel in New York, and Lehman Brothers began branching out into other commodities—petroleum, coffee, and sugar. It also helped finance the start of several banks in the New York area. Emanuel was the inside man, dealing mainly in cotton, Mayer, the outside man, who brought in the customers and guided the firm's expansion.

Although it handled its first underwriting in 1899—of International Steam Pipe, a predecessor of the present-day Studebaker-Worthington—Lehman Brothers remained essentially a commodities house until 1906, when Emanuel's son Philip teamed with Henry Goldman of Goldman Sachs in the first of a series of new issues.

The established investment houses concentrated on rails, steel, and utilities. Lehman and Goldman specialized in stocks that other houses considered undignified, especially retailing. By the time Lehman Brothers celebrated its centennial in 1950, it could boast: "Of today's twenty largest retailing enterprises, Lehman has been or is presently regarded as investment broker for more than half."

By 1914 Philip Lehman and Henry Goldman were Wall Street's "hottest underwriting team," but because of Goldman's pro-German bent, by the end of World War I they no longer were on speaking terms. The partnership was formally dissolved in the 1920s, with Goldman Sachs getting forty-one of the companies the two firms had handled jointly, Lehman Brothers the remaining nineteen. "After the dispute, they became real go-getters," one observer said of Lehman Brothers.

Lehman Brothers, which had severed the remaining ties to its southern cotton brokerage branches, remained a family fiefdom until 1924, when it took in its first non-Lehman partner. Philip Lehman retired in 1925, and leadership of the firm passed to his son Robert and to Mayer's son Arthur. Another of Mayer's sons—Herbert—spent two decades with Lehman Brothers until his election as New York's lieutenant governor in 1928. He went on to greater distinction during four terms as governor and one as United States senator.

In 1928 Lehman Brothers moved to new offices at 1 William Street, the only investment bank fully occupying a building of its own. Its most dynamic partner in this period was John D. Hertz, the Chicago businessman who had started with cabs and limousines, then branched out into the car rental service that still bears his name. At Lehman he put together multimillion-dollar deals involving Paramount Pictures and Fifth Avenue Motor Coach Company. Despite his lifelong involvement with motor vehicles, Hertz's most spectacular success came with a more ancient form of transport—horseflesh. He owned Count Fleet, the 1943 Triple Crown winner.

The details were not disclosed until years afterward, but a Lehman banker played a key, behind-the-scenes role in World War II.

On October 11, 1939, Alexander Sachs, vice president and chief economist of the Lehman Corporation, a wholly owned subsidiary of Lehman Brothers, visited President Roosevelt at the White House.

Sachs's horizons extended far beyond banking. Through his philanthropic work with Jewish refugees, he had made friends in émigré scientific circles. He also had political clout, having helped set up the NRA—National Recovery Administration, the ill-fated "Blue Eagle."

Sachs had been chosen by the scientific community as its intermediary with the nation's Chief Executive on a vital matter. With him, Sachs carried a letter from Albert Einstein, reporting that, as a result of recent experiments with the element uranium, "extremely powerful bombs of a new type may thus be built."

F.D.R. did not seem impressed, but Sachs wangled an invitation to return to breakfast the next morning. This time he tried an historical analogy. He told the President how Napoleon had rejected Robert Fulton's idea of the steamboat, thus dooming his dream of a cross-Channel invasion.

"This is an example of how England was saved by the shortsightedness of an adversary," Sachs said.

F.D.R. finally got the message. He pulled out two snifters and poured—appropriately—Napoleon brandy.

"Alex," he told his old friend, "what you are after is to see that the Nazis don't blow us up."

"Precisely."

The President called in his chief aide, Edwin Watson, handed him Einstein's letter, and said, "Pa, this requires action."

Thus the Manhattan Project was born.

"Bobby" Lehman ran the firm through the 1930s, 1940s, and 1950s, amassing a spectacular art collection while playing polo with the likes of Jock Whitney and Tommy Hitchcock. When he died in 1969, his art collection alone—donated to the Metropolitan Museum of Art—was valued at $100 million, roughly double the entire capital of Lehman Brothers—which suggests that the venerable banking house might have been better off investing in old masters than underwriting new issues.

By then, leadership of Lehman Brothers had passed from the family. But Bobby Lehman—like many strong-willed leaders—had neglected to provide for his succession. Lehman Brothers, always loosely structured, degenerated further into an unwieldy group of rival fiefdoms.

After World War II the firm took in several prominent "public partners"—most notably, General Lucius D. Clay, military governor of Germany, and former Undersecretary of State (and future U.N. ambassador) George W. Ball. In 1973 it added another—former Commerce Secretary Peter G. Peterson. Within a few weeks of his arrival Peterson was promoted to the chairmanship of Lehman Brothers.

At the time, the firm was described as "venerable but financially troubled." Like many securities firms, it had become bogged in a backlog of paperwork during the surging volume of the 1968–69 bull market, and its problems were compounded when it switched to an automated accounting system that was riddled with "bugs." "Lehman was in a real crunch," said one observer. "The operation fell down completely." Indeed, the operation was so confused that the SEC threatened to suspend the firm's registration. Lehman was kept afloat only by a $7 million investment by Banca Commerciale Italiana. A merger with Abraham & Co. brought in another $4.9 million in capital.

In 1977 Lehman merged with Kuhn, Loeb & Co., which was just as venerable and even more financially troubled. Like Lehman, Kuhn Loeb had been started by German-Jewish immigrants—Abraham Kuhn and Solomon Loeb, brothers-in-law who settled in Cincinnati and opened a dry-goods store. In 1867 they moved to New York and with their $500,000 savings started a company "for the transaction of a general banking and commission business."

Kuhn soon returned to Germany, but Loeb stayed on, and the firm flourished under his son-in-law Jacob Schiff, who became a partner in 1875 and ran the firm for forty-five years. Schiff gave Kuhn Loeb its philosophy: "Our only attractiveness is our good name and our reputation for sound advice and integrity. If that is gone, our business is gone, however attractive our show window might be."

For Schiff's first twenty-five years, Kuhn Loeb, according to its official history, was "almost exclusively devoted to providing the finances for the growth of railroads." During the first two decades of the twentieth century, Schiff shifted from rails to foreign financing. Terming czarist Russia "the enemy of mankind," he readily backed Japan in the war of 1904–5. Like Henry Goldman, he sided with Germany against Russia during World War I, and Kuhn Loeb refused to join Morgan and others in a war loan to Britain and France because Lord Reading—the former Rufus Isaacs and future viceroy of India—could not give his assurance that no benefits would accrue to their ally, Russia.

Like Lehman Brothers, Kuhn Loeb was a family fiefdom. Until 1911 there was no partner not related by blood or marriage to Schiff or his partner, Abraham Wolff. After Schiff's death in 1920 leadership of the firm passed to Schiff's son Mortimer, Schiff's son-in-law, Felix Warburg, and Wolff's son-in-law, Otto Kahn.

The younger Schiff was something of a spendthrift and dilettante who ran with what was then called "the international set," but Warburg, scion of a distinguished Hamburg financial family, and Kahn were brilliant bankers. Kahn was a patron of the Metropolitan Opera who gave it $2.5 million over his lifetime and became the first Jew to occupy a box in the exclusive "Diamond Horseshoe."

Warburg's brother Paul, a Kuhn Loeb partner who became the first vice chairman of the Federal Reserve Board, was one of the few to forecast the Great Depression.* He advised Mortimer Schiff to "get out of the market." Schiff barely got started before he died. He left $7.6 million in cash and $28.7 million in securities. By the time the estate was distributed, the value of the stocks had fallen by 54 percent.

After Mortimer Schiff's death leadership of Kuhn Loeb passed to his son John and to Felix Warburg's son Frederick, both great-grandsons of founder Solomon Loeb. Among the younger partners were Lewis L. Straus (who insisted on pronouncing his name "straws"), son-in-law of Jerome Hanauer, the first nonfamily partner, who became Eisenhower's chairman of the Atomic Energy Commission, Benjamin J. Buttenwieser, later assistant high commissioner for Germany, and J. Richardson Dilworth, who was lured from Kuhn Loeb to become chief financial adviser to the Rockefeller family.

By the 1970s Kuhn Loeb had fallen on hard times. It suffered large losses trading in Fannie Mae securities—the Federal National Mortgage Association—and before teaming with Lehman Brothers had talked merger, unsuccessfully, with Shearson Hayden Stone, Paine Webber, and Blyth Eastman Dillon.

In the merger with Lehman Brothers, Kuhn Loeb clearly was junior partner. Although John Schiff was named honorary chairman, Peterson held the posts of both chairman and president, and seven of the ten-member executive committee were Lehman alumni. After all, Lehman came into the merger with $60 million in capital, Kuhn Loeb with only $18 million. But Kuhn Loeb had far greater experience in foreign ventures, so the overseas operation had the name reversed—Kuhn Loeb Lehman Brothers International.

In 1979 L.B.K.L. acquired Sonneblick-Goldman Corp. and moved heavily into real estate sales and financings. Peterson also

* Like Jacob Schiff, Paul Warburg was a son-in-law of Solomon Loeb, which made him his brother Felix's uncle-in-law!

beefed up the firm's trading capability and, for a time, even considered getting into the brokerage business.

"Several wire houses were seeking a merger with us, wherein we would be the surviving firm," he noted. "The more we thought of that, the less enthused we were. The thought of several thousand salesmen in two hundred offices would have changed the very special essence of this firm. So we decided against that option, very deliberately."

Instead, L.B.K.L. relied on about three hundred salesmen in New York and its seven branch offices to handle retail operations. It also beefed up its work in mergers and acquisitions, by 1981 claiming Wall Street's lead in the volume—if not dollar amount—of deals. Peterson even instituted a new products department—not to seek out high-technology companies as candidates for investment, but to develop new financial instruments for clients.

In 1980 an era ended when the expanded firm moved into modern skyscraper offices at 55 Water Street. "It has a view," said one employee, "but it doesn't make up for the mahogany-paneled partners' room on the third floor." Banco Commerciale Italiana took over Lehman's old quarters at 1 William Street.

The **Kidder, Peabody & Co.** of today more properly should be called "Albert H. Gordon & Co." It is a one-man show whose only relationship with the firm founded in Boston in 1863 by Henry Kidder and the brothers Francis and Oliver Peabody is the name.

The original Kidder Peabody was among the six banks targeted in the 1912 Money Trust investigation. It was American correspondent for Baring Brothers and made its mark by handling the original underwritings for AT&T and the Santa Fe railroad. But its leadership lapsed after World War I, and by 1930 it was in deep trouble. The Italian government withdrew an $8 million deposit, and Kidder Peabody owed some $4 million to the Bank for International Settlements. Worse, it had used deposits to underwrite stocks; after the market collapse, it could not meet the demands of its customers.

J. P. Morgan & Co. launched a $15 million bailout operation. As Harold Stanley noted: "If Kidder Peabody had failed—an old firm and it had been a very prominent firm in some ways—it would have shaken confidence and upset everything." Morgan and Chase put up $2.5 million each; First National Bank of Boston, $1.5 million; Bankers Trust and Guaranty Trust, $1 million each; other banks in Boston and New York, sums of $250,000 to $750,000. The Kidder Peabody partners raised another $5 million on their own.

It wasn't enough. On March 6, 1931, the name and physical assets of Kidder Peabody were sold to a new company. Edwin S. Webster, one of the heads of Stone & Webster, the giant construction concern, directed the operation. Although Stone & Webster had its own securities subsidiary, which underwrote the financing for many of its construction projects, Webster Sr. targeted Kidder Peabody as the vehicle for his son's career. Edwin Jr. had been hospitalized after a fall from a horse, and his father thought that investment banking would be a suitable occupation for him.

Joining Webster Jr. as the first partners in the new Kidder Peabody were his Harvard Business School classmate Gordon, then a statistician at Goldman Sachs, and Chandler Hovey, brother-in-law of Webster Sr. None of the partners of the old Kidder Peabody was included.

Webster, Gordon, and Hovey were joined later in the year by G. Herman Kinnicutt, former senior partner of Kissel, Kinnicutt & Co., which had been liquidated. In 1934, when Glass-Steagall took effect, Kidder Peabody acquired the Philadelphia National Company, securities subsidiary of Philadelphia National Bank, and its president, Orus J. Matthews, became a partner. Frederick Moore and Walter Moffitt of the old Guaranty Company were added at about the same time, while Kidder Peabody also took on many of the lower-ranking personnel from the old Chase Harris Forbes and National City companies.

The firm's rebirth was not auspicious. At its inception it had a daily overhead of $5,000 and income of only $1,000. Kidder Peabody responded by withdrawing from general banking—this was three years before Glass-Steagall—to concentrate on underwriting and brokerage, a change symbolized by moving its main office from Boston to New York. It also developed one of Wall Street's strongest selling forces, with outposts in Chicago, Hartford, and Albany, in addition to its home bases in New York, Boston, and Philadelphia.

Unlike Morgan Stanley, which concentrated on blue chips, Kidder Peabody grabbed up the smaller issues. "Under the leadership of Gordon the affairs of Kidder Peabody prospered," Judge Medina noted. "The partners and employees went after everything. . . . No issue was too small, no participation too insignificant." Year after year, Kidder Peabody was among the leaders in the number of underwritings managed—and way down the list in their dollar volume.

"We're not white shoe, we're white sock," a Kidder Peabody banker once remarked. Indeed, the firm sometimes smacked more of the locker-room than of the boardroom. After one annual dinner at the plush Hotel Pierre, a senior partner and a lowly bond clerk got into a fistfight, which had to be broken up by the firm's president, Ralph D. DeNunzio.

Gordon, who almost single-handedly ran the firm for fifty years, relentlessly stalked corporation executives for their underwriting business. His prize catch was Armand Hammer, the unorthodox chairman of Occidental Petroleum.* In 1960 *Fortune* cited Gordon as "Wall Street's most successful underwriter." An arch-Republican —he was a major contributor to Nixon's campaign chest—Gordon carried on a celebrated feud with the New York *Times* in the 1950s because of what he considered its support for Fidel Castro. He yanked all Kidder Peabody advertising from the *Times* and would not permit anyone to bring the paper into his home. At the age of eighty, Gordon, a physical fitness fanatic, decided to enter the London Marathon. He scoured the firm's offices at 10 Hanover Square for a running companion and finally found a margin clerk—who received an all-expenses-paid vacation to Britain.

Webster Jr., who had been a leader of the America First movement in the months before Pearl Harbor, killed himself in 1957. Gordon remains as Kidder Peabody's chairman, though much of the responsibility for day-to-day operations passed to President DeNunzio.

Blyth Eastman Paine Webber, the investment-banking arm of Paine Webber Inc., parent company of the nation's second-largest brokerage, is a prime example of the merger mania that struck securities firms during the 1970s. (See chart.) "Blyth" is the opera-

* However, Occidental's celebrated bid for Cities Service was managed by Goldman Sachs.

tive word of the investment-banking shingle, and its roots sprouted far from Wall Street.

In 1914 Charles R. Blyth and Dean Witter opened a brokerage and underwriting house in San Francisco—Blyth, Witter & Co. Specializing in West Coast utility issues, it soon begat branches in New Orleans, Los Angeles, Portland, and Seattle—and in 1925, New York. Witter resigned in 1924 to form his own firm—Dean Witter & Co., which survives today as Dean Witter Reynolds, the brokerage arm of Sears—but it was another five years before Blyth removed his name from the shingle.

After the stock market crash, Blyth dissolved the brokerage end of the business to concentrate on underwriting. In 1935 he brought

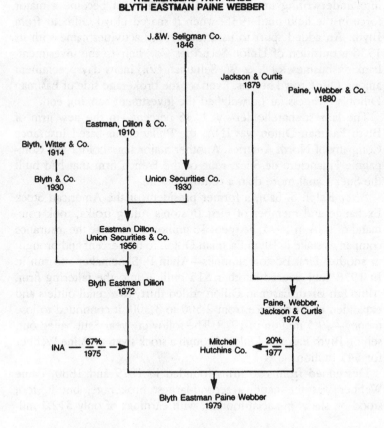

THE MERGERS THAT MADE BLYTH EASTMAN PAINE WEBBER

in Charles E. Mitchell, the slightly tainted former chairman of National City Bank, to head the New York office and Mitchell soon built Blyth & Co. into the big time. By World War II it had offices in twenty-five cities.

Blyth remained in San Francisco, where he became a patron of the arts and a power behind the scenes politically. Over the years he contributed some $25 million to various campaigns managed by Whittaker & Baxter, first of the modern political image makers. He died in 1959 at the age of seventy-six.

In 1972 Blyth & Co., in financial trouble, merged with Eastman Dillon, Union Securities & Co. Founded in 1910 by Thomas C. Eastman and Herbert Lowell Dillon, Eastman, Dillon & Co. began as a regional brokerage in five Pennsylvania cities. It did not get into underwriting until the 1920s and did not become a major force in the field until 1935, when it snared Lloyd Gilmour from Blyth. An added spurt to its underwriting activities came with its 1956 acquisition of Union Securities Co., heir to the investment-banking business of J. & W. Seligman Co., in its day preeminent among Our Crowd houses. Even so, the brokerage side of Eastman Dillon's business far outweighed the investment-banking end.

The largest shareholder—with 36 percent—in the new firm of Blyth Eastman Dillon was INA, the Philadelphia-based Insurance Company of North America. Another major shareholder was Compagnie Financière de Suez, relic of the French firm that had built the Suez Canal more than a century before.

After Ralph S. Saul, a former president of the American Stock Exchange and member of First Boston's ruling troika, took command of INA in 1975, he spent $6 million to increase the insurance company's stake in Blyth Eastman Dillon to 67 percent and brought in another First Boston alumnus—Alvin P. Shoemaker—to run it. In 1978 Saul poured another $15 million into the faltering firm. Although Blyth Eastman Dillon added thirty-five retail outlets and expanded its work force from 2,500 to 3,300, it continued to lose money—$9.5 million in 1978. The following year Saul bailed out, selling Blyth Eastman Dillon through a stock swap to Paine Webber for $45 million.

Descended from two firms founded in 1879 and 1880, Paine Webber was the nation's second-largest brokerage, but it, too, stood on shaky financial footing, with earnings of only $12.7 million on revenue of $384 million. Under Chairman James W. Davant, however, Paine Webber started branching beyond brokerage. It gained research strength in 1977 when it acquired a 20 percent interest in Mitchell Hutchins & Co. Blyth Eastman Dillon—with which it had held abortive merger talks five years before—gave it an active investment-banking arm.

Blyth's employees were unaware of the acquisition until it was announced, and a chagrined Shoemaker soon returned to First Boston. Paine Webber's new underwriting subsidiary was renamed Blyth Eastman Paine Webber—Dillon disappearing into the recesses of financial history.

Blyth Eastman Paine Webber was not noted as a star player in the takeover wars, but in the wake of revulsion over Bendix–Martin Marietta–United Technologies–Allied battle it took out ads boasting of its powers in arranging "quiet acquisitions": "Unfriendly acquisitions make headlines. Quiet ones make money."

However, it was not tabbed to broker the merger most important to its own future—INA's merger with Connecticut General to become Cigna Corp., which was handled by Goldman Sachs.

Paine Webber prospered mightily as a result of the 1982 stock market boom, its income surging 122 percent for the fiscal year. Its stock soared—partly because of its newfound profitability, but primarily because of rumors that Cigna would increase its stake and become a financial supermarket like Merrill Lynch, Prudential-Bache, and Shearson/American Express. Instead, Saul bailed out again, selling Cigna's 24 percent interest in Paine Webber for approximately $100 million in debentures—a divestiture once again handled by Goldman Sachs.

The move left Paine Webber perhaps the most tempting takeover target on Wall Street—with Japan's Nomura Securities cited as the most likely buyer. Another potential raider appeared to be Saul Steinberg, the roly-poly financier who founded Leasco Data and at the age of twenty-nine tried to take over Chemical Bank. In 1968 he acquired Reliance Insurance and merged his operations into a new Reliance Group. At the time Cigna was selling off its shares, Reliance was buying—a 5.7 percent interest in Paine Webber—and Steinberg soon increased his stake to 7.85 percent. But he insisted that it was purely for investment. It apparently was. In June 1983 Steinberg sold his stake—for an $8 million profit.

Like Blyth Eastman Paine Webber, **Drexel Burnham Lambert** —the last name pronounced, as in the French, "lamb bear"—is the product of multiple mergers. (See chart.) Like Kidder Peabody, the firm of today has no relationship, other than name, to the original Drexel & Co. Also, like Kidder Peabody, it is virtually a one-man show—a man named I. W. Burnham II, known to everyone as "Tubby."

The original Drexel & Co. was one of the leading American banks for a century. It was founded by Francis Martin Drexel in 1838 and headed for three decades after the Civil War by his son Anthony. Like Morgan, with which it was affiliated, after passage of Glass-Steagall, Drexel opted for the commercial side of the business and discontinued investment banking. Indeed, Drexel was "the Philadelphia end of J. P. Morgan & Co.," and in 1940 Morgan

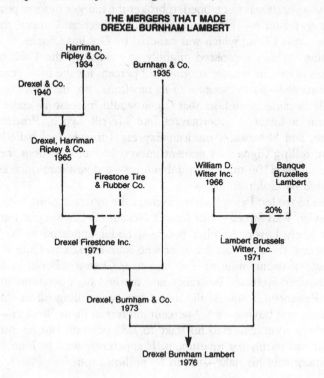

**THE MERGERS THAT MADE
DREXEL BURNHAM LAMBERT**

decided to close the Drexel operation, transferring all its accounts to the Morgan bank in New York.

At that point, a number of former Drexel partners, led by Edward Hopkinson Jr., decided to go into investment banking and acquired the rights to the old Drexel name. Among the founders was Thomas S. Gates Jr., who went on to become Eisenhower's Defense Secretary and, later, chairman of Morgan Stanley. The new Drexel & Co. opened for business on April 1, 1940, with a capital of $1 million. Too small and undercapitalized to be a major force in the industry, the firm probably was named a defendant in the government's antitrust action only because of its time-honored name.

Drexel encountered rough sledding in the 1960s and 1970s. In 1965 it merged with Harriman, Ripley & Co., which had been founded in 1934 when Joseph F. Ripley, former executive vice president of National City Bank, took over the underwriting arm of the private bank, Brown Brothers Harriman & Co., after Glass-Steagall went into effect. Hopkinson and Ripley served as cochairmen of the merged firm of Drexel, Harriman, Ripley & Co.

In 1971 Firestone Tire & Rubber made a $6 million investment in Drexel Harriman Ripley and renamed it Drexel Firestone, Inc. Despite fresh infusions of Firestone money, the firm continued to falter, and in two years Firestone merged it with Burnham & Co., the highly successful brokerage house I. W. Burnham II had founded in 1935. Burnham, scion of a Kentucky distilling family (the "I. W." in I. W. Harper bourbon is from his grandfather, Isaac Wolf Bernheim), started with a nest egg of $100,000—$4,000 of his own and $96,000 borrowed from his grandfather. At the time of the merger Burnham & Co. had $12 million in capital, as opposed to Drexel's $4 million, and clearly was senior partner. Tubby Burnham became chairman of Drexel, Burnham & Co.

The new firm did well, but other brokerages—badly battered by negotiated commissions and the stock market slump—did not. Among them was Lambert Brussels Witter, created in 1971 when Banque Bruxelles Lambert acquired a 20 percent interest in William D. Witter Inc., a resarch firm founded five years before by the son of Dean Witter. So in 1976 Lambert Brussels Witter was merged into what was renamed Drexel Burnham Lambert.

"You've got to have $100 million in capital to make it these days," said Witter, who soon set off on his own again.

Despite massive infusions of Belgian francs, his firm had only $11 million.

The old Burnham & Co. comprised about 80 percent of Drexel Burnham Lambert, but the mergers made what had been essentially a brokerage house a major force in investment banking. Like Kidder Peabody, it conceded the blue chips to larger Wall Street rivals and concentrated on underwriting issues of small- to medium-sized companies. It also carved out a large niche in trading high yield corporate bonds. In 1978 Mike Milken, Drexel's thirty-year-old "Junk Bond King," moved the corporate bond department from Wall Street to Los Angeles—so his children could have "a home and a back yard where they can play every single day without worrying what the weather is going to be like."

Although it started with $35 million less than Witter's prerequisite of $100 million, Drexel Burnham Lambert "made it." By the time Tubby Burnham stepped down as chairman in 1982—he remained as chairman of the parent holding company, Drexel Burnham Lambert Group—estimates of the firm's capital ranged as high as $173 million.

Burnham was succeeded by Robert E. Linton, who had been president and chief executive officer of the house. In an era of M.B.A.s he was among the few to attain the peak of the profession without attending college. Upon finishing high school during World War II, he was commissioned in the Army Air Forces; discharged in 1946, he started at Burnham. Shortly after his selection as chairman, he was elected president of the Securities Industry Association and designated as "point man" in the fight against further erosion of Glass-Steagall.

The "Dillon" of **Dillon, Read & Co.** is not related to the "Dillon" that disappeared when Blyth Eastman Dillon was merged into Paine Webber. In fact, the name originally was Lapowski. Samuel Lapowski was a Polish Jew who emigrated to Abilene, Texas, and opened a clothing store. Later, he went into electrical manufacturing in Milwaukee. He adopted his wife's maiden name—Dillon—and did well enough to send his son Clarence to Harvard, where, according to one account, he majored in poker.

Clarence Dillon started as a salesman in the Chicago office of Wm. A. Read & Co., a venerable firm that had begun in 1830 as Vermilye & Co. He moved to New York and became a Read partner in 1916 and its senior partner in 1920. About a year later his name was added to the shingle. Dillon showed an extraordinary ability for making money—upward of a half-billion dollars, by some accounts.

One of the Wall Street legends has it that Dillon wrote a *personal* check for $137.5 million to acquire the old Dodge Brothers Motor Company. Dillon Read reorganized the company and sold its stock to the public—for a total of $175 million. One observer called Dillon Read's $37.5 million profit "pure water." Dillon also presided over the reorganization of Goodyear Tire & Rubber.

As a purely personal investment Dillon also bought Château Haut-Brion, producer of one of the half-dozen great Bordeaux wines.

Dillon bought his son Clarence Douglas—or C. Douglas, as he preferred to be called—a $185,000 seat on the New York Stock Exchange as a college graduation present. The younger Dillon succeeded to the leadership of the firm after World War II. As late as the 1950s the only shareholders in Dillon Read were the Dillons, father and son.

Two cabinet members, a White House troubleshooter, and a United States senator came out of the firm. James V. Forrestal, Clarence Dillon's right-hand man and the firm's managing director, was tabbed as Undersecretary of the Navy in 1940 and went on to become full secretary and then the nation's first Secretary of Defense.

The younger Dillon served as Eisenhower's ambassador to France and later as Undersecretary of State. Then he was tabbed by J.F.K. for Treasury Secretary—a rare Republican riding the New Frontier. According to Washington legend, he resigned, his dignity ruffled, after L.B.J. insisted on discussing affairs of state face-to-face while perched on the toilet attending to more personal affairs.

Peter M. Flanigan, a Dillon Read vice president, came out of the firm to become assistant to the President in 1969 and soon acquired a reputation as "Richard Nixon's 'Mr. Fixit' when it comes to powerful business interests." He had a heavy hand in arranging the ITT antitrust settlement on terms highly favorable to ITT and helped steer the Postal Service's first bond issue to Dillon Read.

In 1982 New Jersey Governor Thomas Kean gave Dillon Read's managing partner, Nicholas Brady, an interim appointment as United States senator.

Clarence Dillon died in 1979 at the age of eighty-six. By then his son was semiretired. C. Douglas Dillon had fathered only daughters, neither of whom showed an interest in carrying on the family business. So in 1980 he sold the controlling interest in Dillon Read —approximately 80 percent—to Sequoia Ventures, the investment arm of Bechtel Group, the giant California-based construction concern. Most of the remaining shares were owned by Skandinaviska Enskilda Banken, the Stockholm bank of the Wallenberg family, which had entered the fold through a stock swap when Dillon Read acquired its Scandinavian Securities subsidiary. Both the late Marcus Wallenberg and—until his appointment as Ronald Reagan's Secretary of State—Bechtel President George P. Shultz sat on Dillon Read's board.

"Here is Wall Street, growing larger and larger and more conglomerate-type firms doing all manner of things. That's an exciting trend," Shultz said at the time of the sale. "At the same time, there's going to be room for relatively small, high-powered firms to do investment banking things, concentrating on personal, top-level service."

In the fast-moving world of investment banking Dillon Read had remained staid and static. With only $35 million in capital it was too small to compete for shelf registrations. It made only abortive efforts to expand its operations overseas. It didn't even have a research department, fearing that accurate reports might offend established clients. It played no part in the highly profitable takeover wars. It declined to "hustle" clients, preferring to lie back and wait for business. Instead, such long-time clients as Superior Oil and PASNY—Power Authority of the State of New York—left for other houses.

In what was viewed by some as a desperation move, Dillon Read brought in an outsider—John Birkelund, the controversial president of New Court Securities—as its chief operating officer. Birkelund soon plunged into new areas: corporate takeovers, venture capital, and even outright speculation. It may have been too much, too fast. The changes certainly shook up Dillon Read's staff. Within two and a half years, ten managing directors and many more lower-level employees left, either because they could not adjust to the new ways or because they believed that they were doomed to failure. Dillon Read clearly was playing catch-up ball.

"The firm's trying to get back to what Clarence Dillon was doing years ago," one partner explained.

But basically Dillon Read stuck to its bread-and-butter business—underwriting. In October 1982 it had one of its busiest weeks, bringing out a $250 million bond issue for New York's Metropolitan Transportation Authority and $100 million offerings for both Anheuser-Busch and R. J. Reynolds.

Just before Christmas 1982 Dillon Read scheduled a press conference, and Wall Street buzzed with rumors that Bechtel was selling its two-year-old stake in the firm. Instead, Dillon Read announced that it was moving from its longtime nook at 46 William Street to new skyscraper offices at 535 Madison Avenue.

Three months later, after Brady returned to the helm, Dillon Read made the once expected announcement: Its twenty managing directors would buy back a majority interest in the firm, although Bechtel would retain some shares as an investment. Neither the number of shares nor their dollar value was disclosed.

III

SIX DECADES
IN INVESTMENT BANKING

Benjamin J. Buttenwieser's career spans more than six decades in investment banking—with two time-outs for government service during and after World War II. Short, dark, and balding, always impeccably dressed, he bears an uncanny resemblance to Max Aitken, the late Lord Beaverbrook. In his more than sixty years on Wall Street Buttenwieser has seen the winds of change sweep across the world of investment banking, transforming it from the freewheeling era of the "Robber Barons" to the well-regulated markets of the modern money managers, from a period of nib pens and rolltop desks to a transistorized era of Xerox machines, Videcs, and IBM computers, from a time of small family fiefdoms to one of publicly held, globe-girdling conglomerates. Indeed, Benjamin Buttenwieser's career mirrors the history of investment banking through most of the twentieth century.

Let's look at it more closely.

Benjamin Buttenwieser is one of the last remaining Our Crowd members still active in investment banking. His grandfather emigrated from Germany in 1854 and settled in Philadelphia, where he taught at a private academy. The family name derives from the town of Buttenwiesen—somewhere along the way the "en" was dropped.

Buttenwieser's father Joseph, born in 1865, moved to New York and practiced real estate law, taking his fees in parcels of property or participations in land developments. In that era of the city's greatest growth he soon became a millionaire several times over.

"I wasn't born with a silver spoon in my mouth," his son once remarked. "It was platinum, studded with diamonds. My parents were cultured, and they were rich."

However, Joseph Buttenwieser guessed wrong on his most personal investment. He decided that Harlem—not Park Avenue with its still uncovered railroad tracks—would become New York City's next major area for prime residential development. So he settled on Lenox Avenue, where Benjamin—the second son and fourth of five children—was born on October 22, 1900, just in time to usher in the new century.

"My parents had principles—spelled both ways," Buttenwieser said. They instilled in young Benjamin a love of learning and a sense of duty. Theirs was a cultured home, and he grew up speaking German and French, as well as English, and learning about literature, art, and music—even though the elder Buttenwieser had a tin ear.

"Father knew the difference between 'The Star-Spangled Banner' and Beethoven's Fifth Symphony was, if the people got up, he knew it was 'The Star-Spangled Banner.'"

Benjamin breezed through grammar and preparatory schools and entered Columbia College at the age of fifteen. His father promised him a Stutz Bearcat if he graduated before he turned eighteen, but his mother objected to such ostentation, so Benjamin had to settle for a Maxwell. At the time, he was Columbia's youngest graduate since Colonial days—although he didn't formally receive his degree until the following year.

Too young to go on immediately to graduate school, Buttenwieser took a job as a runner at Kuhn, Loeb & Co. He started on October 1, 1918. World War I still had six weeks to run.

"At that time they indoctrinated all beginners alike," he recalled. "They couldn't care less whether you had a college degree or not. You started as a runner. And I started with the large salary of $40 a month, which was considered good pay, I guess, in those days. . . . And I've been working ever since."

By today's standards, Kuhn Loeb in 1918 was a primitive place, more akin to the offices depicted by Dickens than those of *9 to 5*.

"The amount of paperwork was minutely microscopic next to now," Buttenwieser recalled. "The books were all kept in long-hand. We had adding machines, but that was all. The general ledger was handwritten."

All correspondence was handwritten and reproduced on old-fashioned copying presses—a matrix of tissue thin paper, a damp cloth, and the letter to be copied run through the rollers.

"The skill was in wetting those rags just enough so that they were damp enough to cause the copying of the letter onto that thin piece of tissue and not so damp or wet as to make the ink on the letter blur, because in some instances they didn't want to show the letter had been copied," Buttenwieser continued. "And heaven help you, if, after one of the partners had signed a letter, suddenly the whole thing was blurred because you let the copy cloths get too wet!"

In one sense, Buttenwieser has not fully caught up with today's technology of copying: He still asks his secretary to make a "photostat" of his correspondence.

Buttenwieser worked as a runner, bookkeeper, cashier, and clerk. "There was no formal training school," he said, "but you worked at this, and you worked at that. . . . You were more than an apprentice. You were also an available task force for any department."

At the time, Kuhn Loeb had only fifty-two employees—fewer than the number of managing directors of the present-day Lehman Brothers Kuhn Loeb. Except for a slight differentiation between the foreign and domestic departments, the firm was too small to have the compartmentalization of today's investment-banking houses.

"You worked much more closely with the partners, because they were right in on everything, so to speak," Buttenwieser noted. "Now things are much more departmentalized and the number of employees infinitely greater."

The legendary Jacob Schiff still had two years of life left when Buttenwieser joined Kuhn Loeb. Because of the difference in their stations, Buttenwieser had few direct dealings with him, but "I surely do know that he was the boss. No two ways about that. You could tell by the electricity when he walked through the office. He was always pleasant, but he didn't suffer fools gladly."

It was still the age of dollar diplomacy, when presidents and prime ministers alike kowtowed to banks and corporations that had invested abroad. Buttenwieser recalled how Kuhn Loeb had joined N. M. Rothschild & Sons in London on a loan to the Dominican Republic—a loan supposedly secured by the Caribbean nation's customs duties.

A worried Schiff cabled Sir Ernest Cassel, head of Rothschild: "If they don't pay, who will collect the customs?"

Cassel promptly cabled back: "Your marines and ours."

It was a boom time for Wall Street. Commissions were high, and taxes were low. Partners lived on a grand scale in Long Island and New Jersey mansions, collecting art and breeding polo ponies. They also received perks that few of their present-day counterparts enjoy, especially in their capacity as directors of railroads.

"In those days," Buttenwieser said, "directors of railroads traveled free—not only on their own road, but also on every other U.S. railroad—with a private car, to boot. . . . Then came the Interstate Commerce [Commission] rule that you had to pay twenty-six fares for use of a private car. That slowed the K.L.ers up a little bit along that line."

In the years immediately after World War I, Wall Street was a close-knit, comfortable, cozy world.

"We were rivals for business, but one of the more pleasant aspects of Wall Street then—and to a degree now—was that they were all fairly friendly," Buttenwieser noted. "The competition for business is much keener now than it was then. In those days business literally came to you. Also, the large prestigious firms didn't compete with one another. Not that I think they were any more gracious, but probably motivated by the concept, 'He who lives by the sword dies by the sword.'

"We wouldn't have thought of going after J. P. Morgan & Co. business. If there were any companies for which J. P. Morgan, who were our main competitors, were bankers, we wouldn't go near them. And they wouldn't venture near ours, because they didn't want to start any such competition. . . .

"Each [firm] got its business on its reputation for ability, integrity, foresight, knowledge of how to attract the public to invest in securities that it offered, either alone or through a group of firms, usually a syndicate," he continued.

"There was an investigation once at which a memorandum written by someone at Kuhn, Loeb & Co. stated—it even mentioned the other firms—'They're poaching on our preserves.' Well, that didn't make very good reading for KL and company at a congressional investigation."

According to Buttenwieser, there was a hierarchy in underwritings: "In those days, the most prestigious financing was for railroad companies, because their securities were deemed to be the best investment. Little by little, steel companies got to be considered a good investment, somewhat later public utilities. . . . Therefore, the leading firms wanted to do railroad financing."

Morgan was banker for the New York Central; Kuhn Loeb represented its archrival, the Pennsylvania, as well as several Western lines. Once Walter Meyer—brother of banker Eugene, who later bought the Washington *Post*—sued Kuhn Loeb "for allegedly having wrecked" the Denver & Rio Grande. Buttenwieser recalled the trial, at which Meyer's counsel, Samuel Untermyer of the Money Trust investigation, cross-examined Kuhn Loeb's Otto Kahn. Kahn kept answering, "I don't remember."

An exasperated Untermyer finally elicited from Kahn that "I make it a studied practice, that when I'm in a transaction, I try to know all about it. I just don't rely on my assistants."

"Well, how do you account for the fact that you handled this transaction fifteen years ago, and you don't seem to recall anything about it?" Untermyer asked.

Kahn replied: "I reiterate: While I'm making a transaction, I make it a studied practice to know as much about it as possible. Then as soon as it's over, I similarly try my best to purge my memory of every bit of knowledge about it, so as to be ready for the next one."

Untermyer turned to the judge—Martin T. Manton, later convicted of corruption on the federal bench—and said: "Your honor, I'll refresh Mr. Kahn's memory."

Kahn cut him off: "I'm sorry, Mr. Untermyer. If I have no recollection, you can't refresh it."

As Buttenwieser noted, "That stood up, and that was the end of that lawsuit."

During this period, Leonor F. Loree, head of the Delaware & Hudson, acquired ambitions of transforming the line into a fifth railroad link between New York and Chicago. He instructed Kuhn Loeb to buy up the outstanding shares of three connecting lines—the Lehigh Valley, Western Maryland, and Wabash. When Samuel Rea of the Pennsylvania learned that his railroad's banker was financing a potential rival, he was furious and demanded a showdown with Loree and Kahn.

"In those days," Buttenwieser noted, "you did business primarily with the president or chairman of the board, whichever was the chief executive officer."

Things came to a head one Saturday morning—in an era when all of Wall Street worked a five-and-a-half-day week, with at least one Kuhn Loeb partner reporting for duty on Saturday. Kahn, a great patron of the Metropolitan Opera, had come to the office that morning also to mediate a dispute between the Met's general manager, Giulio Gatti-Casazza, and one of his prima donnas. His solution was to put Rea in one room, Loree in another, Gatti-Casazza in a third, and the soprano in a fourth.

"Mr. Kahn would sort of commute from one room to another," Buttenwieser recalled. "And I must say, he satisfied all four."

Kahn taught Buttenwieser that sometimes a banker's best work is done, not with his brains or his hands, but with his buttocks: "You make more money with the seat of your pants than you do with the top of your head: Buy good securities and sit on them."

He also showed Buttenwieser how to answer authors who press their unwanted books upon friends: "Let me teach you something: If you get a book that you don't want to read, but the author—a friend of yours—thinks you should, just quote something from the last or next to last chapter, so the author will think you read it."

Throughout the mid-1920s Buttenwieser, primarily because of his fluency in German, worked mostly in Kuhn Loeb's foreign department. In 1927 he was assigned to New Court, Rothschild's London headquarters, and later to M. M. Warburg & Sons in Hamburg, where Kuhn Loeb also maintained correspondent offices.

"From 1922 through 1927 there was a great deal of international arbitrage, especially in gold." Arbitrage is the simultaneous buying and selling of stock or commodity on different markets to profit on the minute variations in price. Buttenwieser found himself trading not only in British pounds and French francs, but in Dutch gulden and even Greek drachmas and Romanian crowns.

Because of the time difference between Europe and New York, some of Buttenwieser's Wall Street rivals slept with bedside telephones to receive early morning calls—a rare luxury in an age when most American homes did not have a single phone.

"We didn't believe in that," he said of Kuhn Loeb, "because the people who were young enough to get up that early would find that the major factotums of the firm didn't arrive till somewhat later, and we weren't allowed to take positions of over $1 million without the approval of someone more senior than I was at the time."

In 1927 Buttenwieser—not yet a partner—was promoted to head of the foreign department and dispatched to Bremen, where he arranged the financing for North German Lloyd's construction of the *Bremen* and *Europa*, which soon became the fastest liners to ply the North Atlantic. Buttenwieser conducted the negotiations in German, while Chester McLain of Cravath, Henderson & deGersdorff (now Cravath, Swaine & Moore), Kuhn Loeb's Wall Street law firm, drafted the documents and McLain's wife Sally coded them for cabling to New York. The head of North German Lloyd was so impressed with Buttenwieser's work that he promised the young banker free passage in the *Bremen*'s presidential suite for his honeymoon.

Trouble was, Buttenwieser had not yet found a bride—nor even a bride-to-be. But the following year, dressed in white tie and tails at a six-day bicycle race at Madison Square Garden, he proposed to Helen Lehman, daughter of Arthur Lehman, one of the heads of Lehman Brothers. It was to be a Kuhn Loeb–Lehman combination that preceded the formal merger by nearly fifty years.

During their engagement, Lehman Brothers was about to float shares in its investment trust, Lehman Corporation. Otto Kahn, who wanted to be cut in on the offering, summoned Buttenwieser to his office.

"You go down the street," Kahn told him, "and tell your future father-in-law that I want to get ten thousand shares of that stock, and if not, the engagement is off."

Kahn got the stock, and Buttenwieser and Helen Lehman got married on October 3, 1929—a date that had to be moved up several days because the *Bremen*'s first eastbound crossing had been rescheduled.

"There were the obvious snickering questions, such as, 'When may we look forward to the baby?' We took quite a lot of ribbing," Buttenwieser recalled. But, "I call myself blessed every day since then."

The newlyweds sailed for Europe in the presidential suite. Before the voyage was over, however, someone discovered a clause in the maritime regulations forbidding free passage. Buttenwieser was forced to fork over the minimum fare—$197.50.

Another German client was Eugenio Cardinal Pacelli, then nuncio in Bavaria and later Pope Pius XII, for whom Kuhn Loeb invested $200,000 in United States Steel. A few years later, after Pacelli had become the Vatican Secretary of State, the SEC launched an investigation into Kuhn Loeb's trading in Big Steel and demanded a list of its customers. In an attempt to avoid publicity and possible embarrassment to the Vatican, Kuhn Loeb provided the commission with a list arranged, not by dollar amount, as customary, but alphabetically, giving only last name and initials— "Pacelli, E. C."

"And it got by," Buttenwieser boasted.

During this period Buttenwieser also had dealings—briefly— with Ivar Kreuger, the Swedish "Match King." Kreuger came to Kuhn Loeb to present a proposition for financing his latest venture. Buttenwieser and Leonard Kessing, then head of the foreign department, sat in on his meeting with Mortimer Schiff.

After Kreuger left, Schiff asked Buttenwieser for his opinion.

"Two things," he replied. "First, methinks the maiden doth protest too much.

"Second, I would have been much more impressed if at some point he had said, 'Now this particular venture went bad.' . . . I just don't believe that anyone in business bats a thousand."

Kessing chimed in with a similar assessment.

"I couldn't agree with you two more," Schiff said. "This is not for us."

Kreuger's house of cards collapsed in 1932, and he shot himself in a Paris hotel room. The Boston banking firm, Lee, Higginson & Co., which had backed Kreuger after Kuhn Loeb backed out, was brought to its knees and never fully recovered its stature among investment houses.

On another occasion, Mortimer Schiff was working with Thomas L. Chadbourne, the prominent attorney, in what turned out to be an abortive attempt to put together a Little Steel amalgamation, just as J. P. Morgan had done with U.S. Steel three decades before. Seven companies were to be merged into a new North American Steel Corporation. Buttenwieser and Frederick Warburg labored through the night preparing a multicolored chart—showing what each of the seven companies would contribute to the merged entity—for Schiff to use in his presentation. Schiff came into the office the next morning, took one look at their handiwork, and, according to Buttenwieser, "turned every color of the zodiac." Then he exclaimed:

"Damn it, Freddy! Didn't you and Ben know I'm color-blind?" Buttenwieser hadn't.

Although Buttenwieser was still a salaried employee and not yet a partner, he was doing well financially. Times were good, the market was booming, and the bonuses just kept coming.

But the dam was about to burst. A few saw it coming—among them, Buttenwieser's father. During the summer of 1929 he phoned his son from his summer retreat at Poland Springs, Maine:

"Sell every security I own—stocks and bonds—and put all the proceeds into tax-exempt securities. This speculative bubble must soon burst."

The elder Buttenwieser escaped disaster, but his sons were not so prescient. Clarence and Benjamin Buttenwieser wound up owing $250,000 each after the crash. Their father made good the debt, but he told them:

"This is it. My advice to you is: Don't ever have a margin account. And what is more. You can have any debt you want to in the future, but don't come to me again to help pay it. That's it."

"It was a lifelong lesson to both of us," Buttenwieser said. "I've never bought five cents worth of anything on margin since. And I never will."

Buttenwieser became a partner of Kuhn, Loeb & Co. on January 1, 1932. It was not a propitious time to reach the pinnacle of the profession. The depression was nearing its depths, and banks were bolting their doors. Soon the Pecora investigation would destroy the public's perception of the morality—and even the intelligence —of the financial community. Buttenwieser himself spent a day before the Senate committee defending Kuhn Loeb's handling of a $90 million Chilean bond issue in the 1920s. And on March 4, 1933, Franklin Delano Roosevelt took office proclaiming that "the money changers have fled their high seats in the temple of our civilization." Then came the torrent of New Deal legislation—the Glass-Steagall Act, the Securities Act of 1933, the Securities Exchange Act of 1934, and more—all of which changed the course of investment banking.

"The ground rules were completely different," Buttenwieser said. Indeed, he divides investment banking into two phases—before the SEC and after the SEC.

Buttenwieser, a Democrat, was one of the few on Wall Street who welcomed the New Deal's securities legislation, which he called "a very great boon and of great advantage to the securities industry, to the public, to the borrowers, to the lenders, to all concerned.

"Of course, they changed the concept of the securities business by supplanting the principle of *caveat emptor* with the principle of *caveat vendor,*" he continued. "From 1933–34 the seller had to beware, rather than the buyer. Up to the time of the Securities Act, the prospectus describing the security being offered was rather sketchy. Therefore, the public wasn't any too certain as to what they were buying. Also, the rules concerning trading pools and the like were drastically changed. Therefore, I think the securities business, in general, is in much better shape now than it was then."

For Kuhn Loeb, Glass-Steagall had little impact. The firm had not engaged in commercial banking. Mainly as a convenience to clients, it had maintained a few deposit accounts, which were easily closed or transferred to commercial banks. Buttenwieser worked out a scheme whereby Kuhn Loeb could have gone into commercial banking, while spinning off an investment-banking subsidiary, but it never materialized.

The Securities and Securities Exchange acts were another matter, for they enmeshed underwriters—and their lawyers—in a flood of paperwork that has scarcely subsided in the fifty years since. Buttenwieser recalled Kuhn Loeb's handling of a Republic Steel issue in the mid-1930s.

"By this time we were confronted with the requirements of the Securities Act and the Securities Exchange Act," he said. "To illustrate our frustration at all the meticulous requirements of the SEC —no matter what we wrote, we'd always get a 'deficiency letter'— we decided to pile all the documents, one on top of the other, right in front of the entrance to the SEC. We then took a photo of the pile with Tom Girdler, [chairman] of Republic Steel, standing right beside this mountain of papers, which towered over Girdler, who was only about five-feet-six. And we submitted the photo with the documents."

Buttenwieser couldn't recall whether or not the ploy worked.

During the depression stock issues were far fewer than they had been during the boom years of the Roaring Twenties, and competition for them became keener. Halsey, Stuart & Co. broke the gentlemen's agreement among investment bankers by raiding a rival's client—the Chicago & Northwestern Railway—saying, in effect, "Whatever Kuhn Loeb offers for the issue, we'll pay more."

"And they were read out of that group in no uncertain terms," Buttenwieser said—an assertion that lends credence to Harold L. Stuart's testimony as the government's chief witness in the antitrust trial.

Kuhn Loeb got other Northwestern issues, but never again included Halsey Stuart in their syndication.

"Since then," Buttenwieser continued, "competitive bidding for railroad and public utility security issues has become the usual procedure, but via sealed, fixed, stated bids—not 'we'll pay higher,' which is tantamount to public open auction."

During this period Buttenwieser also had some slight dealings with the Duke of Windsor, but he was not impressed with the quondam king: "From what little I know of [him] and have heard about his spouse, I surely wouldn't have wanted them as acquaintances, let alone as friends."

While bearing and raising four children, Helen Buttenwieser attended NYU law school. Upon graduation, she became an associate at Cravath—one of the first women at a major Wall Street law firm. It surely did not hurt that her husband was a partner at one of Cravath's major clients—or her uncle the governor of New York.

Buttenwieser recalled how he'd once worked until 2 A.M. with Cravath's Alexander Henderson drafting a "declaration of intent" for some Kuhn Loeb transaction. When he finally got home, his wife was not there. Nor did she return for several hours more. It turned out that she'd been among the Cravath associates drafted to plod through the night finishing the paperwork on the declaration of intent. The question at Cravath, she told her husband, was, "Which son of a bitch at Kuhn Loeb figured that out?"

"And she said to me," he added, " 'You know, your name came into prominent discussion.' "

Like her husband, Mrs. Buttenwieser still remains active—in her case, as a senior partner in the midtown law firm, London & Buttenwieser.

By the end of the 1930s Buttenwieser had soured on the Roosevelt administration. "My greatest criticism of the New Deal is that, for the first time in our history, it has sought to array class against class," he said at the time. In the 1940 Presidential election he supported Wendell Willkie, and he remained a Republican for the next dozen years.

When the Japanese bombed Pearl Harbor, Buttenwieser, over-age at forty-one, immediately volunteered for active duty. He had been a leader in William Allen White's Committee to Defend America by Aiding the Allies and felt that one who had urged others to enter the conflict had an obligation to serve himself.

Commissioned a Navy lieutenant, he served as second in command of a dive-bomber squadron aboard the aircraft carrier *Lexington* and flew several missions as a tail gunner. His unit saw combat at Guam, Palau, Saipan-Tinian, and Iwo Jima, receiving a Bronze Star citation. Buttenwieser was discharged as a commander.

He returned to Kuhn Loeb after the war and was named vice chairman of the steering committee that coordinated the seventeen investment banks' defense in the government's antitrust action. To Buttenwieser it was a classic case of what John W. Davis once termed "monopoly by addition": "If one adds up enough firms doing business in one industry, their total volume, ipso facto, will constitute a monopoly."

By the time the case came to trial, however, Buttenwieser was gone, off on a second stint of government service. In 1949 John J. McCloy appointed Buttenwieser as his assistant high commissioner for Germany. McCloy was a Cravath alumnus with whom Buttenwieser had worked in the 1920s and 1930s.

"I can't marshal enough superlatives to do him justice," the banker said. "He's just a great guy and a great friend."

"Men should go into public service during their careers, not after them," Buttenwieser told columnist Sylvia Porter. "I've made enough money out of this country. It's time I gave something back in return. And I want to get into government while I'm still young enough to be of some use."

Buttenwieser flew to Europe in a DC4—"I could have swum almost as fast"—and helped supervise Germany's economic recovery and transition to democracy. "The most interesting two-and-a-half years I spent in my life," he recalled. But many criticized McCloy's administration for not pressing denazification enough and for restoring industrial cartels like Krupp and I. G. Farben.

From another flank, Buttenwieser fielded flak from the McCarthyites when his wife became one of Alger Hiss's appellate attorneys, but he stood up for Hiss's right to counsel—and her right to be it. He also had a celebrated run-in with McCarthy aides Roy Cohn and G. David Schine, who managed to have Theodore Kaghan, one of the high commission's press officers, sacked—supposedly for past leftist associations, but primarily because Kaghan had called them "junketeering gumshoes."

Years later, at a Columbia University function, when Buttenwieser was introduced to Cohn—a fellow alumnus—he refused to shake hands. He cited the Kaghan case as his reason.

In 1952 Buttenwieser initially backed Dwight D. Eisenhower for President, but when the general deleted a statement of support for George C. Marshall from a prepared speech in order to appease McCarthy, he switched to Stevenson and has remained in the Democratic fold since.

Buttenwieser returned to Kuhn Loeb in 1953 but as a limited partner. He decided to devote most of his time to charity work—"to pay back this city for some of what it has given me." Long active in the Federation of Jewish Philanthropies—he had served as its president in the 1930s, as his son Lawrence would in the 1970s

—he continued to work with the umbrella organization. He also served as a trustee of the Police Foundation, Charles H. Revson Foundation, Lenox Hill Hospital, New York Philharmonic, and Columbia University, which awarded him an honorary doctorate in 1977. On the political front, Governor Averell Harriman named him as a commissioner of the Port Authority of New York & New Jersey. In business, he continued part-time at Kuhn Loeb and served as a director of Revlon, Chock Full O' Nuts, and Tishman Realty & Construction.

Buttenwieser's method was to work quietly, behind the scenes. But his wife hit the headlines in 1963 when she forfeited $60,000 bail she had posted for Dr. Robert Soblen, a convicted Soviet spy. Facing life imprisonment, Soblen jumped bail and fled to Israel. Arrested and extradited, he committed suicide on the flight back.

In 1977 Buttenwieser watched from the wings, while his more active junior partners negotiated Kuhn Loeb's merger into Lehman Brothers.

"It was a natural fit," he observed. "We supported and supplemented each other. I think it's been a happy marriage, as far as I can judge at this point."

Now in his eighties, Buttenwieser remains mentally alert and physically active. In his younger years he was an ardent skier and tennis and squash player. He still works out regularly and walks to the office every day—which he regrets is a much shorter walk since he has moved from Lehman Brothers Kuhn Loeb's new headquarters at 55 Water Street to its uptown annex at 660 Madison Avenue. Even in the harshest winter weather he does not wear an overcoat.

From his perspective of more than sixty years in investment banking Buttenwieser sees the industry in an era of increasing consolidation and conglomeration.

"I think that's becoming increasingly necessary," he noted, "because we've got to be what are termed full-service firms, which means we've got to have brokerage, investment banking, international banking, and—less essential though often desirable—money management investment advisory.

"Investment banking subsumes the purchase and sale of practically every type of security you can think of—and they're becoming increasingly varied. There are industrial securities, public utility securities, conglomerate securities, U.S. and foreign government and agency securities, state and municipal and their agency securities, and so ad infinitum. All this requires a large staff and subsistence capital.

"Also, for the distribution of securities of any of these entities a large, active trading department is essential, because many of these new issues are nowadays sold in large measure to life insurance companies, pension funds, savings banks, savings and loan associations, and investment trusts, which are the chief reservoirs of investment funds. . . .

"So that's why I think these full-service firms are needed," he continued. "Also, there's a lot more to investment banking than what I've just described. There is an increasing use of investment bankers to governments, governmental and state agencies, corporations, etc. One of my major activities is being financial adviser to corporations on a retainer or ad hoc basis.

"And you've got to have the backup. You've got to have a large research staff . . . I did mention the international part of our business, which I think will continue its growth. . . . Commercial paper is also a significant part of our day-to-day activity. Also, trading in puts and calls, futures, or options to buy or sell stocks or commodities, is also growing.

"Some of this, I think, is overdone, because there is even trading in futures on futures," he added. "I fear some of this far-out trading may have some atmospheric fallout from Las Vegas or Atlantic City to Wall Street. . . .

"I think there will be more mergers," Buttenwieser concluded, predicting that Wall Street could wind up with perhaps eight to ten full-service investment houses, possibly themselves parts of even larger financial supermarkets.

IV

A BEVY OF BANKERS

Time was, investment bankers were bald, portly, and sported walrus mustaches. They sat around in overstuffed chairs, smoking cigars and drinking port. They worked traditional bankers' hours but served a long apprenticeship; few became partners before middle age.

Today, investment banking is a game for young men on the go. Men—there are still only a handful of women in the profession—in their thirties may earn incomes well into six figures. They also must work long hours under intense pressure. Many burn out before fifty.

The gallery that follows is an arbitrary selection—not necessarily the best or the richest or the most powerful. Rather, it is designed to be representative, to illustrate the variety of the breed—investment bankers in their many manifestations.

Here, then, in alphabetical order, a bevy of bankers:

They are not listed in Who's Who in America. They don't give interviews and their portraits rarely appear in the papers. They are ascetic, all business, rarely going out—and certainly not to the glittering night spots. After sixty years on Wall Street their very names are all but unknown, except to a handful of financial insiders.

Yet they are affluent enough to be included in *Forbes'* listing of the four hundred wealthiest Americans. Their investment house is among the richest on Wall Street. And they have put together headline-making deals worth hundreds of millions of dollars.

They are **Charles R. Allen Jr.**, his brother **Herbert Allen**, and Herbert's son, **Herbert Anthony Allen Jr.** The phrases used to describe them include "obsessively secretive," "publicity shy," "reclusive," while their firms have been depicted as "shrouded by a passion for privacy . . . so Byzantine are its inner workings and so eccentric its folkways."

This much is known: Charles Allen was born in 1903 in a coldwater flat on Manhattan's Columbus Avenue. Herbert followed five years later. Charles began his career on Wall Street as a runner at the age of fifteen. In 1923—with $1,000, a desk, and a telephone—he founded Allen & Co. and started trading in bonds. Herbert joined in 1928. By 1929 they had made $1 million—which they promptly lost in the stock market crash.

Undaunted, they pressed on. Herbert concentrated on running the office, while dabbling in oil and mining deals. Charles, guiding genius of the company, specialized in medical and electronics stocks. His modus operandi was to seek out small companies with a potential for growth, invest heavily, guide their development—and wait for the stock to soar.

Forbes said that Charles Allen "may be the canniest investor of all time." Herbert Jr. was less uncertain: "My uncle is the greatest picker of stocks in the history of equity markets."

Charles Allen's greatest coup came in 1958 with an $800,000 investment in a small pharmaceutical concern called Syntex Corp. Within a few months Syntex became the nation's largest manufacturer of the Pill. Ten years later Allen & Co. sold $48 million worth of Syntex holdings—while still retaining shares worth another $50 million!

Now semiretired, Charles Allen is short and wiry. He neither smokes nor drinks, never takes a vacation, and seldom ventures far from his office or his suite at the posh Hotel Carlyle. He is cold and reclusive. "Shaking his hand is like clasping an electrode," *Fortune* noted.

A rare venture into the public eye came in 1978, after the New York *Times Magazine* dubbed him "the godfather of the new Hollywood," implying that he had Mafia connections from a long past investment in a Bahamian gambling casino. Allen's Hollywood deal making included buying RKO from Howard Hughes and selling it to General Tire & Rubber, as well as buying Seven Arts and merging it into Warner Brothers, then merging Warner Brothers–Seven Arts with National Kinney to form the conglomerate that is now Warner Communications. Allen threatened the *Times* with a $150 million libel suit, and the paper was forced to print a rare retraction.

Herbert Jr.,* two years out of Williams College, came on the scene in 1964, when Charles and Herbert Sr. decided to spin off their investment-banking operation to their children and some veteran employees for the bargain basement price of $1 million. Herbert Jr. and the founders' four other children—none active in the business—bought 51 percent interest in this new Allen & Co., Inc. Around the office, Allen & Co., still controlled by Charles and Herbert Sr., is called "the partnership"; Allen & Co., Inc., headed by Herbert Jr., is "the corporation."

The younger Allen once described himself as "a throwback to the entrepreneurs of one hundred years ago." He turned the corporation into a miniature of the partnership, while he, in many ways, became a carbon copy of his uncle. He keeps to a spartan regimen, rising at 5:30 A.M. and retiring before ten. Like his uncle he is a nonsmoker—he won't even permit an ashtray in the office, a touch that often hastens the pace of decision making—and his consumption of alcohol is limited to a glass or two of wine with dinner. Divorced and the father of four, for several years he was seen in the company of glamour girls like Jennifer O'Neill and heiresses like Amanda Burden, stepdaughter of CBS Chairman William S. Paley. He now dates "exclusively" Ann Reinking, star of Broadway's *Dancin'* and Hollywood's *All That Jazz*.

The corporation has a capital of some $30 million, about half its own, the rest from a roster of clients that includes Harvard University. Unlike other Wall Street houses, Allen requires its traders and bankers to pay their own expenses—including travel, secretarial salaries, and office furnishings—and they are required to put a stake of their own money into any deal they recommend. But Herbert Jr. calls the shots.

* Technically, Herbert A. Allen Jr., is not a "junior," since his father has no middle name, but they use the affixes to differentiate themselves.

Like his uncle, Herbert Jr. specializes in small, high-tech companies. An $850,000 investment in Genetic Systems grew to $3.3 million, and $350,000 in Tie/Communications netted $4 million in profits. Herbert Jr., the two senior Allens, and two "corporation" bankers teamed with a retired oilman named Reeves Lowenthal to form a concern to prospect for petroleum. Their combined stake in Allegheny & Western Energy Corp. was $100,000. By the time the company went public in 1981, their investment was worth $5 million.

Herbert Jr.'s most sensational deal came, not by putting together a small scientific concern for a "hot issue," but with a bold plunge into a supercolossal, publicly traded company—Columbia Pictures. In 1973, when Columbia teetered on the brink of bankruptcy, Allen & Co., Inc. bought a 6 percent stake in the studio—about $2.5 million worth—for about $4 a share.

It was enough to give Allen control of the company, and he promptly installed an Allen banker, Alan Hirshfield, as president. Hirshfield, in turn, picked a new chief of production, David Begelman. Under Begelman, Columbia started to turn out money-making movies like *Taxi Driver, The Deep,* and *Shampoo,* and the studio's stock edged upward.

In 1977 it turned out that Begelman had forged an endorsement on a $10,000 check supposedly issued to actor Cliff Robertson. More Begelman forgeries soon surfaced, and the question of what to do with him was up to Allen. The normally decisive Allen, known to make multimillion-dollar decisions in as little as thirty seconds, waffled. Begelman was out . . . then back in . . . finally out for good. The scandal, with its panorama of front office backbiting, should have been enough to put any company on the rocks. But . . .

Within a few weeks, one of Begelman's pet projects hit the screen—*Close Encounters of the Third Kind.* It proved to be one of the most successful movies of all time, and Columbia's stock soared. In 1981 Allen successfully fought off Kirk Kerkorian's bid to buy the studio for $50 a share. Most observers thought that Allen was crazy not to sell. Instead, he turned around and sold Columbia to Coca-Cola for $70 a share! On its $2.5 million investment Allen & Co., Inc. reaped a profit of $40 million. *Fortune* called it "a vindication of the way he ran a corporate show that often bordered on soap opera."

Once again, the Allens had prospered mightily by ignoring the rule book. But then, as Herbert Jr. once noted, "We don't play by Wall Street's rules. We're not members of the club."

The rumor swept Wall Street even before the market opened. By 10 A.M. the switchboard at Salomon Brothers was jammed with inquiry calls. By 10:20 the floor of the New York Stock Exchange was buzzing, and even though there was no official word, the Dow Jones industrial average was up five points. At 10:41 Salomon confirmed the rumor:

> SPECIAL NOTICE: Recent events in the economy and financial markets necessitate a fresh look at the prospects for U.S. interest rates. These events suggest that the present decline in interest rates will continue. . . .

The prose was scarcely scintillating, but the message was clear: **Henry Kaufman,** Salomon's chief economist, at long last, had predicted that interest rates would come down.

With that, the biggest buying binge in Wall Street history was underway. By the time the Big Board closed on Tuesday, August 17, 1982, more than 92 million shares had changed hands, and the Dow Jones index had shot up 38.81 points, its greatest one-day jump ever. The *Daily News* parodied *Variety*'s famous 1929 headline:

WALL STREET LAYS
A GOLDEN EGG

The buying frenzy continued—a record-shattering 132 million shares on Wednesday, though profit taking sent the Dow down nearly two points. The following week saw four successive days on which the volume exceeded 100 million shares, with Thursday's mark of 138 million breaking the week-old record. In nine trading days the Dow Jones average gained 91 points. Never in the history of Wall Street had so many spent so much on the say-so of one man.

Who was this Henry Kaufman? And what was his power to move otherwise prudent money managers?

To Wall Street bears, Kaufman and Albert Wojnilower, his opposite number at First Boston Corporation, were "Doctor Doom" and "Doctor Gloom." For years they had predicted that interest rates would go higher . . . and higher . . . and still higher, as government borrowing dried up the well of money available for private capital. Kaufman's predictions were uncannily accurate—so accurate that the market reacted accordingly. On at least a half-dozen occasions in 1980, '81, and '82 his pronouncements were followed immediately by stock market slumps. As the New York *Times* noted on January 6, 1982:

> Stock prices fell sharply yesterday after Henry Kaufman, an influential Wall Street economist, said that an economic recovery this year will be marred by another spurt in interest rates to record or near-record levels in the second half of 1982.

So when Kaufman, at long last, saw a rosy glow on the economic horizon, the bears were avid to become bulls. (First Boston had released Wojnilower's similar forecast the day before Kaufman's, but it did not have the same impact on the market.) Ironically, Kaufman's forecast that interest rates would fall was postulated, not on the nation's economic recovery, but on its continued recession. The traders chose not to notice it, but Henry Kaufman was still Doctor Gloom.

Kaufman was born in Germany in 1927, the only child of Jewish parents who fled to the United States a decade later. They settled in Manhattan's Washington Heights—a haven for German-Jewish refugees like Henry Kissinger's family—where Henry learned English and went to school. Although his father held a lowly job in a relative's meat-packing plant, it was a "given" that Henry would go on to college.

He studied economics at NYU and went on to get an M.S. from Columbia. In 1949 he went to work in the credit department of a neighborhood bank; within two years he was the credit manager. Meanwhile he studied nights for his Ph.D. in economics at NYU, learning to get by on five or six hours' sleep a night. In 1957, his doctorate in hand, he got a job in the research department of the

Federal Reserve Bank of New York and got married. He is now the father of three.

At the Fed, Kaufman met Charles Salomon, then a leading partner of his family's firm, and in 1961 Kaufman joined Salomon Brothers. He started in the research department under Sidney Homer. Among his tasks was preparing a weekly memo for Homer on the Fed's actions. His first consisted of a mere twelve typewritten lines. Word of Kaufman's insights spread through the firm, and other partners asked to see his memos. Soon, someone suggested that they be sent to Salomon's clients and customers. Thus, *Comments on Credit* was born—a weekly newsletter that now has a circulation of 13,000.

Kaufman became a Salomon partner in 1967, chief of research in 1972, and a member of the executive committee the same year. He now directs three research divisions with a total staff of ninety.

The immigrant economist first came to national notice in the early 1970s, when he kept predicting that interest rates would rise. In October 1974 he forecast that they would peak—and in two weeks they did. "I was fortunate," he said modestly. From 1977 to 1982 he forecast another upward trend, with occasional dips, but with each peak hitting a new high. Once again, he was dead on the mark.

"He has practically always been a bear," Harvard economist Otto Eckstein said in 1981. "And since the market has deteriorated for almost twenty years, he looks good."

"Henry Kaufman has done a Nobel Prize-winning job in catching some of the long-term trends," said Jay N. Woolworth of Bankers Trust. "Anyone who has a better than average record, like Henry, deserves a following."

Indeed, Kaufman soon became an economic guru with a cult following—which posed an ethical problem for Salomon Brothers: Since Kaufman's words had the power to move the market, were he and his partners entitled to act on advance knowledge of what he would say? "There probably ought to be an iron wall between him and his trading desk," said one Wall Street analyst.

Kaufman insisted that there is: "Any time I give a major speech or release a major document, we make an effort to synchronize its distribution very carefully to avoid any conflict of interest. Our salesmen and traders are not given an advance look."

And yet . . . In the days before Kaufman made his bullish projection on interest rates, Salomon reportedly bought $400 million worth of Treasury bond futures on the Chicago Board of Trade. Once Kaufman's prognostications became public, they zoomed in price. Unlike the stock or bond markets, futures trading does not carry strictures against the use of inside information—if Kaufman's forecasts were such—thus relieving Salomon of the necessity of facing the ethical question. Salomon, which has a public policy of not making public policy pronouncements, declined to comment on the report.

In the flesh, Kaufman is a short, balding man who favors elegantly tailored suits and large, gold-rimmed glasses. At the office he insists on being addressed as *"Doctor* Kaufman." He has no hobbies, other than work, although he has cultivated a taste for fine food and French wine. Salomon's sale to Phibro netted him $10.6 million—making him perhaps the world's richest economist—but he remains a workaholic. He has never taken a vacation of more than eight days. And he still rises before 6 A.M., arrives at the office at 7:30, and stays until 6 P.M. Weekends at his New Jersey home are devoted to research and writing, which he finds a lonely, agonizing discipline.

Nearly a year after he touched off the stampede of the big bull market, Kaufman agonized over new economic figures. The July 29, 1983, *Comments on Credit* predicted that demand for borrowed money would force federal interest rates back up from 9 1/2 percent to 10 or 11 percent. The market responded with a selling spree; in one day the Dow Jones industrial average plunged 17 1/8 points. Henry Kaufman had reverted to form.

They are the Odd Couple of investment banking, a Mutt-and-Jeff combination who seem more suited to comic strips than to corporate suites. **Joseph Perella** stands a rail thin six-foot-four and is nearly egg-bald. Always impeccably dressed, he is garrulous, ebullient, and down-to-earth. **Bruce Wasserstein** is short, tubby, and has a shock of wild reddish hair—a face and figure uncannily akin to those of Metropolitan opera conductor James Levine. He can be brash, rough-edged, irritating. Wasserstein thrives under pressure; Perella gets nervous backaches that have to be treated by acupuncture. Together, they head the mergers-and-acquisitions department of First Boston Corporation and constitute the hottest takeover team in town.

Their backgrounds are as dissimilar as their physiques and personalities. Perella, born in 1942, grew up "a crazy kid from Newark," the son of Italian immigrants. He started on Wall Street as a $6,500-a-year accountant, toting municipal bonds in the third subbasement of a brokerage house. Bored and dissatisfied with his prospects, at the age of twenty-eight he hied himself to Harvard Business School, paying for his first year of graduate study out of his meager savings. Goldman, Sachs & Co. gave him a scholarship so he could finish his second. But Goldman Sachs didn't offer him a job, so in 1972 Perella signed on at First Boston for $18,000 a year.

A year later, after being told that he was "too old for a regular career path here," Perella took over First Boston's fledgling mergers-and-acquisitions department. The firm had little taste for such work, having been badly burned by the Bangor Punta case. First Boston had handled Bangor Punta's successful bid for Piper Aircraft, but Chris-Craft, the rejected suitor, sued and won a $38 million judgment, most of it First Boston's liability. The award eventually was overturned by the U.S. Supreme Court, but "M&A was a dirty word around here in the early 1970s," Perella noted. However, he persuaded George Shinn, First Boston's new chairman, that there was a future in it.

If Perella was a late bloomer, Wasserstein was a whiz kid. Six years Perella's junior and the son of a well-to-do New York textile manufacturer, by the age of twenty-four he had breezed through the University of Michigan, earned both law and M.B.A. degrees from Harvard, as well as a graduate degree in economics from Cambridge University. He became a "raider" for Ralph Nader, concluding one study by asking: "Whatever happened to antitrust?" Within a few years he would be brokering the biggest corporate mergers in history.

Wasserstein's views have "matured," but, "A lot of those comments are still valid. The world has changed. The posture of General Motors isn't as awesome as it had been. I never was—and never purported to be—a knee-jerk anything."

In 1976 Wasserstein was an associate at the Wall Street law firm of Cravath, Swaine & Moore assigned to work on Combustion Engineering's $66 million purchase of Gray Tool. Perella was the First Boston banker on the deal. Despite their differences, the chemistry clicked. Perella asked Cravath to assign Wasserstein to the First Boston account, but the firm—in its prearranged rotation—shifted Wasserstein to finance. So Perella made Wasserstein an offer he couldn't refuse: Come to First Boston at double his $50,000 salary.

"M&A had four people," Wasserstein recalled. "We had no transactions for six months."

Then two plums fell into the team's lap. First Boston represented Kennecott in its acquisition of Carborundum, and Combustion Engineering on its takeover of Vetco. The two deals netted First Boston $3 million in fees in a single month—as opposed to a measly $100,000 for its years of travail with Bangor Punta. Sniffing the scent of profit, First Boston beefed up the department to eighteen men, and in 1979 Wasserstein became cochairman with Perella.

Perella is the out-front man who usually deals with the clients; Wasserstein, the behind-the-scenes strategist. Every takeover battle calls for a different game plan. "You have to throw out the cookie cutter," Wasserstein once said. "Tactics in this business are like the old child's game of rock, paper, and scissors. Every tactic is designed for a particular situation, and the tactics are changing rapidly."

In 1981 Perella and Wasserstein played key roles in the two biggest corporate mergers in American history. First, they advised white knight Du Pont on its rescue of Conoco from the clutches of Mobil. Hard on the heels of that contest, they represented target Marathon Oil, fending off Mobil once again, until they finally found a white knight in U.S. Steel.

First Boston received $14 million in fees from Du Pont and a record $17.9 million from Marathon Oil. Though their department was only half the size, in 1981 Perella and Wasserstein actually outpaced the takeover trendsetter, Morgan Stanley. Merger billings —which did not include the Marathon fee—accounted for a major portion of First Boston's 1981 record earnings of $46.3 million and 1982's new record, $93.4 million.

In 1982 Perella and Wasserstein received last-minute calls for relief pitching in two more titanic takeover battles. Along with Lehman Brothers Kuhn Loeb, they helped Cities Service repulse Mesa Petroleum's raid, arranged its abortive acquisition by Gulf, and then led the subsequent search for a white knight that finally resulted in Cities Service's purchase by Occidental Petroleum.

Before the Cities Service contest was concluded, they were called into action again—this time by Bendix to assist Salomon Brothers in what became a four-way contest among Martin Marietta, United Technologies, and Allied Corp. (See Chapter 7.) Bendix, which had launched the battle by bidding for Martin Marietta, encountered a tenacious "Pac-Man defense" and had to be rescued by white knight Allied.

"Seventy-five percent of our business comes from people who are not our clients," Wasserstein noted. "What we sell is, basically, 'We do the job better.' "

By 1982 First Boston's mergers-and-acquisitions department had so much business that Perella and Wasserstein no longer were able to work in tandem on every case, while their administrative load became so heavy—the staff had grown to forty-four—that they added a third codirector of the department—Bill G. Lambert, known throughout the office as "The Legend."

Lambert, a thirty-five-year-old high school classmate of Wasserstein's, is a bushy-bearded former securities analyst who frequently shows up at the office wearing a plaid shirt and blue jeans. Some of First Boston's more staid elders were put off by his appearance, but Shinn said: "That young man has earned a lot of money for this firm. He can wear whatever he wants." And to show his support, Perella himself grew a beard.

Lambert's position is unique in investment banking, even in the freewheeling world of mergers and acquisitions—"creative director," a title that seems more appropriate for an advertising agency. While Wasserstein plans the strategy and Perella executes it, Lambert selects takeover targets for clients—and potential clients.

It takes a killer instinct to succeed—even survive—in the cutthroat world of corporate-takeover wars. Dominating Joseph Perella's corner office forty-two stories above Park Avenue is a painting of a shark—all jaws. It's the symbol of the breed.

When he was booted out of President Nixon's cabinet after the 1972 election and eased into exile as foreign trade representative, **Peter G. Peterson** explained that he had flunked the physical: "I'm too fat at the calves. I can't click my heels fast enough." Within a few months he had a far loftier perch from which to watch the wheels of international finance—as chairman of what is now Lehman Brothers Kuhn Loeb.

The son of Greek immigrant parents—the name originally was Petropolous—Peter George Peterson grew up working at his father's restaurant in Kearney, Nebraska, and went on to the local state teachers college. After a year he jumped to MIT, but soon realized he lacked spatial perception and dropped out. He finished at Northwestern University, graduating *magna cum laude.*

His business career started with Market Facts, Inc., an advertising research organization, while he studied nights for an M.B.A. at the University of Chicago. In 1953 he went to McCann Erickson, the giant advertising agency, and before long was a vice president of the company and general manager of the Chicago office.

One of McCann Erickson's clients was Bell & Howell, the optics and electronics company. The up-and-coming Peterson attracted the attention of another boy wonder, Charles Percy, who had become president of Bell & Howell at the age of thirty. Percy found that Peterson was "a brilliant and creative mind and a thinker about the future who could project an idea out to its ultimate conclusion twenty years hence."

In 1958 Percy persuaded Peterson to leave the ad game and join Bell & Howell as executive vice president. When Percy stepped down in 1961 to pursue a political career—he was elected to the U.S. Senate five years later—Peterson succeeded him as president and chief executive officer at the age of thirty-four. In time, he became Bell & Howell's chairman. He was an outspoken advocate of civil rights, which caused several Southern communities to threaten boycotts of Bell & Howell products.

One of Peterson's professors at the University of Chicago had been George Shultz—now the nation's Secretary of State. In 1971 Shultz, then Nixon's Labor Secretary, recommended Peterson for a White House post, as assistant to the President for International Economic Affairs. Peterson played a key role in persuading Nixon to devalue the dollar and to impose wage and price controls.

Within a year he was promoted to Secretary of Commerce—replacing Maurice Stans, who had resigned to head the fund-raising for Nixon's reelection campaign. Before long, Nixon was telling

Peterson that he was the greatest Secretary of Commerce since Herbert Hoover.

But there was a flippant side to Peterson that alienated Nixon and the Berlin Wall—Haldeman and Ehrlichman—that surrounded him. He once told Nixon that "the rocks in my head fill up the holes in yours." "Nor did Commerce Secretary Peter Peterson's flirtation with 'the Georgetown cocktail party set' endear him to the President," William Safire observed. Peterson was too friendly with the "enemy." He had listened to soundings from CBS about succeeding Frank Stanton as the network's president. He was a crony of liberal columnist Tom Braden and his wife Joan. Worse, he had attended a dinner party at the home of Washington *Post* publisher Katharine Graham. "With that," Theodore H. White noted, "Peterson was out."

He had a half-dozen offers from industry, including two to head aluminum companies, but he couldn't conceive of devoting the rest of his career to a single product. Wall Street was much more attractive. He considered offers from Salomon Brothers and Lazard Frères before settling on Lehman Brothers for his "fifth career."

Peterson clearly was being groomed for eventual leadership, but it came sooner than anyone expected. Five weeks after his arrival, at a midnight meeting at George W. Ball's duplex apartment at the U.N. Plaza, the nine senior partners picked Peterson as their new chairman.

"Lehman was in a real crunch," said one observer. "The operation fell down completely." "Lehman was like a wolf pack," said another. "They weren't pulling together." A third called it "a jungle."

P.G.P—as he quickly became known from the signature on the steady stream of memos flowing from his office—started knocking heads. "Peterson tamed and unified a temperamental and individualistic band of investment bankers," *Fortune* observed. "He introduced management techniques, such as cost accounting, that were new to the business. He fired people who failed to perform and brought in capable younger bankers." He functioned less as a traditional investment banker like Harold Stanley than as a corporate administrator like Harold Geneen of ITT. Like Geneen, he soon started empire building.

In 1978 Peterson engineered Lehman's merger with Kuhn, Loeb

& Co. As he had five years before, P.G.P. immediately started lopping heads. Some two hundred employees—most of them Kuhn Loeb alumni, including several partners—got the ax, while others were demoted. For Peterson, the prize in the merger was Kuhn Loeb's international division, one of the few areas were Lehman was weak and Kuhn Loeb was strong. The following year he engineered another acquisition—Sonneblick-Goldman Corp., which put L.B.K.L. into the real estate business.

Wall Street's "fast track" took its personal toll. After more than twenty years and five children, his marriage broke up. He remarried Joan Ganz Cooney, creator of *Sesame Street*.

Peterson is a dark-complexioned man with straight, dark-brown hair. He wears horn-rimmed glasses and speaks with a deep, almost gruff voice. Critics have commented on his propensity for namedropping—especially that of his old White House colleague Henry Kissinger.

On the political front, Peterson organized a Bi-Partisan Budget Appeal—headed by six former cabinet members and endorsed by some five hundred former public officials, educators, lawyers, bankers, and businessmen, calling for a $25 billion cut in defense spending and $60 billion less for nondefense items—as well as a $60 billion boost in taxes!

"The federal budget is now out of control," they warned. "It is primed to generate immense deficits, year after year, for decades ahead—deficits far larger than any in our history. This fiscal course is senseless."

In 1983, after ten years on the job, Peterson decided to share the load. Henceforth, according to the announcement, he and President Lewis L. Glucksman would split the title and duties of Lehman's CEO—chief executive officer. Peterson stressed that this did not mean a step-up in his outside activities: "Lew Glucksman and I both have every indication of spending the rest of our careers working together at Lehman Brothers."

Only two months later, in a power ploy that stunned Wall Street, Glucksman seized sole command of the firm. He reportedly told Peterson that he had devoted his whole life to Lehman Brothers and wasn't satisfied with sharing leadership. Instead of squelching the threat, rallying support among the partners or battling back,

Peterson surrendered without a fight.*On July 26, almost ten years to the day since he assumed leadership of Lehman Brothers, Peterson announced that he was stepping down as chairman and co-chief executive officer, phasing out his departure between October and January, to join Los Angeles financier Eli Jacobs in merchant banking—"the investment of money in promising businesses."

It was as if the heavy had said to Gary Cooper, "This place ain't big enough for the both of us"—and Cooper meekly boarded the next stagecoach out of town. But no cowpoke ever rode off into the sunset with $15 million stuffed in his wallet—the settlement in equity, bonuses and promised investment in his new venture that Peterson reportedly received when he left Lehman.

He's been called "Felix the Fixer," "the Wizard of Lazard," "the Henry Kissinger of the financial world." He's short, dark, wiry, and speaks with a staccato, high-pitched voice. He's often casually clad, even at the office or away counseling clients. Hardly the image of the traditional investment banker. But then, as one financial writer observed, "Every time Felix Rohatyn gets his name in the paper, the traditional investment bankers cringe."

They must be doing a lot of cringing, for **Felix Rohatyn** (pronounced roe-a-tin) probably gets his name in the papers more than any investment banker in town.

He was born in Vienna of Russian-Jewish parents in 1928. His father had what is described as "a small credit business"—that is, he was a moneylender. After Hitler's *Anschluss* the family fled to France, where the senior Rohatyn managed a brewery. When the Nazis overran France, the family fled again—with young Felix stuffing their hoard of gold coins into toothpaste tubes—first slipping across the border to Spain, then, via Casablanca and Rio de Janeiro, to the United States, where they settled in New York.

Felix, quickly Americanized, studied physics at Middlebury, a small college in Vermont, and had every intention of pursuing a

* One of Glucksman's first moves was commissioning retiring Brigadier General Peter M. Dawkins to head Lehman's public finance group, an area in which the firm traditionally was weak. "Pete" Dawkins bore a name more familiar to readers of sports pages than of stock tables. As captain of West Point's 1958 football team, he was an all-American halfback and winner of the Heisman Trophy. Whether the newcomer to Wall Street could run broken-field through the "jungle" to which Lehman reverted after the Glucksman-Peterson showdown remained to be seen.

scientific career. Then he took a summer job at Lazard Frères & Co. Except for a stint of Army service during the Korean War, he's never worked anywhere else.

Despite its name, Lazard is an American firm, not the American branch of a European one; Lazard's Paris and London offices are the branches. The firm was founded by Lazare, Alexandre, and Simon Lazard as a dry-goods business in New Orleans in 1848. Later they moved to San Francisco, branched into banking, moved again to New York, and finally opened offices overseas.

Lazard's European image was enhanced by its leadership for nearly forty years by the late André Meyer, a courtly Frenchman of the old school. Adept at investments, currency exchange, and international banking, he amassed a fortune estimated at more than $200 million. But his true specialty was corporate mergers. Under Meyer's direction, Lazard bankers fused Fiat and Citroën, McDonnell and Douglas.

Yet the firm remained small. "Lazard has no backup," said one observer. "They live by their wits. They have no gremlins in the back rooms churning out the numbers to support their gut feelings."

With Rohatyn in the fold, there would be many, many more mergers. As Meyer's protégé, he supervised United Technologies' acquisition of Otis Elevator and plotted Textron's unsuccessful takeover of Lockheed. In all, he masterminded more than three dozen mergers or corporate takeovers. But he spurned Bernard Kornfeld's bid to rescue his scandal-tainted IOS—Investors Overseas Services. "A great firm is known by the business it can turn down," Rohatyn explained.

His most noteworthy work was done for ITT. In 1961 Lazard had bought money-losing Avis Rent A Car. Meyer and Rohatyn brought in the unorthodox executive Robert Townsend and Donald Petrie from Hertz's Chicago office to run the company.* Aided by an aggressive advertising campaign—"We try harder"—within four years the concern was in the black. When Harold Geneen, chairman of ITT, came to Lazard looking for companies to con-

---

* Petrie later became a Lazard partner. He once delivered a lay sermon at Chicago's First Unitarian Church in eight minutes—and found that the service could not continue. The organist and choir members, used to their pastor's more ponderous homilies, were out in the alley on a smoke break.

glomerate, Rohatyn had a ready candidate. Avis was sold to ITT in 1965 for $52 million.

Over the next five years Rohatyn supervised ITT's wholesale absorption of widely diverse concerns—everything from Brownell Business College and the Nancy Taylor Secretarial and Finishing School to ABC—an acquisition blocked by the Justice Department.

ITT's acquisition of Hartford Fire Insurance—then the largest corporate merger in American history—brought in Justice's trust-busters once again, and Rohatyn fielded flak at a Senate hearing because he had interceded with then-Deputy Attorney General Richard Kleindienst to keep the merger intact. To many, he seemed linked to the scandals of Dita Beard and ITT's effort to overthrow the Allende government in Chile. Lazard's dealings with ITT also came under SEC scrutiny. After a six-year investigation Lazard signed a classic consent decree, under which it denied that it had done anything wrong—and promised not to do it again.

By then, Rohatyn was off on other missions. After the 1969–70 stock market crash, when many brokerages teetered on the brink of bankruptcy, he was tabbed to head the New York Stock Exchange's crisis committee. But what really brought him into the public eye was the New York City fiscal crisis. In 1975 Governor Hugh Carey named the Lazard banker to head a blue-ribbon panel to devise ways of dealing with the city's worsening plight. Rohatyn was the visionary, the catalyst of the panel. One attorney who worked with the group observed: "Rohatyn would say, 'This is what has to be done'—and then the lawyers would look for ways to do it."

Although he once quipped that a New York City bankruptcy would be like "rearranging the deck chairs on the *Titanic,*" Rohatyn devised the mechanism that kept the Big Apple from going under—Big MAC, the Municipal Assistance Corporation. Under MAC, the city's sales tax was shifted to the state and used to secure MAC's bonds, which gave the city funds to stay afloat. Within a few months MAC raised more than $8 billion dollars.

Rohatyn served without pay as MAC's chairman, and Lazard acted as its investment banker gratis. Rohatyn estimated that Lazard's billing for its services would have cost the city $2.5 million. In 1979, after Rohatyn stepped down as chairman, MAC negotiated a $250,000-a-year fee with Lazard. But Mayor Edward Koch, with whom Rohatyn had been friendly, denounced the deal as "a moral conflict of interest," and Lazard withdrew. *The Economist* called the Mayor's action "biting a helping hand."

In recent years Rohatyn has spoken out on national and international issues, often using an unlikely forum for an investment banker—the left-wing *New York Review of Books.* In 1980 he called for a $20 billion budget cut, a wage and price freeze, and a gasoline tax of at least 50 cents a gallon. More recently, the man who saved New York City from bankruptcy called on international bankers to let Poland go under.

Unlike bankers of previous generations, Rohatyn spurns the trappings of wealth. His almost jail cell-sized office is bare and unadorned. His only outerwear is a battered trench coat. Instead of a banker's homburg, he wears a safari hat. Likely as not, he'll show up at a business conference in a turtleneck sweater.

Rohatyn relaxes by skiing and playing tennis. His first marriage to Jeanette Streit, daughter of Atlantic Unionist Clarence Streit, ended in divorce; he has since remarried.

A middle-of-the-road Democrat, Rohatyn is a charter member of the so-called Regency Mafia, a power-brokering group of bankers, businessmen, lawyers, and labor leaders who breakfast regularly at the posh Regency Hotel on Park Avenue.

"He wins your confidence because he plays no games," said another "Mafia" member, Victor Gotbaum, head of New York City's municipal employees' union. "You might not like what he tells you, but it's always the clear-eyed truth."*

Rohatyn himself dissented: "People say I'm a good persuader. But that's wrong. Facts are persuaders."

Even though he was Meyer's protégé, Rohatyn showed no interest in succeeding him and was passed over in favor of Donald C. Cook, a former SEC chairman. "What I do for this firm, I do in my head," Rohatyn explained. "I can do it from here [Lazard's headquarters in Rockefeller Center], or from Morgan Stanley, or my apartment at the Alrae."

---

* Gotbaum's son Joshua subsequently became a vice president at Lazard. "You gotta have some kids that go wrong," the union leader quipped. The younger Gotbaum and another Lazard vice president, Eugene Keilin, executive director of Big MAC under Rohatyn, worked out the financing under which the workers bought National Steel's plant in Weirton, West Virginia.

Some investment bankers find fame and fortune by brokering mergers for client corporations. **Sanford I. Weill** did it by brokering them for his own. They propelled him, first, to the peak of the profession—literally, for he operated out of a 106th-story aerie atop Manhattan's World Trade Center—and then out of the industry, for he now serves as president of the financial empire that is American Express.

It was a long climb for a middle-class Jewish boy from Brooklyn, but a rapid one. Sandy—even his secretary calls him "Sandy"— Weill studied business and economics at Cornell and started his career on Wall Street as a lowly runner at Bear Stearns & Co. He soon became a broker at what was then Burnham & Co. Tubby Burnham remembered him as "one of our best salesmen."

In 1960, at the age of twenty-six, Weill left to launch his own firm—Carter, Berlind, Patoma & Weill. "I contributed $30,000 of the original $215,000 in capital," he noted, "and I borrowed one third of that from my mother." Over the years the firm name evolved into Cogan, Berlind, Weill & Levitt—"C.B.W.L.," for short, or, according to Wall Street wags, "corned beef with lettuce."

C.B.W.L. soon became a fat sandwich—with lots of lettuce. While President Arthur Levitt Jr., son of New York's six-term state comptroller and now president of the American Stock Exchange, concentrated on running the firm, Chairman Weill set out boldly to expand it. His first acquisition—Bernstein-Macaulay, an assets-management house—came in 1967. By then, C.B.W.L. had $18 million in capital, and the firm's focus shifted from venture capital to retail brokerage. By 1969 it no longer had to clear its purchases through Burnham & Co.

In 1970 Weill made a much more significant acquisition—the venerable firm of Hayden, Stone & Co., which had suffered large losses on investments in the fraudulent Four Seasons Nursing Home chain and which had been badly battered by the "paper crunch." At the stroke of a pen C.B.W.L. went from a one-branch to a thirty-branch operation.

The merged entity was renamed—briefly—CBWL–Hayden Stone. Weill recalled that the Hayden Stone people wanted the Cogan Berlind name because their own was so tarnished, "but when you have living partners in the name, that name is subject to

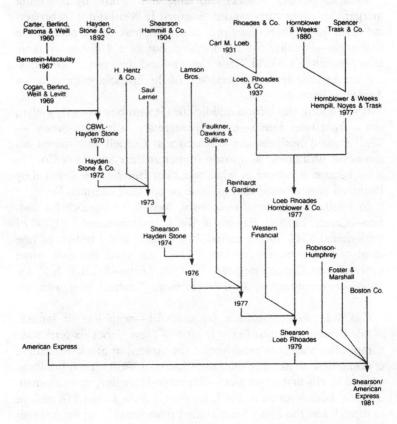

THE MERGERS THAT MADE
SHEARSON/AMERICAN EXPRESS

change, because you have egos. We wanted an institutional presence. We didn't think it was important to have our name on the
door." In 1972, after going public, Weill and Levitt modestly
dropped their own initials in favor of the time-honored Hayden
Stone name.

More acquisitions followed—too many to list here. (See chart.)
C.B.W.L. had brokered Saul Steinberg's acquisition of Reliance Insurance and collected a $750,000 fee. Weill was determined not to
incur such expense, so he brokered his own conglomeration.

"We did it all ourselves," he boasted.

In 1974 the firm acquired Shearson Hammill & Co. and went

through another shingle metamorphosis, to emerge as Shearson
Hayden Stone, the nation's fifth-largest brokerage house. But Weill
was frustrated in his effort to acquire Kuhn, Loeb & Co. and trans-
form Shearson into a full-service house with an active investment-
banking arm. Kuhn Loeb wound up being absorbed by Lehman
Brothers.

"That left us still that opening in investment banking," Weill
noted. He filled it in 1979 by acquiring Loeb Rhoades, Hornblower & Co., itself the product of multiple mergers,* and the firm
then went through its fifth name change in less than a decade to
become Shearson Loeb Rhoades, the nation's second-largest brokerage. In 1980 Weill persuaded ex-President Gerald Ford to
adorn the board of directors.

The new name turned out to be as short-lived as those of its
predecessors. In late 1980 Weill and American Express Chairman
James D. Robinson III—known on Wall Street as "Jimmy Three
Sticks" because of the Roman numerals after his name—launched
discussions about a proposed joint "platinum card," akin to Merrill
Lynch's Cash Management Account. While negotiations were in
progress, Prudential announced its $285 million acquisition of
Bache Group, putting it in the ranks of financial supermarkets.

* The Loebs of Loeb Rhoades are not related to the Loebs of Kuhn Loeb, although
the family backgrounds are similar. The son of a German-Jewish dry-goods merchant, Carl Morris Loeb started as a clerk in the Metallurgische Forschungsgesell-
schaft G.m.b.H. cartel. In 1892, at the age of seventeen, he was sent to its subsidiary
in St. Louis, American Metal Co. Within a decade he was the company's president.
The other directors deposed Loeb in 1929 and forced him to sell back 80,000 shares
of the company's stock. In a few months the crash came, and American Metal's value
fell by 50 percent. Loeb's son John then suggested that his father buy a seat on the
New York Stock Exchange, and the firm of Carl M. Loeb opened for business in
1931. Six years later it merged with the faltering old-line firm of Rhoades & Co.
John L. Loeb, who had married into the Lehman family, ran the firm for more than
forty years. According to one observer, he achieved "the kind of influence and
presence that has not been seen on Wall Street since the days of Jacob Schiff." He
was one of the last of the independent entrepreneurs. "Old John Loeb could do a
deal because he could write a check," another observer noted. Perhaps his greatest
coup came in 1958, when he sold off millions of dollars worth of Cuban sugar
holdings—only the day before Fidel Castro seized power! Loeb also was a rare
Democratic casualty in the fallout from Watergate. He pleaded no contest to con-
cealing $18,000 in illegal contributions to Hubert Humphrey's 1972 presidential
primary campaign through the use of dummy donors and was fined $3,000. By the
time of Loeb Rhoades' merger with Shearson, Loeb had retired from active management of the firm. His son John, also a Loeb Rhoades partner, served as Jimmy
Carter's ambassador to Denmark.

"I saw there was a bigger playground out there," Weill noted.

"We felt that American Express added more of a dimension to our business than anybody else," he added. "It wasn't in Hartford, it wasn't in Chicago like Sears, it was here in New York. The merger gave credence to the philosophy that a big financial institution could be, should be, would be interested in a brokerage operation."

All-day negotiations started in earnest over the Easter weekend of 1981. In the end American Express shelled out $915 million to acquire what was renamed Shearson/American Express. Initially, Weill remained as chairman of the new subsidiary, but it was the first time in more than twenty years that he reported to anyone other than himself.

"I think it's been terrific," he said. "That's the fun part of doing something different, taking on a different kind of challenge."

"We don't look at this as a sellout," he said at the time. "The merger allows us to leapfrog what would have taken us years to do."

With its acquisition of Shearson, American Express also became a financial supermarket. Weill was quick to see the possibilities: "Our goal [is] to make sure that our customer will need to make only one call—to us—whenever he requires cash, investment advice, credit, insurance, estate planning, home ownership financing, or travel planning."

In the flesh, Sandy Weill is short and trim, with a hawk nose and curly black hair flecked with gray. He's a constant cigar chomper and a compulsive tape watcher, with a video display terminal always aglow on his desk—"My rattle," he calls it. To some subordinates, he's a tough taskmaster, "a nitpicker who's always second-guessing."

Although his career was spent on the retail side of the business, Weill lists himself in the Manhattan telephone directory as "investment banker" and, under his leadership, Shearson/American Express moved into the ranks of the top dozen underwriters. Nor did Shearson's acquisition by American Express curb Weill's merger mania. Within a year the firm acquired three more regional firms—Robinson-Humphrey in Altanta, Foster & Marshall in Seattle, and the Boston Company—while Weill continued to stay on the lookout for others, especially in the Sunbelt.

For Weill, the merger with American Express meant coming down in the world—some 750 feet, from the top of the World Trade Center to American Express' fortieth-floor executive offices at 125 Broad Street. Leaving Shearson's destiny in the hands of his thirty-six-year-old protégé, Peter A. Cohen, Weill became, first, chairman of American Express' executive committee, then in 1983, president and number two man in the company, while other Shearson alumni moved into key positions at American Express.

Among Weill's new responsibilities was planning for the new headquarters of both American Express and Shearson/American Express, to be built in Battery Park City, the giant landfill in the Hudson River.

V

MA BELL
DONS A GREEN SHOE

Morgan Stanley & Co.'s third underwriting—back in 1935—was a $43 million issue for AT&T. In June 1981 Morgan Stanley served as lead manager for what was then the largest stock offering in history—an 18.15 million share, $1 billion issue for Ma Bell. Morgan Stanley's share of the sale was approximately $3 million.

Within less than two years Morgan Stanley sold another $16 billion in AT&T shares, including two issues of more than $1 billion each, each successively the largest offerings in American history.

The man who managed these issues was Thomas A. Saunders III, the forty-six-year-old manager of Morgan Stanley's capital-market-services group. Spindly and bespectacled, Saunders, who speaks with a soft Virginia drawl, trained as an electrical engineer at VMI and worked on defense research for Allis-Chalmers before returning to school, this time to take his M.B.A. from the University of Virginia. Upon graduation in 1967, he started at Morgan Stanley.

"It was really moving out into a size issue that was never done before," Saunders said of the June 1981 offering. "We were really going into uncharted waters. No one had done one of these. You had difficult conditions. [The stock market was still in its pre-Kaufman doldrums.] The most important thing, quite frankly, was assessment of the market."

Facing the impending divestiture of its twenty-two regional operating companies and needing capital to launch "Baby Bell," its new high-tech subsidiary,* AT&T seemed certain to return to the well for further financing—all of which would mean more profit for its longtime lead underwriter, Morgan Stanley.

But an ominous cloud loomed on the Washington and Wall Street horizon, especially for firms like Morgan Stanley: "shelf registration."

In February 1982 the Securities & Exchange Commission adopted the controversial new Rule 415, for an experimental nine-month period starting on March 16. The plan, dubbed "shelf registration" and devised by Lee B. Spencer Jr., director of the SEC's division of corporate finance, had been incubating for two years.

Under shelf registration, a company that filed regular reports with the SEC would not have to prepare a prospectus for secondary stock issues; its filings would be "incorporated by reference" into an imaginary prospectus. The company merely would file a registration statement listing how much stock it expected to sell over the next two years. Whenever it wished—normally at a time when it deemed market conditions most advantageous—it could sell any or all of the stock, if need be, directly to investors, whether individuals or institutions.

According to the SEC, shelf registration would eliminate red tape and paperwork. According to most investment bankers, it would also eliminate the middlemen—themselves. As good capitalists, they might espouse free enterprise for others, but when it came to their own bottom line, they sought government protection.

The investment banks feared that giant corporations, most of which were hearty proponents of shelf registration, would sell their shares directly to such institutional investors as pension funds, insurance companies, and bank trust accounts. "Proposed SEC rule

* As the result of a subsequent court order that forced AT&T and its subsidiaries to surrender use of the Bell name and logo to the operating companies, American Bell was rechristened AT&T Information Systems and both it and AT&T exchanged the familiar Bell logo for a globe. However, most of the divested companies shunned both "Bell" and "telephone" in favor of nondescript or high-tech terminology like "US West," "Nynex," "Pacific Telesis," and "Ameritech."

on New Financing May Kill Gentlemanly Art of Syndication," the *Wall Street Journal* headlined.

To most investment bankers, selling stocks off the shelf was an off-the-wall idea. Just as the securities industry had lined up against the introduction of negotiated commissions nearly a decade before, it now arrayed itself in opposition to adoption of Rule 415.

More than any other house, Morgan Stanley had the most to lose. The first companies to take advantage of Rule 415 included some of its biggest blue-chip clients—AT&T, Du Pont, Exxon, and General Electric subsidiaries. Morgan Stanley's President Robert H. B. Baldwin mounted what SEC documents described as an "intense lobbying campaign" against adoption of Rule 415.*

Other houses quickly joined the fray. John C. Whitehead of Goldman Sachs called Rule 415 a "regression to the 1929 precommission days" when investors bought blindly. John E. Gutfreund of Salomon Brothers wondered "whether the underwriter [First Boston] would have discovered problems with Penn-Central under today's instantaneous shelf procedure." The Securities Industry Association, then headed by Kidder Peabody's Ralph D. DeNunzio, made a futile, last-ditch effort to keep Rule 415 from going into effect.

Of major investment houses, only Lehman Brothers Kuhn Loeb and Dean Witter Reynolds gave even qualified support to shelf registration. Lehman's Francois de Saint Phalle called it "a clear plus as a matter of public interest."

When the shelf was cleared, corporations scrambled to climb aboard. Citicorp/Citibank was first out of the starting gate with a $500 million filing on March 26, to be marketed through any of ten

---

* The day after the experimental rule went into effect, SEC Chairman John S. R. Shad's own dealings with Morgan Stanley were called into question. When Shad, formerly vice chairman of E. F. Hutton, joined the Reagan administration, he placed his assets in a blind trust with Barton M. Biggs of Morgan Stanley. Among the assets were 200,000 Hutton shares. Since neither Shad nor the trust could have holdings in a company he regulated, Biggs sold the shares—to Brooks, Harvey & Co., a Morgan Stanley subsidiary. At the time of the shelf registration vote, Brooks Harvey still owed Shad some of the $7.8 million from the sale. Shad protested that he—like the other SEC commissioners—had adopted Rule 415 *despite* Morgan Stanley's opposition, but by June he bowed to the rising furore and recused himself from further consideration of shelf registration. In November the House Oversight Committee found that there was "no wrongdoing" in Shad's or Biggs's dealings. Said Shad: "It has taken seven months and $70,000 in personal legal fees, but I am glad to get it over with."

underwriters; in December it filed a $2 billion registration—the largest ever, though it was doubtful that all the shares would be offered for sale at once. Other corporations followed suit. Even Merrill Lynch, which had called for a delay of shelf registration pending further study, submitted a $300 million filing for its own shares. And Canada filed a shelf registration for $500 million in government bonds.

To the surprise of many observers, most corporations continued to market their shares through the investment banks. After all, they had been dealing with the banks for years, and most of them lacked direct contact with institutional investors and, perhaps even more important, the intuitive knowledge of market conditions that would determine when and for how much they should offer their shares.

In the first sale under shelf registration, AT&T sold $110.8 million worth of stock—to Morgan Stanley, for resale to institutional investors. But for the underwriters the old days of predictable profit had disappeared. Instead of taking a set fee on every share, the banks had to put up their own money—and take their chances on the open market.

In August 1982—three months after Ma Bell's initial shelf registration offering—Morgan Stanley led a consortium of some twenty-five other houses in a second AT&T sale under Rule 415—this time 8 million shares for $457.4 million. Morgan Stanley had changed its sales strategy because many houses had complained that they had been frozen out of the offering.

"We want to make it available to the whole street," Saunders explained. "The whole street should participate in telephone offerings."

AT&T also generated $13.5 billion in additional financing internally. Another $2.56 billion came from shareholder and employee stock purchase plans. And, in addition to the $568 million realized through the shelf registration sales, $400 million was raised through sales to European investors.

Although the rules had been changed, the investment banks played by the new ones. As one Wall Street lawyer observed, "If the SEC passed a rule saying you had to do underwritings in Watertown, New York, in the snow stark naked, these guys would take the next plane up." Virtually every house prepared elaborate brochures explaining Rule 415 to corporate clients and sent its bankers scrambling after shelf registration business.

The banks had to scramble to sell, waiting for what Lehman's Peter G. Peterson—deliberately mixing his metaphors—called "the brief window of opportunity," the fleeting moment when the price was right, the bank had the cash on hand and the buyers lined up. "What has been pure investment banking business now becomes competitive banking," observed A. G. Becker Paribas' John G. Heimann.

Shelf registration transactions were swift; usually, an entire issue was bought and resold in less than a day. Syndications were few—and small. AT&T's 1981 issue had been handled by a syndicate of 255, its May 1982 issue solely by Morgan Stanley, its August 1982 issue by a syndicate of twenty-five.

"In the main, they're not being syndicated," observed Robert E. Linton of Drexel Burnham Lambert. "The good deals that are easy to place are not being syndicated, so the moment you're invited into a syndicate, you raise your eyebrow."

The big losers in shelf-registration were the smaller houses, regional brokerages, and individual investors. Smaller houses lacked both the capital to bid for entire issues and the broad base of institutional investors to buy the shares. Regional brokerages, cut off from instantaneous communication with the New York money markets, had no opportunity to bid for shelf registration issues and generally were frozen out of the few syndicates that were formed to peddle them. Similarly, because almost all shelf registration sales were made to institutions, individual investors had little or no opportunity to get in on the action.

Ultimately, as some critics of unbridled capitalism contended, shelf registration could create that longtime bogeyman—concentration of economic power among a handful of investment banks and institutional investors, rather than spread through that broad base of "widows and orphans" that Ma Bell had always claimed as its mainstay.

By November 1982, according to a survey conducted by Merrill Lynch White Weld, 175 companies had filed shelf registration statements, and 126 issues, worth $12.8 billion, had been brought to market. On October 7 alone sixteen issues worth $1.8 billion had been sold. As expected, Morgan Stanley led the pack with twenty-five issues worth $3.3 billion, followed by Goldman Sachs, Salomon Brothers, Merrill Lynch, First Boston, Lehman Brothers Kuhn Loeb, and Kidder Peabody.

According to *Forbes,* the cluster at the top was even tighter. The Big Five—Morgan Stanley, Goldman Sachs, Salomon, Merrill Lynch, and First Boston—"monopolized" shelf registration. Their share of managing issues rose from 50 percent of syndicated offerings in 1981 to 70 percent of shelf registrations in 1982.

"A classic pattern of deregulation is being played out again," the magazine noted. "Simply put: The strong get stronger, and the hangers-on, whom overprotection had kept alive, get eaten up or hung out to dry."

By the time the shelf registration experiment came up for renewal, Morgan Stanley—strongest of them all—had muted its opposition. Saunders asked the SEC to "extend the Rule as a temporary rule for a reasonable period of time to explore its impact on the capital raising process more fully."

Saunders spoke in June. In less than two months the market was soaring, institutions went on a buying binge, and new issues—both old-fashioned syndications and shelf registrations—came pouring out of the hopper like water over Niagara.

On September 1 the SEC voted to extend shelf registration for another year beyond the scheduled expiration date of December 10, 1982. The commission had been unanimous on its original vote; the second time around the measure didn't even receive a majority of the five-member board—only 2 to 1. Commissioners John Evans and Bevis Longstreth voted in favor, arguing that the rule should be made permanent, Barbara Thomas dissented, and Chairman Shad—true to his promise—abstained. The fifth seat was vacant.

In June 1983, however, the commission voted unanimously to solicit public comment on whether the shelf registration rule should be extended again, either temporarily or permanently, beyond its scheduled expiration date of December 31, 1983.*

---

* According to a study prepared by the SEC's Office of Chief Economist (Charles Cox, nominated by President Reagan to become an SEC commissioner), nineteen corporations that used shelf registration cut their stock-issuing expenses by 29 percent. The commissioners got the message. On November 10, 1983, by a 4-to-1 vote, they made shelf registration permanent but limited its use to the largest and most

It remains to be seen if shelf registration becomes a permanent revolution in investment banking or merely a temporary aberration. Most observers figured the former. As John Heimann predicted: "It's good for the issuer, so it will stay around." Or, as Lehman's Peterson put it, "You can't fight progress."

To most corporations, $16 billion is a staggering sum, but it wasn't enough to meet AT&T's needs of starting up Baby Bell or financing the divestitures of its operating companies. So in November Ma Bell decided to return to the money markets for new equity financing. Virginia Dwyer, AT&T's vice president and treasurer, explained that the money—originally pegged at $990 million—would be used for "general corporate purposes."

Once again, Morgan Stanley was named as lead manager on the issue, with Saunders in charge. The comanagers were Blyth Eastman Paine Webber, First Boston, Merrill Lynch White Weld, and Salomon Brothers.

To some, it seemed that Ma Bell, by mixing its managers from issue to issue, was merely spreading the business around, but AT&T Assistant Treasurer Lawrence Prendergast insisted:

"We approach each issue on an individual basis and try to put the best possible team together. For a given issue, for a given set of market conditions, we have varied the participation of the comanagers, but not solely on the basis of spreading the business around."

Behind the team of five comanagers was a syndicate of some 255 banks and brokers.

Unlike the previous two AT&T issues, the November offering was made through traditional syndication, rather than shelf registration. "It's one thing for them to put a toe in the water by using the shelf rule for a two-million-share, or even eight-million-share, issue," one underwriting executive explained. "But when you're dealing with double that amount of stock, it's time to pay a fee and let the pros handle it."

For Thomas Saunders, the big question was whether the market could withstand such another gargantuan claim on its capital re-

credit-worthy companies—those with at least $150 million in stock held by outside investors. The lone dissenter was Mrs. Thomas, serving her last day on the job.

sources. At first, the issue was pegged at 15 million shares, but as Morgan Stanley's battery of analysts—largest on Wall Street—studied market conditions, they decided that an even larger issue could be brought to market, and Ma Bell's offering was increased to 16.5 million shares.

But Morgan Stanley included in its prospectus the so-called Green Shoe Option—named after the Green Shoe Manufacturing Co., which first used it in the 1950s—under which a corporation could issue an additional 10 percent of the initial offering, if conditions warranted.

AT&T's second billion-dollar issue was fully subscribed before noon on the first offering day, December 1. But only 1.2 million of the 1.65 million shares available under the Green Shoe Option were sold, netting Ma Bell only $1.062 billion, rather than its potential of $1.089 billion—but still the largest stock sale in history.

After the sale Gerald Morgan of Prudential-Bache opined that "this offering will take care of all the necessary funding requirements for the operating subsidiaries prior to the divestiture."

How wrong he was! Within three months, Ma Bell was back at the well. AT&T's top financial officers—William S. Cashel Jr., vice chairman and chief financial officer, Mrs. Dwyer, and Prendergast —were seeking to raise another $1 billion. Once again, according to a Bell spokesman, the money was to be used for "general corporate purposes," including "costs relating to the preparation" for the divestiture of its operating companies.

"We came to the next issue with the same question on the table," Saunders recalled. "Could we raise $1 billion, especially as we had just raised $1 billion? We were concerned about coming back to the market that quickly.

"We agreed that it would be very important to indicate that this was the last common stock that AT&T would offer into the common market in 1983, the last offering before divestiture.

"That was a very critical decision and that, as much as anything, accounts for the success of the issue."

According to Saunders, it was not a decision that could be based on facts and figures ground out by the traditional "gremlins in the back room," but "a judgment that had to be made in the blind." It was the highest of high finance, flying by the seat of the pants.

However, two major factors influenced Morgan Stanley's and Ma Bell's decision to go ahead. First, as AT&T's last issue of 1983, "it would create demand." Second, "We liked what was going on in the economy—inflation and interest rates."

The decision was thrashed out over the weekend of February 26–27, with Saunders and his staff cloistered in a thirty-second story conference room at Morgan Stanley's office in Rockefeller Center conferring constantly by telephone with the AT&T officials at their soon-to-be-abandoned headquarters downtown at 195 Broadway.

"We went back and forth a zillion times," Saunders noted.

Few of the participants worked the traditional "bankers' hours."

"The most important decision that we made was the size of the deal and to go off with a Green Shoe," Saunders said. "The second —and clearly as critical—was that this was the last offering of its kind and to communicate that to the marketplace. It's a very complicated and not easily determined decision. In the dark, you draw on your own experience and judgment."

On Monday, February 28, AT&T announced the new $1 billion offering and said that it would be issued through an underwriting syndicate. "The bigger the offering, the more we feel we need the strength and experience of an underwriting syndicate to sell the stock," a telephone company spokesman explained.

The lead underwriter was not named, but few on Wall Street doubted that it would be Morgan Stanley, Ma Bell's banker for fifty years. The speculation was confirmed four days later—on Friday, March 4, when the preliminary prospectus was filed with the SEC— with Morgan Stanley as lead manager, the issue to be comanaged by Goldman Sachs, E. F. Hutton, Merrill Lynch White Weld, and Salomon Brothers.

In the interim, Morgan Stanley had been busy with two chores that, by then, had become fairly routine—assembling the syndicate and preparing the prospectus.

In the main, the syndicate duplicated the one that had been formed for the AT&T issue three months before and, because it was so large, included virtually every investment banker and broker of consequence. But there was one important difference: In the March issue special stress was laid on including European houses, the first time that a significant share of Bell stock was peddled abroad.

Similarly with the prospectus. "Putting together the prospectus went along in a very professional manner and was not a particular problem, given the fact that there just was one three months ago," said Karen P. Robards, a principal* in Morgan Stanley's corporate finance department. "It's a lot different from never having done an offering.

"With the way prospectuses are being done now, where you can incorporate documents by reference, prospectuses are, indeed, fairly short documents," she continued. "Certainly, AT&T has a staff whose job it is to keep all their information up-to-date—their registration department."

The next question: How to sell the stock?

"It's not only structuring the issue, but developing a market strategy, timing, communicating with institutions," Saunders explained. "You really are developing a game plan. Without a well-thought-out program, it's a tremendous undertaking to raise a billion dollars. There's an awful lot on your platter."

On a previously syndicated AT&T issue Morgan Stanley and Ma Bell had put on a "road show," sending bankers and telephone company officials flying to twenty-three cities to present their case. On another, they had produced a closed-circuit telecast from AT&T's headquarters, with Saunders, Mrs. Dwyer, Prendergast, and others making presentations and fielding questions from other underwriters and institutional investors.

For the March issue, Morgan Stanley and AT&T decided that the most important consideration was to move quickly. A luncheon for approximately one hundred institutional investors was held Tuesday, March 8, at the University Club—the first facility available on such short notice—with the speeches and questions communicated by conference calls and speaker phones to similar gatherings in Boston, Chicago, and San Francisco.

The big issue was scheduled for Thursday, March 10. The "tombstones" had been placed, in the New York *Times* and *Wall Street Journal* (see Illustration, p. 13). The institutional investors were primed to purchase their massive blocks of stock. Customers' men from some 255 houses hovered over their telephones, poised

* At Morgan Stanley, an intermediate level between vice president and managing director.

to make the hard sell to Ma Bell's traditional ownership of "widows and orphans."

Then disaster boded.

Moody's Investor Service, one of two major agencies that rate corporate and municipal bonds (the other is Standard & Poor's, a division of McGraw-Hill) unexpectedly reduced its ratings on the bonds of AT&T, Western Electric, and twenty-three of Ma Bell's operating companies. Previously all but two had been rated Aaa, the highest possible, which meant that the companies could borrow at the lowest interest.

Moody officials explained that divestiture would force the operating companies to absorb many expenses previously passed along to AT&T's Long Lines operations, but that state regulatory agencies might be reluctant to add the costs to customers' bills, thus reducing the companies' rate of return. In addition, Moody officials doubted that Ma Bell, Western Electric, or its new Baby Bell subsidiary, accustomed to nearly a century of government-protected profit, were primed to contend in the competitive arena with more experienced rivals.

The table indicates Moody's 1983 ratings for the Bell System's debt:*

	LONG-TERM DEBT (IN MILLIONS)	OLD RATING	NEW RATING
AT&T	$9.800	Aaa	Aa1
Bell of Pennsylvania	1.700	Aaa	Aa2
Cincinnati Bell	130	Aaa	Aa2
Chesapeake & Potomac (D.C.)	230	Aaa	A2
Chesapeake & Potomac (Md.)	690	Aaa	A2

* In descending order, Moody's ratings are: Aaa, Aa1, Aa2, Aa3, A1, A2, A3, Baa1, Baa2, Baa3.

Cincinnati Bell and Southern New England Telephone, only partially owned by AT&T, were not affected by the divestiture order. Bell of Nevada, which was, is a wholly owned subsidiary of Pacific Telephone with no debt of its own and, thus, was not included in Moody's ratings.

Three weeks later, Standard & Poor's revised its ratings of the Bell units. Approximately half the operating companies retained their triple-A ratings, while the others were revised downward, but not by as much as Moody's. Both AT&T and Western Electric retained the highest triple-A ratings.

	LONG-TERM DEBT (IN MILLIONS)	OLD RATING	NEW RATING
Chesapeake & Potomac (Va.)	710	Aaa	Aa3
Chesapeake & Potomac (W.Va.)	250	Aaa	A3
Diamond State Telephone	112	Aaa	Aa2
Illinois Bell	1.400	Aaa	Aa3
Indiana Bell	804	Aaa	Aa2
Michigan Bell	1.400	Aaa	A3
Mountain States Bell	2.200	Aaa	A2
New England Telephone	1.800	Aaa	Aa3
New Jersey Bell	1.300	Aaa	Aa1
New York Telephone	3.700	Aaa	Aa3
Northwestern Bell	1.300	Aaa	Aa3
Ohio Bell	915	Aaa	A1
Pacific Northwestern Bell	1.000	Aaa	A1
Pacific Telephone	5.700	A3	Baa1
South Central Bell	2.300	Aaa	A1
Southern Bell	4.800	Aaa	A1
Southern New England Telephone	625	Aa2	Aa2
Southwestern Bell	4.900	Aaa	A2
Wisconsin Telephone	510	Aaa	Aa3
Western Electric	231	Aaa	Aa1

AT&T's Cashel called Moody's action "harsh" and "not justified," and some speculated that it might scuttle the big stock issue.

"Prices of Bell System bonds outstanding dropped as much as $15 for each $1000 face value following Moody's action early yesterday," the *Wall Street Journal* reported on Friday.

But at AT&T's financial center there was no panic, no consternation, no frantic calls to the front office or urgent messages for the bankers at Morgan Stanley.

"On the day of the announcement, the trading in Bell bonds was light," Prendergast recalled. "Some of them did sell off—it varied by company and bond issue. The fair estimate of the range was ten to fifteen points [per $1,000], depending on what issue you were looking at. A day or two later most of them came back to the preannouncement level. So the marketplace didn't agree with Moody's. That's what it amounts to.

"In terms of what effect did it have on the stock issue," Prendergast continued, "the price went up"—50 cents—to $66.75 a share.

"It was our judgment at the time that the debt and equity markets are fairly separate," he added. "We didn't feel that there'd be much of a reaction or an impact on the equity side. And it turned out that was the case.

"So we went ahead with the issue. From the equity standpoint, it turned out to be a nonevent."

At Morgan Stanley, however, the bankers were not so sanguine. Ensconced in Rockefeller Center, they waited to see how the market would react.

"That was the big event," Miss Robards said of Moody's rerating. "The thought was that you needed to let it settle a little, and there was a lot of information all during the day about the downgrading. Finally, we thought it was disseminated well enough, and the book was holding up well enough to price it."

In the early afternoon Tom Saunders made the crucial decision to go ahead—at $66.25 a share, 50 cents under the day's closing price. The figure, however, was not printed in the "tombstones" or on the prospectuses until the following morning.

By midday Friday, March 11, the entire issue had been subscribed, and Saunders decided to exercise the Green Shoe option, the underwriters buying 1.6 million shares at discount ($64.95 each) and reselling them, either directly to investors or on the open market.

By the closing bell on Friday, March 11, 17.6 million shares in Ma Bell, worth $1.166 billion, had been sold. It was the biggest issue in Big Board history, even though about a tenth of the sales had been placed overseas.

In 1977, in a rare moment of exuberance, Morgan Stanley bankers broke out a bottle of champagne to celebrate a successful sale. On Friday March 11, after the third billion-dollar Bell issue, there was no champagne—only the usual "closing dinner" some weeks later.

But Morgan Stanley had good cause to celebrate. It and the four other comanagers, allotted 1,055,200 shares each, each received commissions of $1,371,760 ($1.30 a share), plus expenses (estimated at $400,000), plus whatever profits they earned on the shares sold under the Green Shoe option.

The *Wall Street Journal* for Monday March 14—the first edition published since the sale of the AT&T issue—noted the news. It cited the offering as "the largest in history" and quoted Saunders as calling it "real testimony" to the strength of the company. Both comments were buried deep inside another story—announcement of a $250 million debt offering by South Central Bell.

Time marches on—and so do the stock and bond markets.

VI

THE RISE AND FALL OF
A HOT HOUSE

In March 1981 *Newsweek* hailed "Ray Dirks' Rebirth on Wall Street" as the guiding genius of John Muir & Co., hottest of the houses in bringing out new issues. Two months later Dirks's alma mater, De Pauw University in Greencastle, Indiana, awarded him an honorary degree—which put him in the same league as former British Prime Minister Harold Macmillan. Within another two months John Muir & Co. had filed for bankruptcy, Dirks was out of work and out of pocket some $2.1 million, while both Muir and its guiding genius faced a slew of stockholder suits and investigations by both the SEC and Justice Department.

In the flesh, Raymond L. Dirks seems an unlikely candidate for such fame—or notoriety. He looks more like the neighborhood grocer than a Wall Street wheeler-dealer. He's short and pudgy, a "Kewpie doll of a man," according to the *Wall Street Journal.* Now nearing fifty, he has long light-brown hair and wears black horn-rimmed glasses. He dresses casually—if not sloppily—and maintains none of the usual trappings of wealth. He and his second wife live in a rented apartment in a Greenwich Village coach house, which Jessy Dirks herself plasters and paints. He's never owned a car or carried a credit card. He's a workaholic who never takes a vacation and who only recently has learned to relax with a few weekend rounds of tennis.

Dirks's financial wheeling and dealing started in college, buying and selling shares of Standard Oil of Indiana, Grumman, and Gulf, Mobile & Ohio. In ninety days he ran $800 into $1200. "I thought I was a genius," he said. So he hied himself to Wall Street, where in twelve years he worked at a half-dozen banks and brokerage houses, including Bankers Trust and Goldman Sachs. He was an iconoclast in the financial community, an admirer of antiestablishment crusaders like Clarence Darrow, Gandhi, and later Ralph Nader. He hasn't voted since 1956; since Adlai Stevenson "there's no politician I have liked." During this period he also had his first clash with the authorities. While at G. A. Saxton & Co., he was censured by the New York Stock Exchange for trading securities without going through a Big Board member.

Once, he dropped out for a year to try his hand at speculating and playwriting. Both bombed.

"I'm a gambler by nature," he once observed. "There was a period in my life when I would bet on two dozen basketball games a week. My gambling streak was reflected in my business decisions. . . . I did a lot of speculating. I tried to make countless short-term gains. Often I succeeded, but sooner or later I would have a loser— the kind of loser that can wipe out all your gains. On one occasion, I went broke. I learned that you can make money fast for a while, but not forever."

In 1969 Dirks and his brother Lee formed Dirks Brothers Ltd., an investment advisory service. Dirks was a securities analyst specializing in insurance company stocks. In his newsletter *Insurance Confidential* he blew the whistle on possible hanky-panky in ITT's acquisition of Hartford Fire Insurance.

"Ray's a gadfly, a skeptic who doesn't mind being a pain in the rear to those guys whose companies he analyzes," said one of his clients. "He's not your typical analyst; he's a specialty player who provides warning signals to guys like me."

By 1973 he had merged Dirks Brothers into Delafield Childs Inc., a broker-dealer serving institutional investors. On March 6, 1973, he received a telephone call from Ronald Secrist, who recently had been fired from Bankers National, a subsidiary of Equity Funding Corporation of America. Secrist, who believed that neither federal nor state authorities would act on his information, tipped Dirks that there was massive fraud at Equity Funding. It was a hot tip, for in barely a decade Equity Funding had come out of no-where to become one of the nation's leading life insurance companies. Its stock was highly favored by institutional investors.

Dirks met with Secrist later that day, then began his own investigation. He met with other former employees and by March 21 had bearded Equity Funding's top management at its Los Angeles headquarters. By then, he was convinced that Secrist's tip was true: Equity Funding had inflated its earnings by carrying on its books millions of dollars worth of phony life insurance policies.

Along the way, Dirks briefed William Blundell, Los Angeles bureau chief of the *Wall Street Journal.* Blundell began his own investigation, with similar results. On March 26 Blundell contacted the SEC, which had failed to act previously on rumors of irregularities at Equity Funding. The next day Dirks started filling in the commission. On the same date, after Salomon Brothers complained of "disorderliness" in the market for Equity Funding shares, the New York Stock Exchange suspended trading in the stock. In less than two weeks Equity Funding had fallen from $26 a share to less than $15. In the hours before trading was stopped it lost another $3.

On April 2, the same day that the *Wall Street Journal* published a front-page story that won Blundell a Pulitzer Prize nomination, the SEC filed a civil complaint against Equity Funding. Three days later the company filed for bankruptcy. The court-appointed trustee eventually found that some 60,000 policies supposedly worth more than $100 million had been falsified. It was, in Dirks's words, "the most monumental money swindle of modern times." A financial writer called it "the fraud of the century."

In due course, the Justice Department brought criminal indictments against twenty-two persons—twenty Equity Funding officers and employees and two outside auditors. There also were state indictments in California, Illinois, where the company was chartered, and New Jersey, headquarters of Bankers National. Most of the defendants pleaded guilty. Stanley Goldblum, Equity Funding's chairman and president, was sentenced to eight years in prison; Fred Levin, the executive vice president, to seven. Eventually, the stockholder suits were settled for $57 million—15 to 20 cents on the dollar.

Dirks saw himself as "the Ralph Nader of Wall Street." But the SEC viewed his dealings differently. Between March 20 and 26

Dirks had tipped five Delafield Childs clients about the brewing scandal at Equity Funding. As a result, Boston Company Institutional Investors unloaded all its Equity Funding holdings—nearly $8 million worth. Also acting on Dirks's tips, Dreyfus Corporation got rid of a $500,000 debenture, Towlin, Zimmerman & Parmelee, $457,000 worth of holdings, Manning & Napier, $90,000 worth. John W. Bristol & Co., which had bought the $8 million Boston block six days before, sold it on the basis of Dirks's information. Dirks also tipped officials of Loews Corporation, a nonclient, which, in turn, had bought the Boston block. By then, it was too late; Loews was stuck with the stock.

Dirks later tried to justify his actions:

> My job was to make the stock sell where it belonged as quickly as I could. In the process of getting it from here to there, someone unfortunately was going to get hurt. It was a game of musical chairs—the opposite of musical chairs; whoever wound up with some shares was the one who would be stuck. . . . It didn't seem to make any great moral difference as to who would be stuck. . . . The important thing was to get the stock suspended.

The SEC contended that Dirks had saved his firm's clients millions of dollars by feeding them inside information in violation of the securities laws. Charges were filed against Dirks and the five investment houses that had acted on his tips. The administrative law judge ruled against all six of them. Of the corporate defendants, all but Dreyfus were censured. Dirks was ordered to be suspended from any association with any broker or dealer for sixty days.

Both Dirks and the SEC's Division of Enforcement, which sought stiffer sanctions, appealed the judge's ruling to the SEC commissioners. In 1981 the SEC upheld the administrative law judge's findings of fact, but reduced Dirks's penalty to censure. Even though it was the mildest sanction the SEC could impose, Dirks, who had retained the Washington law firm of Arnold & Porter and who eventually would spend more than $500,000 in legal fees, appealed again—to the U.S. Court of Appeals for the District of Columbia.

The following year the court found that:

Largely thanks to Dirks one of the most infamous frauds in recent history was uncovered and exposed, while the record shows that the SEC repeatedly missed opportunities to investigate Equity Funding.

But it sustained the commissioners' censure!

Undaunted, Dirks filed for Supreme Court review.*

Meanwhile, Dirks was out of work, suspended from securities dealing by the New York Stock Exchange while the SEC considered his case. He worked for a while as director of research at Bernard Herold, Inc., and cowrote a book on the Equity Funding scandal. Then in 1976 John Sullivan, the managing partner, invited him to join John Muir & Co., and Dirks accepted.

It was to be a wild and woolly ride. Under Dirks's leadership, John Muir became to investment banking what the Marx Brothers were to grand opera.

John Muir & Co. had been the Merrill Lynch of its era, the five-and-dime of brokerage houses. As a youth, Muir left his native Toronto, went west to Chicago, and studied stenography. He became secretary to Allan Pinkerton, founder of the detective agency that still bears his name, but Muir soon decided that there was a brighter future in railroads. He started as a shipping clerk and rose to become right-hand man to Collis P. Huntington, president of the Southern Pacific and preeminent among the Robber Barons.

In 1898 Huntington told Muir: "John, I'm going to give you a seat on the New York Stock Exchange." Thus, John Muir & Co. was born. Muir, a poker-playing crony of John W. "Bet-A-Million" Gates and "Diamond Jim" Brady, proved an aggressive salesman and an innovative broker. He became known as "the odd-lot king" and originated both installment purchase of bonds and "baby bonds"—under $100—both of which later played so large a part in financing World Wars I and II. In 1918, however, both Muir and his son were suspended from trading for a year for taking in a partner in violation of stock exchange rules.

Muir died in 1935, and for forty years, according to Dirks, "the firm meandered without any great distinction." By 1976, when

---

* The case produced a rare open split in the Reagan administration. Justice refused to support the SEC, contending that Dirks's information wasn't "inside" or "confidential." It also argued that sustaining the SEC would deter future whistle-blowers.

Dirks joined, it was what one financial writer called "a fading old-line brokerage firm," a small house, almost unnoticed among the giants of Wall Street. Dirks soon changed all that, transforming Muir from a backwater brokerage into an aggressive investment bank.

There was an anomaly in Dirks's situation. He was still barred from holding any supervisory post with any house on the stock exchange, so he officially operated as a sort of firm within a firm—Raymond Dirks Research. Soon Raymond Dirks Research was generating 90 percent of Muir's revenue, and Dirks, in fact if not in name, was running the show.

But the formalities had to be preserved. According to one former salesman: "One time Ray wrapped up an underwriting of a technology company, but, of course, he wasn't empowered to sign the agreement. So he had a Muir partner sign it. A few minutes later the partner came over to me and asked, 'What did I sign? What does that company do?' "

Once the SEC acted on his case, the stock exchange suspension was lifted, and Dirks became one of three Muir partners in May 1981. By then, the eighty-three-year-old firm had less than three months of life left.

Dirks's specialty became new issues—taking small, privately held companies public. They were nickel-and-dime stocks, most of them traded over the counter, that the big boys at Morgan Stanley and Goldman Sachs wouldn't touch. Muir underwrote its first new issue in 1977—Tri-American Corp., an insurance company. The issue was small—only $1.7 million—but, according to the Chicago *Daily News,* it was the only new issue of the year's third quarter. It also was Muir's only new issue of the year. Tri-American proved to be a bonanza for its investors: the stock shot up from 4½ to 11 before the company was acquired by Scottish & York Holdings, Ltd.

Muir handled only three underwritings the following year—Knogo Corp., a manufacturer of magnetized tags to prevent shoplifting, and two more insurance companies—and none at all in 1979. Then . . .

"In 1980 we started doing more exotic companies," Dirks recalled.

By then, there was a booming market for new issues, especially of high-technology companies, as investors scrambled to get in at the ground floor of the next Xerox, Texas Instruments, or Apple. According to one former salesman, "People would call in and say, 'Put me down for 10,000 shares of each of your next five issues.' They wouldn't even ask for the *names* of the stocks." Muir handled twenty new issues in 1980 and twenty-five during the first seven months of 1981, by then a rate of roughly one new issue a week.

The table lists the new issues underwritten by John Muir & Co.:*

COMPANY	ISSUE DATE	ISSUE PRICE	PRICE DEC. 24, 1982	PCT. GAIN OR LOSS
Tri-American	9/14/77	4 1/4	11 1/2[1]	+ 171
Knogo	9/14/78	5 1/2	12 3/4	+ 132
Celina Financial	10/4/78	11	6	− 46
Aneco Reinsurance	11/28/78	6	2 9/16	− 57
Danelcor	1/31/80	4 1/4	6 1/2	+ 44
Universal Fuels	4/10/80	5	1 5/8	− 68
Nitron	5/29/80	5	7	+ 40
International Capital Equipment	6/12/80	5 1/4	6 3/4	+ 23
Empire Oil & Gas[2]	6/19/80	1	3/32	− 91
Energy Clinic[3]	7/1/80	1	1 3/16	+ 18
Digital Switch	7/29/80	6	70	+1300
Griffin Petroleum[4]	8/29/80	1	7/8	− 12
Mid Pacific Airlines	9/16/80	5	6 1/2	+ 30
Numax	9/17/80	4	.06	− 98

* By June 1983, with the Dow Jones industrial average soaring upward another 200 points, some of Muir's issues showed even more spectacular gains. Adjusted for a stock split, Digital Switch went from a low of 2 5/8 to 160; Scientific Leasing from 4 5/8 to 34. "A rising tide," *Forbes* noted, "floats all ships." Even Dirks's; he held about $9 million in Digital Switch warrants. But those who held on a few weeks longer lost most of their paper profits. As the result of an FCC rate ruling affecting MCI, Digital Switch's biggest customer, both stocks were badly battered in August 1983. In eight days 30 percent of Digital's shares changed hands and the price fell from 48 to 27 3/4.

COMPANY	ISSUE DATE	ISSUE PRICE	PRICE DEC. 24, 1982	PCT. GAIN OR LOSS
American Pacific International	9/30/80	1 1/2	1 19/32	+ 6
Little Prince Productions	10/7/80	2	1 1/2	− 25
Meridan Productions	10/20/80	3/10	.06	− 80
Solid Photography[5]	10/30/80	5 1/2	7 3/4	+ 41
Custom Alloy[6]	11/18/80	12	12 3/8	+ 3
Security America	11/20/80	6	0	− 100
SAI Group	11/26/80	2	3/4	− 63
Cayman Islands Re	12/17/80	1	3/16	− 81
Basic Earth Science Systems	12/18/80	7 1/4	1 9/16	− 89
Brady Energy-preferred	12/19/80	10	2	− 80
Superior Care	1/6/81	3	3 1/2	+ 17
Metal Arts	1/22/81	1	7/16	− 56
Datavision	1/29/81	2 1/2	2 7/8	+ 15
Enterprise Radio	2/3/81	5	0	− 100
Balance Computer	2/5/81	2	1 13/16	− 10
American Syn-fuels	2/11/81	1	2 3/8	+ 138
Micros Systems	2/12/81	2 1/2	2 3/4	+ 10
Scientific Leasing	2/17/81	6	16	+ 167
Energy Clinic[3] (secondary offering)	2/2/81	1 1/2	1 3/16	− 21
Bio-Energy Systems	3/6/81	3/4	9/32	− 63
Atours	3/10/81	1 1/2	1 7/8	+ 25
Star Brite	3/26/81	2	1/8	− 94
Henry Energy	3/31/81	1	7/32	− 78
American Fiber Optics	4/1/81	6 1/2	8	+ 23

COMPANY	ISSUE DATE	ISSUE PRICE	PRICE DEC. 24, 1982	PCT. GAIN OR LOSS
Cyber Diagonistics	4/8/81	1	.06	− 94
Neighborhood Realty Group-USA	4/12/81	1	.02	− 98
Aero Services International	4/14/81	3	1 3/4	− 48
Central Corporate Reports Service	4/30/81	3	1 5/8	− 46
Cogenic Energy Systems	5/21/81	1	6 1/2	+ 550[7]
American National Petroleum	6/4/81	1	1/2	− 50
North East Insurance	6/16/81	4 1/2	2 7/16	− 46
Wind Baron	6/23/81	1	7/8	− 13
Air Chapparral	7/8/81	1	22/32	− 31
Ferrofluidics	7/16/81	2	3	+ 50
Quickprint of America	7/23/81	5	3 25/32	− 24

Data adjusted for stock splits.
1. Of 7/13/81, cash received in acquisition by Scottish & York Holdings, Ltd.
2. In bankruptcy
3. Acquired by Servmatic Solar Systems, 1 for 1
4. Acquired by MGF Oil, 1 MGF for 4.27 Griffin
5. Name changed to Robotic Vision Systems
6. Name changed to Custom Energy Services
7. Includes spin-off, 1 National Energy Capital for 5 Cogenic

Muir's was a heady atmosphere—exhilarating and exhausting. Dirks estimated that he worked eighty to one hundred hours a week—with time off only for a ten-day honeymoon when he remarried in 1979.

To peddle the flood of new issues, Dirks assembled a "boiler room" of 150 salesmen at Muir's offices at 61 Broadway. Some were Wall Street veterans, but most were newcomers to the market, the flotsam of Greenwich Village: out-of-work actors, unpublished poets, sometime waitresses, and ex-airline stewardesses, some of whom suddenly found themselves making as much as $50,000 a week in commissions.

Muir reveled in a go-go atmosphere akin to a college pep rally, more *Animal House* than Auchincloss. There was no dress code, either written or unwritten, and Muir's salesmen were far from pinstripers. Many showed up for work in sweat shirt and blue jeans. On one salesman's birthday, he was greeted with a Strip A Gram—an ecdysiast who peeled and jiggled at his desk—surely a sight never seen in the staid preserves of Morgan Stanley & Co.!

"I missed it," Dirks lamented, adding—almost ruefully—that she hadn't gone "all the way."

But Dirks acknowledged: "We tried to create an open atmosphere where everybody had an opportunity to participate and make money."

According to one account, Dirks himself climbed atop a desk and exhorted his salesmen: "Get it while you can!"

"I never climbed on top of a desk," Dirks insisted. Then he added: "There wouldn't be anything wrong with that."

While they could, Muir's staff lived high off the hog. They flew first class—two salesmen even took their girlfriends to Europe via the Concorde SST and wrote it off as a "business expense"—and rode in chauffeured limousines. There were "near fistfights" over use of the firm's limousine.

According to a former employee, "The guys wanted to take their girlfriends out, but they would tell Ray, 'I've got a heavy customer in town tonight. I need the car.' When a couple of salesmen threatened to quit if they couldn't use the limo, Ray finally got rid of it."

The staff also attended lavish parties at Windows on the World—the posh restaurant atop the World Trade Center—at which clients and wealthy customers were entertained. But Muir's pregame party in Miami Beach for the 1979 Super Bowl proved a near disaster. The liquor flowed freely, and the guest list was stocked with what were euphemistically described as "stewardesses." Then it was learned that Carl Lindner, founder, chairman, and president of American Financial Corp., and his wife planned to attend. Not only was Lindner the largest investor in Muir—with some $5 million—

he was a strict Baptist who didn't drink, smoke—or chase around. The "stewardesses" were quickly hustled away from the party, while sentries were posted in the hotel lobby to head off late arrivals.

Muir's was a heady atmosphere—literally. A New York Stock Exchange examiner—virtually a fixture in Muir's office—noticed that along about 3 P.M. many of the sales staff complained of headaches. He called in a city health inspector, who took air samples—then took his findings to managing partner John Sullivan: There were 150 persons working in a room that had air enough only for 138. Sullivan was confronted with a choice of thinning out the room or installing a costly new ventilation system.

After the inspector left, Sullivan scanned the staff roster and told the receptionist to send twelve persons to his office. They were the lowest producers in the shop.

"You people are breathing too much air," Sullivan told them. "You're using up too much oxygen. You have a half hour to clean up your desks and leave."

One salesman protested: "I've been with John Muir for fifteen years. I'm a pro. I'm doing a good job."

"You smoke a pipe, and that pipe uses up oxygen, too," Sullivan shot back. "You have a half hour to clean up your desk and get out."

Thus, the departing dozen.

There was also the Dirty Dozen, a varying stable of ten to fifteen shapely young women, "whose duties included things other than brokerage," according to a former employee.

One specialized in cultivating CEOs—chief executive officers—who were clients or potential clients. Once, she persuaded an oil company president to take her out for a drink after work. According to his account, the drink escalated into dinner . . . then a lift home in a cab . . . next a nightcap in her apartment. Once there, he excused himself to go to the bathroom. When he emerged, he found his hostess sprawled naked on the couch. The shocked oilman protested that he was a married man—and fled.

She was more successful in the case of a congressman from upstate New York—also married—who gave her a couple of thousand dollars to invest for him. She promptly marched to the trading desk and placed an order: "Buy me one hundred shares of Dynatech at sixteen."

"The stock's only fifteen," the trader informed her.

"That one point's for me," she replied.

The trader placed the order, then announced over the intercom to Muir's sales staff: "———— has now become a discount broker." She got one eighth—a $12.50 commission.

Two of the Dirty Dozen—Dirks's traveling companions until his remarriage—were nicknamed the Gold Dust twins. Dirks eventually got them registered as salesmen and gave them accounts to manage. One month later both of them sashayed into the office wearing full-length mink coats.

By all accounts, Muir's sales staff included the largest lot of oddballs and screwballs assembled this side of Bedlam. Among them:

One salesman, who habitually carried a whip and pinned the panties of his conquests on the office wall above his desk. Every two or three days a new pair of panties replaced the old. Every twenty or thirty minutes, he'd pull out the whip, give a yell, and swat the panties.

Another salesman was an obscene telephoner. At first, he called women in other parts of the boiler room—until one belted him with a book. Then he started calling outside. His favorite ploy was to introduce himself as a police sergeant and tell the woman to expect an obscene call, but keep the man on the line as long as possible so the police could trace the call. Then he'd hang up, call back—and babble away to his horny heart's content. Or he'd pretend to be the husband's psychiatrist and tell the wife that a necessary part of the therapy was for *her* to go out and have sex with the first man she met. Once he came under suspicion, he was called into the front office and ordered to take a lie-detector test. "I resign," he announced—and walked out. He was never charged.

Yet another was an obese man who wore his hair in a black and gray ponytail—by name, John McLanahan, although he liked to pass himself off as a scion of the Du Pont family. Even after his imposture was exposed in *New York* magazine, he was able to maintain personal friendships and business relationships with folksinger Peter Yarrow (of Peter, Paul and Mary) and TV personality Dick Clark. He constantly shifted his base of operations between New

York and Southern California, where he worked out of a poolside cabana at the Beverly Hills Hotel surrounded by an admiring coterie. McLanahan (a.k.a. "John du Pont") eventually was charged with evading $40,800 in taxes on $126,000 in income from Muir for the years 1978–80—which gives an indication of the earnings the firm's employees enjoyed.

Then there was the salesman who married his assistant. A few weeks after the wedding they showed up at the office—he, head wrapped in a bandanna and earrings dangling from his lobes, she in a pin-striped pantsuit, shirt, and tie. They were experimenting with role reversal, they explained. A few weeks later she showed up with a black eye, he with scratches on his face. Within another week he showed up with a new sales assistant. Before long he divorced assistant number one to marry assistant number two. When they returned from their honeymoon, he peddled videotapes—at $25 each —of both the ceremony and the consummation.

And more . . .

But no oddball at John Muir got as much attention—in-house or out—as Jerry Rubin, the onetime Yippie leader and charter member of the Chicago Seven, whose antics had included wearing a Revolutionary War uniform to a congressional hearing, trying to "levitate" the Pentagon during a march on Washington, and nominating a pig for President at the 1968 Democratic National Convention. "The most militant, unpredictable, creative—and therefore dangerous—hippie-oriented leader available on the New Left," according to Norman Mailer.

Could a onetime Yippie sell stock on Wall Street?

Ray Dirks thought so. A Muir salesman told him that Rubin was interested in coming to Wall Street. Dirks, curious, arranged to invite him for lunch. "He came to lunch, and I hired him on the spot," Dirks noted. Rubin started on salary—reportedly $50,000 a year—and later took the examination and became a registered dealer.

"Money is power," Rubin said, explaining his conversion to capitalism. "If I'm going to have any effect on my society and the world in the next forty years, I must develop the power that only money can bring."

Rubin added that he was interested in searching out "companies of the future," like those in solar energy. But, according to Dirks, "he was never a salesman, he was more an organizer"—which may explain Muir's eventual collapse.

After a while, Rubin started holding "salons" at his apartment—wine and cheese parties paid for by Dirks, at which potential customers could rub elbows with celebrities. According to Dirks, "They brought in a tremendous amount of business."*

According to other accounts, Rubin's arrival also drove away business, especially Muir's customers in conservative Texas. Other Muir salesmen agitated for his ouster, and Dirks finally was forced to give in.

But for the remaining three months of Muir's existence, Rubin managed to remain on the payroll. The official explanation was that he had left to form his own investment advisory firm—though it was not explained why anyone would seek expertise from a one-time Yippie with barely a year's experience on Wall Street.

During this period Dirks launched an ill-fated business venture of his own. He joined Michael Goldstein, former publisher of the *SoHo Weekly News*—and, briefly, a member of Muir—in issuing the *Wall Street Final*, an afternoon stock sheet. Undercapitalized, understaffed, undercirculated—under-everythinged—it quickly folded.

Dirks's method of producing stock sales was as unorthodox as his sales staff. He promoted fierce rivalry—indeed, cutthroat competition—among Muir's dealers. Weekly results were publicly posted—a practice rare on Wall Street, but not uncommon in the insurance companies Dirks had so long surveyed.

No salesman's accounts were safe from the prying eyes—or grasping hands—of his office neighbors. The firm's top producers surrounded themselves with "satellites" to whom they farmed out pieces of their business. At the office these top salesmen were literally surrounded, for the satellites' desks were clustered around those of their mentors—"like a whole bunch of little forts around the citadel"—to protect the accounts from rivals.

Dirks's solution was to rearrange the desks. "Ray spent a quarter to a third of his time rearranging desks," commented a former colleague.

The stock exchange examiner—the same man who called in the

* After Muir's collapse Rubin continued the "salons" at the trendy disco, Studio 54 —at $6 a head. Rubin supposedly had started as a raiser of venture capital, but, as Dirks noted, "In the end he became the recipient of venture capital."

health inspector—once noted that if a broker tried to talk to him alone, he'd report that man to the office manager—and usually the errant broker would be sent packing. On his first day at Muir three women propositioned him, and fifteen men offered him gifts. "There was so much, I didn't know what to do," he reported. It turned out that the would-be bribers weren't trying to cover up their own misdeeds—they were trying to induce the examiner to take action against their office rivals, so they could take over their accounts!

Mario Andretti, the champion auto racer, had invested $350,000 in Muir and was a limited partner in the firm. When he competed in the Canadian Grand Prix, Muir threw a lavish party at a Montreal hotel. One broker showed up with his girlfriend, but at the party he paid more attention to two of his best customers—members of the Kerr family, of Oklahoma oil fame.

Suddenly, he noticed another broker walking out of the party with his girlfriend. He chased after them, but missed them at the elevator. He scoured the hotel for a half hour, to no avail. Crestfallen, he returned to the party—only to find that a third broker had walked off with his customers!

The two rivals in love occupied adjoining desks in the boiler room. Before the party, the first broker and his girlfriend had been photographed snuggling on a couch. His colleagues blew up the picture to poster size, but superimposed a head shot of the successful rival over his face. They hung the composite over the unlucky broker's desk. He was in the office for two hours before he noticed the poster. Then he let out a roar and started for his rival. He had to be physically restrained.

"Ray wouldn't move their desks," a colleague noted. "He thought it would create good competition."

Many Muir dealers kept empty briefcases in their desks—insurance against the day when the SEC descended upon the shop; then they could sweep their account cards into the briefcases and make a hasty departure with clients in tow for the next shop where they'd work. In the spring of 1982 that day loomed closer and closer.

The prices of many Muir issues nose-dived far below the initial offering price, prompting a series of suits by irate stockholders claiming that Muir failed to make full disclosure in the prospectuses. The SEC wallowed in their wake, giving special attention to several issues. Among them: Empire Oil & Gas, issued at 1 in July 1980, which fell to 3/32 after the company filed for bankruptcy; Security America, an insurance company stock issued in November at 6, which soon proved untradable at any price; and Basic Earth Science Systems, which went on the market in December at 7 1/2 and plummeted to 1.

Digital Switch, a Virginia-based computer company that later relocated in Texas, also was singled out for scrutiny. The issue had been troublesome for Muir because a number of its officers and employees already owned stock in the company. John Fedders of Arnold & Porter—now director of the SEC's Division of Enforcement and Dirks's No. 1 nemesis—was counsel to Muir on the underwriting. He called the Digital Switch prospectus "the worst piece of shit I've ever seen in my life" and refused to allow Arnold & Porter's name to appear in it. However, the firm submitted a bill for more than $100,000.

Later, at a hearing before the National Association of Securities Dealers on the Digital Switch issue, Sullivan became so incensed with Fedders that he tried to choke the attorney.

Ironically, Digital Switch turned out to be the stellar performer of all Muir issues. It went on the market in July 1980 at 5 and soon fell to 2, but then it soared to 49 1/2—an appreciation of nearly 1000 percent—and by the end of 1982 it hit 70. In both 1981 and 1982 Digital Switch was among the New York *Times*'s listing of the ten best-performing stocks.

Perhaps the most questionable of all Muir issues was Cayman Islands Reinsurance Corp.—Cayman Re, for short—issued in December 1980 at $1 a share. According to the SEC, the prospectus failed to disclose that the company's chairman had a criminal record in Canada for stock fraud or that Dirks and a Muir broker named Carl John Peterson allegedly pressured Cayman Re's board into using the money raised by going public to buy into—and thus prop up the prices of—at least ten other issues brought out by Muir.

To one former employee, however, "the worst thing he [Dirks] ever did was Little Prince Productions." A friend of Dirks's owned the stage rights to Antoine de Saint-Exupéry's classic, *The Little Prince,* but lacked the funds to mount a production. So Dirks underwrote a $1.5 million stock issue—"the first Broadway show to go public," he boasted—and, under threat of dismissal, pressured Muir's employees into investing in the company. In time, the $1.5 million was dissipated, and the stockholders became "angels" in a play that was never mounted. The value of Little Prince stock fell from the offering price of $2 to 50 cents.

As the stockholder suits mounted and the investigations were announced, the flood of Muir's new issues slowed to a trickle—only one in May 1981 and three each in June and July. Muir's dealers found themselves stranded without stocks to peddle. Many saw the handwriting on the wall.

"We're going out of business," Dirks predicted as summer approached. "Our brokers are wearing business suits to the office"—so they could interview for other jobs during the lunch hour.

Dirks still blames the house's woes on the SEC: "I think ultimately the SEC was the real villain in the piece. They had a vendetta against me. I think the whole thing adds up to a very intensive effort by the SEC to discredit someone who's trying to raise money for small companies.

"Ultimately, when the publicity turned extremely negative, there was nothing we could do to counteract it. All our customers got negative feelings about the firm and withdrew their accounts. Negative publicity is the worst thing that can happen to you in the United States."

Exacerbating Muir's problems was its rapid expansion. In little more than a year it had ballooned from a one-office firm to a ten-branch brokerage—Boca Raton, Denver, Fort Lauderdale, Houston, Los Angeles, North Miami Beach, Palm Beach, Phoenix, and Washington, in addition to its New York base on lower Broadway. It was too much too soon. New York accounted for more than three quarters of Muir's revenue; the branches merely added overhead without producing profits.

These problems were merely the tip of the iceberg. The twenty-five bankers in Muir's corporate finance department were as fiercely competitive as the firm's brokers. They didn't confide in each other, only in Dirks, who approved or disapproved their deals, and no one else in the firm knew what they were up to.

Shortly before the end, one banker came back to the office with a "letter of intent" for underwriting a cable television company in Chicago. Sullivan and Robert Smith, the third Muir partner, becoming wary of Muir's highly speculative issues, refused to sign the document. The banker then took it to Dirks, who signed, and the banker then departed for Chicago to get the cable company executives' signatures—and a check for Muir's $25,000 fee. Sullivan tried, without success, to head him off with a phone call to the airport.

The next morning Sullivan called Chicago and told the cable company officials that the letter was "invalid" and that they shouldn't sign it. He told them to tell the banker to "rip up the letter of intent and don't come back to the office." However, he came back, and Dirks promptly rehired him. The issue was unresolved when the firm went under.

Fearing that the investment-banking side of the business was getting out of hand, Sullivan and William Bonilla, Muir's general counsel, finally called a meeting of the twenty-five bankers and discovered, to their amazement, that they had issued more than five hundred letters of intent for future underwritings worth more than $6 billion. Even in the best of times, it would have been beyond Muir's capacity.

As the liquidity crisis worsened, the firm began to cut back. During the first week in August it announced that it no longer would underwrite new issues. Dirks poured $1.5 million of his own money into the faltering firm, and Lindner's American Financial made a $5 million loan. It wasn't enough. Dirks estimated that another $5 to $10 million would have been needed to keep Muir afloat, but "we couldn't raise capital because of the unfavorable press."

The crisis came to a head over the weekend of August 15–16, when Muir discovered that it did not have enough cash on hand to meet a deadline for funding legally segregated customer accounts. A last-minute plan to sell off nonliquid assets had to be abandoned because another deadline loomed the following week, and Muir would be "back in the same kettle."

At about 9 P.M. Sunday Dirks emerged from his office and announced to the handful of employees on hand, "That's it. We're not going to open for business Monday morning."

Within an hour more than one hundred Muir employees were swarming over the office, cleaning out their records. According to one observer, "The place was picked clean."

The following morning John Muir & Co. filed for bankruptcy. Muir's customer accounts were transferred to Rodney, Pace Inc., while Harvey R. Miller, the bankruptcy specialist at the Fifth Avenue law firm of Weil, Gotshal & Manges, was appointed trustee for Muir's remaining assets. After eighty-three years on Wall Street John Muir & Co. had closed its doors. The hottest of the hot houses was dead.

Fourteen months after Muir's collapse Harvey Miller still was trying to unsnarl the firm's tangled affairs. By October 1982 he had successfully repatriated about 60 percent of Muir's accounts, though in about a half-dozen cases he had to sue customers who had inadvertently received refunds of more than the $500,000 limit under the Securities Investor Protection Act. Miller and law enforcement officials also scoured the files for any trace of some $200,000 in bearer bonds that mysteriously disappeared when Muir went bust. Miller's surgery wasn't painless. The industry-funded Securities Investor Protection Corp. (usually called by its acronym, "Sippic") poured more than $18 million into Muir, primarily to pay off loans that had been collateralized by customers' securities.

The SEC filed a civil suit over the Cayman Re issue, seeking to bar Dirks permanently from the securities business. Cayman Re signed a consent decree accepting guidelines for investment of its assets. Carl John Peterson accepted a three-year suspension. Cayman's former chairman, Michael Scott, remained in Canada, exempt from extradition in a civil case. Only Dirks chose to fight.

Midway through the trial, Dirks, who had invoked the Fifth Amendment during pretrial depositions, insisted on taking the stand—"I'd like to tell what I believe is the truth"—and fired his counsel, Stanley Arkin. He sought out two other lawyers, neither of whom could continue the case on such short notice, then returned to Arkin—but he remained off the stand.

When the defense argued that Cayman Re would have made $872 if it had held on to the stocks recommended by Dirks, Judge William Conner was not impressed. He rounded off the figures—$1,000 on an investment of $1 million.

"That's one percent," he snorted. "They could have done better at any savings bank and got a free toaster."*

Six months later Judge Conner ruled that Dirks had violated the securities laws in the Cayman Re issue, but declined to impose any penalty, not even the usual stricture enjoining him from future violations. Dirks's counsel called the decision a "significant victory," but added that he would appeal the guilty finding, anyway.

Dirks and Sullivan also faced administrative action by the SEC on charges of running a firm with less capital than the rules required; again, the maximum penalty would be revocation of their brokers' licenses. Meanwhile, the SEC continued another investigation into Muir's handling of the Security America issue. Two Security America officials were accused of falsifying company records and the stock prospectus; no one at Muir was charged. Muir's partners also faced possible liability for the $18 million advanced by SIPC—the stock market surge made payoff a possibility—while Dirks faced a slew of stockholder suits that threatened to keep him in court for years and tie up his few remaining assets.

But Dirks wound up not only victorious, but vindicated. After his nine-year vendetta with the SEC, the U.S. Supreme Court, in a landmark decision handed down on July 1, 1983, ruled that he was right all along to blow the whistle on the financial hanky-panky at Equity Funding.

Speaking for the majority, Justice Lewis F. Powell, Jr., said: "The test is whether the insider personally will benefit, directly or indirectly, from his disclosure. Absent some personal gain, there was no breach of duty to stockholders. And absent a breach by the insider, there is no derivative breach."

He noted that Secrist, who had tipped Dirks to the scandal, "was motivated by a desire to expose the fraud"—not personal profit—and therefore breached no duty when he informed Dirks. Dirks, undaunted by the years of legal furor, even returned to the security business. His new vehicle was Raysearch Associates. Operating out of his Greenwich Village coach house as a Connecticut partnership —with Kenneth Kirshon, a Shearson/American Express broker— Raysearch managed investment portfolios. Dirks limited his cus-

* The judge's arithmetic was off: $1,000 is one tenth of one percent of $1 million.

tomers to fewer than fifteen, thus obviating another "Shad row"—registration and regulation by his old nemesis, the SEC.

"Some people seem to have nine lives," commented Theodore Focht, general counsel of SIPC.

Raysearch was at least Ray Dirks's third life in high finance. Could be that sometime soon the financial writers once again will he hailing "Ray Dirks' Rebirth on Wall Street."

VII

PAC-MAN, CROWN JEWELS, AND GOLDEN PARACHUTES

Martin Lipton, the takeover specialist at the Park Avenue law firm of Wachtell, Lipton, Rosen & Katz, likened corporate takeover battles to the feudal wars of the Middle Ages. The corporate chairman is the count in the besieged castle. The lawyers are his mercenaries.

> The investment bankers are the clergy. They consult the scriptures by Moodys and Standard & Poors and damn the takeover bid as unfair or inadequate. They review the household accounts and bless the continued independence of the Castle. They comfort the serfs. They strengthen the resolve of the Count and the Council. They know the Bishops of Wall Street and can read the signs as they appear on the tape. They know the mercenaries and can reach them at any hour of the day or night. If the need arises, they act as emissaries to the neighboring Castles in the sometimes desperate last minute quest for a White Knight.

In recent years, however, the clergy have come out of the sanctuary and started manning the ramparts. With experience, judges stopped sustaining technical or trivial objections to takeover bids, taking the attitude—as jurists put it in the Bendix battle—"a plague on both your houses" and "let them fight it out in the marketplace." Investment bankers, perfecting their sophisticated skills, superseded the legal mercenaries as the strategists of tender-offer raids and the tacticians of takeover defense.

Although a Louis Auchincloss character complained, "Even the vocabulary gets me down. Terms like 'bear hug,' and 'blitzkrieg' and 'shark repellent'!" the investment bankers also enriched the language. To such Liptonesque locutions as "Saturday-night special" and "white knight" were added such colorful coinages as "two-tier tender," "crown jewel option," "Pac-Man defense," "double-barreled two step," and "golden parachute"—verbal shorthand to describe complex strategic maneuvers.

The takeover wars revolutionized investment banking, transforming mergers-and-acquisitions departments from back room operations that were maintained as "loss leaders" or services for established clients into operations that came to rival corporate-finance departments in size—and profits.

From the age of J. P. Morgan down to today's Felix Rohatyn, investment bankers have been merger brokers. But the era of tender-offer raids and takeover battles is relatively recent, barely a decade old.

Like the blue-chip law firms, most investment banks long scorned tender-offer raids as grubby and undignified. Until Robert F. Greenhill took over Morgan Stanley's mergers-and-acquisitions department, the firm maintained the old school's gentlemanly hands-off policy toward advising raiders on "hostile" tender offers. Then in 1974 Greenhill advised International Nickel of Canada on its takeover of EBS Inc., a Philadelphia battery maker—and the stampede started.

"He got into the merger business and changed the whole nature of the business and the whole nature of the firm," said one Wall Street observer. "Everybody else is an imitator. He made aggressive action respectable."

Those who got there first got the most. Joseph Flom—"King of the Takeovers"—and Lipton locked up the legal business of the takeover wars. In investment banking, three houses wound up with most of the action—Morgan Stanley under Greenhill, Merrill Lynch under Carl Fehrenbach, and First Boston under Joseph Perella and Bruce Wasserstein.

Their head start had a cyclical effect. The more battles they fought, the more expert they became. The more expert they became, the more business they got. The more business they got, the

more battles they fought. . . . Seeing how lucrative takeover battles became, some of the old-line houses hastened to get in on the
action. But they found themselves playing catch-up ball.

As the stock market slumped in the 1970s and the well of underwritings dried up, fees from mergers and acquisitions became a
much more significant part of the investment houses' income. In
Fortune's listing of the fifty "Biggest Deals of 1982" only two were
issues of common stock—both for AT&T—fifteen were for deben-
tures of the Federal National Mortgage Association (Fannie Mae)
and all the rest were mergers and acquisitions, many of them "hostile" takeovers.

Tender-offer raids themselves were a symptom of the sagging
market. During the go-go years of the 1960s, when stocks sold for
fifteen to twenty times earnings, few companies had the resources
to offer thirty to forty for another's shares. Even fewer would be so
profligate as to make such a bid. But when stocks fell to five or six
times earnings and often traded for less than a company's book
value, tender-offer raids became financially feasible. The outlay
could be recouped in a half-dozen years—or even sooner, by selling
off some of the acquired assets.

As interest rates and construction costs soared, it became more
economical to buy than to build. If Universal Conglomerate wanted
to expand into the wingding market, it was far cheaper—and
quicker—to acquire Independent Wingding in a tender-offer raid
than to build, equip, and man its own wingding plant from scratch.

"Today most major acquisitions are at the end of a well-thought-
out strategic plan, and the company has made a fundamental decision that they can achieve an objective most effectively by making
an acquisition within a certain set of parameters," said Merrill
Lynch's Fehrenbach. "It's a quick and often well-thought-out way of
accomplishing goals. To the extent it's well executed, well thought
out, and they make it work, it works to everybody's benefit."

Perhaps. But—as we shall see—the urge to merge sometimes
springs from the machismo factor, ego-tripping by a corporate executive eager to show off his empire building prowess.

For stockholders of the target company, tender-offer raids offered
the prospect of a quick buck—sale of a stock far above its market
price. But some saw long-term dangers in taking the money and
running.

"Stock buyers are only thinking about a quick buck," said Richard E. Cheney, a vice president of Hill & Knowlton, who handled the public relations in many takeover battles. "They're not thinking about putting money into something that's going to mean money to them five years from now. Their attitude has an impact on the economic system because management comes to think the way investors want them to think."

In any event, the merger mania showed no sign of abating. Mergers and acquisitions, a $23.7 billion business in 1969, swelled to $82.6 billion in 1981. That year also saw the two biggest mergers in American history, both of which were completed only after titanic takeover battles.

The first was the three-way struggle for Conoco, the nation's ninth-largest oil company. Seagram, advised by Lazard Frères and what was then Shearson Loeb Rhoades, Du Pont, advised by First Boston, and Mobil, the nation's second-largest oil company, advised by Merrill Lynch—all bid for Conoco. The bidding started at $87.50 a share and soon soared to Mobil's $120.

Even though its bid was lower, Du Pont offered a two-tier cash-or-stock option—the "double-barreled two step"—that was more attractive to many investors. Perhaps more crucial to the outcome was its public relations campaign, geared to the slogan, "Nine into two won't go." Conoco, advised by Morgan Stanley, accepted Du Pont's offer. Du Pont won, but because of the stock swaps, Seagram wound up as the largest shareholder in the Delaware chemical concern.

The dust barely had settled on the Conoco battlefield when the fight over Marathon Oil began. Mobil, again advised by Merrill Lynch, started it by offering $5 billion—$85 a share—for the Ohio oil company. Marathon resisted. Its lawyers threw up antitrust objections, while its bankers searched for a white knight. First Boston contacted thirty-five companies before it found a willing gallant in U.S. Steel, badly battered by German and Japanese competition and seeking to diversify into more lucrative fields.

U.S. Steel, advised by Goldman Sachs, jumped into the fray, offering $105 a share—a total of $6.36 billion. In one day Marathon shares shot up 27 1/4 points. But analysts noted that the reserves in Marathon's West Texas Yates oil field alone were worth $6 billion.

Losing virtually every round in the courts, Mobil tried another tactic, announcing that it intended to purchase 15 to 25 percent of U.S. Steel to "coerce" the white knight into withdrawing from the battle. But Big Steel carried the day—at a final price of $6.7 billion.

1982 saw another titanic struggle for an oil company, this time Cities Service. After Mesa Petroleum, advised by Donaldson, Lufkin & Jenrette, made a "friendly" offer for 15 percent of Cities Service, Cities Service decided to launch a preemptive strike. Advised by First Boston and Lehman Brothers Kuhn Loeb, it bid $380 million—$17 a share—for 51 percent of Mesa.

Mesa then went public with a "hostile" tender offer of $45 a share for 15 percent of Cities Service and called in relief pitching— Lazard Frères. The two companies started buying each other's shares.

Meanwhile, Cities Service had been searching for a white knight and found one in Gulf. The day after Mesa got the go-ahead to buy Cities Service shares, Gulf and Cities Service announced that they had agreed to a $5.04 billion—$63 a share—takeover. In a highly unusual action for a deal of such size, Gulf acted as its own investment banker.

But the deal suddenly fell through when the Federal Trade Commission raised antitrust objections. Rather than fight, Gulf threw in the towel. A day after the announcement Cities Service stock plummeted to 37 1/4.*

First Boston and Lehman, which had stood to split $20 million for brokering the merger with Gulf, started searching for another white knight, sounding out six other major oil companies, chemical concerns, and "smokestack" industries. Occidental Petroleum, ad-

---

* On paper, the biggest loser in the battle was Ivan F. Boesky & Co. The son of a Detroit postman, Boesky studied law and accounting at night school and plunged into Wall Street in the 1970s. He soon emerged as the boldest player in the high stakes game of risk arbitrage—buying large blocks of stock in takeover targets in the expectation that the final tender would fetch a far higher price. "What Boesky does," said a Wall Street observer, "is much closer to what Mr. Goldman and Mr. Sachs did one hundred years ago than a guy who takes a quarter on an underwriting or a guy who takes a check for putting together a deal." Working eighteen-hour days, in seven years Boesky parlayed a $4.1 million investment into a firm with assets of more than $300 million. He made an estimated $40 million on Conoco, but got creamed on Cities Service. Estimates of his Cities Service holdings, acquired at $52 to $55, ranged up to 3 million shares—which translated into a one-day paper loss of up to $52.25 million!

vised by Goldman Sachs, finally came to the rescue, but it was touch and go for a while. The final price was $4.05 billion—$55 a share for half the stock, securities worth $50 for the remainder.

Martin Lipton likened corporate takeover battles to the feudal wars. A corporate executive called the one he witnessed "the closest thing to combat I've seen since World War II." But unlike medieval mercenaries or twentieth-century dogfaces, the investment bankers who fight corporate takeover battles don't get killed. Win or lose, they just get richer. And the fees they command make Herschel Walker and Reggie Jackson look like paupers. But the fee structure contributes to the brutality of the battles.

To switch analogies: An investment bank that rides a loser collects only a "saddle up" fee; the winning jockey gets the purse. Merrill Lynch received a reported $1 million from Mobil in the Conoco battle; had Mobil won, the fee would have been $12 million. First Boston, which rode the winner, collected $14 million from Du Pont. The bank that represents a target company is paid a percentage of the purchase price, which sometimes induces it to touch off a bidding war for the client.

"The level of fees is so different, depending on what happens, and that's the unhealthy element," said Lazard's Felix Rohatyn. "All the dynamics are to fight. The company will do better for the shareholders by fighting, and with the investment bankers and lawyers, you have egos and fees involved."

Like military campaigns, corporate takeover battles are fought by young men. Only a handful of grizzled veterans have reached the age of forty, while men in their twenties may earn six-figure incomes. But they must endure the ordeals of battle—weeks of eighteen-hour days and periods when weekends, vacations, and personal commitments go down the tubes. The battle scars are ulcers, broken marriages, and burnout.

Conoco, Marathon, Cities Service—all were grueling battles. But they pale by comparison with what may have been the Armageddon of corporate takeover battles—1982's epic four-way contest among Bendix, Martin Marietta, United Technologies, and Allied. When the smoke cleared, the carnage was complete—a rubble-strewn battlefield, the reputations of captains of industry and their investment-banking advisers tarnished, corporate coffers sadly depleted. And there came a postwar hue and cry for regulatory reform.

In one sense, Bendix is not representative of corporate takeover battles, for four strong-minded principals overshadowed the supporting players. In Liptonesque terminology, the counts came out of their castles to tilt personally with the besieging knights.

If—as Lipton said—corporate-takeover battles are the contemporary equivalent of the feudal wars of the Middle Ages, Bendix is the only idyll with a Queen Guinevere.

According to one participant, the full story of Bendix will never be told: "The only guy to talk to is Agee, and he isn't talking to anybody."

Perhaps so. But the role of the investment bankers in creating the carnage of the Bendix battle is worth examining.

The story starts and ends with William M. Agee. The forty-four-year-old chairman of Bendix—the Southfield, Michigan, automotive parts, electronics, and aerospace concern—began as a protégé of W. Michael Blumenthal and succeeded him as chairman when Blumenthal became Jimmy Carter's Treasury Secretary. In the business world he was regarded as a brash manipulator who "runs Bendix like a stock portfolio," with an eye to quick profits, rather than long-term planning.

Agee also was one of the few captains of industry to hit the gossip columns—because of his relationship with Mary Cunningham, who rose rapidly through the ranks to become a Bendix vice president. When tongues clucked that her advancement might have been due to more than business acumen, Agee indignantly denied the rumors. But Miss Cunningham soon departed to become a vice president of Seagram.

Agee set his sights on companies to conquer. He met with the bankers at Salomon Brothers, but the Bendix account was assigned, not to J. Ira Harris, Salomon's chief merger maker, but to the relatively junior Jay F. Higgins, who drew up game plans for Agee. Bendix was code-named "Earth," RCA "Wind," and Martin Marietta "Fire."

In March 1982, after Bendix bought 7 percent of RCA and Agee seemed poised for a tender-offer raid, Thornton Bradshaw, RCA's chairman, snorted: "Mr. Agee has not demonstrated an ability to manage his own affairs, let alone someone else's."

Agee and Miss Cunningham were married in June, and Agee turned from "Wind" to "Fire." Bendix started buying shares of Martin Marietta—the Maryland-based aerospace and defense contractor—and by midsummer owned about 4.5 percent of the company. On Wednesday, August 25, Agee tried to phone Martin Marietta Chairman Thomas G. Pownall at his Bethesda headquarters, but failed to reach him. According to the official account, Pownall was tied up at a meeting; according to another, he suspected what was coming and refused to take the call. In any event, a messenger arrived a few minutes later with formal notice of Bendix's bid— $1.5 billion, or $43 a share, for 45 percent of Martin Marietta. Bendix stock, presumably, would be swapped for the remaining shares.

The official announcement appeared in the next morning's newspapers (see p. 149).

This was a tacit two-tier tender—tacit, because the second step was not explicitly stated, only "The purpose of the offer is to acquire shares for cash as a first step towards acquiring the entire equity interest in the company."

The two-tier tender is a device increasingly favored by bankers in takeover bids—cash for controlling interest, a stock swap for the remaining shares. Two-tier tenders are said to be "front-end loaded," because the cash offer is worth more than the stock swap. The idea is to create a stampede of shareholders tendering controlling interest by the proration date—in the case of Martin Marietta, September 4.

Two-tier tenders have been criticized for favoring institutional investors, who presumably follow business developments more closely than small stockholders and are therefore more likely to tender their shares and reap the maximum benefit. Small stockholders were given some protection under a 1968 law requiring that, if more shares than sought are tendered, purchases must be prorated.

In the wake of the Bendix battle—in December 1982—the SEC broadened this protection. By a 3 to 2 vote, it extended the proration date through the entire twenty-day tender period, thus giving small stockholders more time to tender their shares.

As soon as he received the Bendix bid, Pownall summoned Mar-

Notice of Offer to Purchase for Cash

Up to 15,800,000 Shares of Common Stock

of

Martin Marietta Corporation

at

$43 Net Per Share

by

The Bendix Corporation

> THE PRORATION PERIOD EXPIRES AT 12:00 MIDNIGHT, NEW YORK CITY TIME, ON SEPTEMBER 4, 1982. THE WITHDRAWAL DEADLINE IS AT 12:00 MIDNIGHT, NEW YORK CITY TIME, ON SEPTEMBER 16, 1982. THE OFFER WILL EXPIRE ON SEPTEMBER 23, 1982, AT 12:00 MIDNIGHT, NEW YORK CITY TIME, UNLESS EXTENDED.

The Bendix Corporation, a Delaware corporation (the "Purchaser"), is offering to purchase up to 15,800,000 shares of Common Stock, par value $1.00 per share (the "Shares"), of Martin Marietta Corporation, a Maryland corporation (the "Company"), for $43 per Share, net to the seller in cash, upon the terms and subject to the conditions set forth in the Offer to Purchase dated August 26, 1982 (the "Offer to Purchase") and in the related Letter of Transmittal (which together constitute the "Offer").

The Offer is not conditioned upon any minimum number of Shares being tendered.

The purpose of the Offer is to acquire Shares for cash as a first step towards acquiring the entire equity interest in the Compan~~y~~ ~~intends to acqui~~ ~~control of~~ ~~the~~ ~~Company~~

~~tender~~ ~~the Offer~~

~~being made to the Company for the use of its stockhold~~ ~~security position listings~~ for the purpose of disseminating the Offer to stockholders. The Offer to Purchase and the related Letter of Transmittal will be mailed to record holders of Shares and will be furnished to brokers, banks and similar persons whose names appear or whose nominees appear on the stockholder list or, if applicable, who are listed as participants in a clearing agency's security position listing for subsequent transmittal to beneficial owners of Shares.

The Offer to Purchase and the Letter of Transmittal contain important information and stockholders are urged to review them carefully before making any decision with regard to the Offer.

Requests for copies of the Offer to Purchase and the Letter of Transmittal may be directed to the Information Agent or the Dealer Manager as set forth below, and copies will be furnished promptly at the Purchaser's expense.

The Information Agent is:

D.F. KING & CO., INC.

One North LaSalle Street	60 Broad Street	400 Montgomery Street
Chicago, Illinois 60602	New York, New York 10004	San Francisco, California 94104
(312) 236-5881	(212) 269-5550	(415) 788-1119
(Call collect)	(Call collect)	(Call collect)

The Dealer Manager for the Offer is:

Salomon Brothers Inc

One New York Plaza
New York, New York 10004
(212) 747-6114
(Call collect)

August 26, 1982

tin Marietta's investment banker—Martin A. Siegel of Kidder Peabody, who came winging to Washington for a strategy session with the company's top executives and lawyers.

Siegel had "cultivated a reputation as a takeover defense coach," selling Kidder's services, for a $75,000-a-year retainer, to potential targets before they attracted the eye of a raider—"shark repellent," in the jargon of the trade. Approximately one hundred companies enrolled; Martin Marietta had signed up the year before.

Among his ploys was an "early warning system"—monitoring every major purchase of Martin Marietta stock. "We spotted Bendix accumulating long before they ever surfaced, so we quietly arranged with bankers to take down a lot of money in an emergency," Siegel said. "When Bendix launched their offer last August, they acted partly on the normally sound advice that we'd never be able to get enough money quickly enough to launch a credible counter-offer. But we were waiting with $1 billion."

After five frantic days—on Monday, August 30—Martin Marietta's board met and resolved to fight. It damned Bendix's bid as "inadequate" and called its front-end load "discriminatory." It then announced that *it* would bid for Bendix—another tacit two-tier tender of $75 a share for just over 50 percent and Martin Marietta stock valued at "approximately $55" for the remainder.

This was the so-called Pac-Man defense, named after the popular video game, "where my client eats yours before yours eats mine."

Martin Marietta's board also voted to give "golden parachutes" to twenty-nine top executives—guarantees of salary and perks should they lose their jobs after a takeover. Although their legal validity is under court challenge, companies increasingly are giving golden parachutes, often far in advance of a takeover threat. Sometimes the benefits are so great that they depreciate the target's value and deter a potential raider.

Formal announcement of Martin Marietta's offer came the following day (see p. 151).

The battle was joined. It was to be brief, brutal, and bloody. The *Wall Street Journal* predicted that the ultimate result "could be a stalemate," with both Bendix and Martin Marietta owning substantial chunks of each other.

In the postmortems, Salomon Brothers was charged with making several key errors. First, it underestimated Martin Marietta's will

Notice of Offer to Purchase for Cash
Up to 11,900,000 Shares of Common Stock
of

The Bendix Corporation

at

$75.00 Net Per Share

by

Martin Marietta Corporation

The Proration Period Expires at 12:00 Midnight, New York City Time, on Thursday, September 9, 1982. The Withdrawal Deadline is 12:00 Midnight, New York City Time, on Tuesday, September 21, 1982. The Offer Will Expire on Tuesday, September 28, 1982, at 12:00 Midnight, New York City Time, Unless Extended.

Martin Marietta Corporation, a Maryland corporation (the "Purchaser"), is offering to purchase up to 11,900,000 shares of Common Stock, par value $5 per share (the "Shares"), of The Bendix Corporation, a Delaware corporation (the "Company"), for $75.00 per Share, net to the seller in cash, upon the terms and subject to the conditions set forth in the Offer to Purchase dated August 31, 1982 (the "Offer to Purchase") and the related Letter of Transmittal, which together constitute the "Offer").

The Offer is not conditioned upon any minimum number of Shares being tendered.

The information required to be disclosed by Rule 14d-6(e)(1)(vii) of the General Rules and Regulations under the Securities Exchange Act of 1934 is contained in the Offer to Purchase and is incorporated herein by reference.

A request is being made to the Company for the use of its stockholder list and security position listings for the purpose of disseminating the Offer to stockholders. The Offer to Purchase and the related Letter of Transmittal will be mailed to record holders of Shares and will be furnished to brokers, banks and similar persons whose names appear or whose nominees appear on the stockholder list or, if applicable, who are listed as participants in a clearing agency's security position listing for subsequent transmittal to beneficial owners of Shares.

The Offer to Purchase and the Letter of Transmittal contain important information which stockholders are urged to review carefully before making any decision with respect to the Offer.

Requests for copies of the Offer to Purchase and the Letter of Transmittal may be directed to the Information Agent or the Dealer Manager as set forth below and copies will be furnished promptly at the Purchaser's expense.

Information Agent

MORROW & CO.

345 Hudson Street	39 South LaSalle Street
New York, New York 10014	Chicago, Illinois 60603
(212) 285-7400	(312) 444-1150
(Call Collect)	(Call Collect)

The Dealer Manager for the Offer is

Kidder, Peabody & Co.
Incorporated

10 Hanover Square
New York, New York 10005
(212) 747-5163

August 31, 1982

and financial capacity to resist. Second, it undervalued Bendix's bid —an error that was not rectified until September 7, when the offer was increased to $48 a share. Third, and most important, it failed to account for differences in the laws of Maryland—where Martin Marietta was chartered—and Delaware—where Bendix was chartered. Thus, Bendix wound up buying Martin Marietta, but found itself unable to exercise control immediately, and Martin Marietta, in effect, was able to buy itself back.

Worse, Salomon's bankers often were kept in the dark by their own client, excluded from meetings and not privy to vital decisions. Agee, holed up with his wife at the Helmsley Palace Hotel, the posh new hostelry rising above the Villard Houses on Madison Avenue, kept meeting with "everybody on Wall Street"—a steady stream of lawyers, bankers, and businessmen—in what came to be called "The Bill and Mary Show."

"The problem," said one banker, "was: What did Agee want to do?"

No one knew.

Martin Marietta had determined on a "scorched earth" policy and denied that it was searching for a white knight. But Siegel soon found what came to be called "the Gray Knight." On Tuesday, August 31—the day after Martin Marietta's board met—he called Harry J. Gray, the United Technologies chairman whose string of acquisitions for the Connecticut conglomerate included Otis Elevator and Carrier air conditioners, and sounded him out about joining the fray—not as a white knight riding to the rescue, but as a fellow predator splitting the spoils.

Gray had his investment banker, Felix Rohatyn of Lazard Frères, talk to Siegel, and two days later Pownall and Gray met in Martin Lipton's Park Avenue law office—Wachtell Lipton was counsel to both United Technologies and Kidder Peabody. In two and a half hours they agreed to carve up Bendix, with United getting the automotive division, Martin Marietta the aerospace and electronics operations.

On Tuesday September 7—the day after Labor Day—United formally entered the arena, matching Martin Marietta's $75-a-share offer (see p. 153).

Faced with this new threat, Bendix panicked. Its board, meeting three days later, voted golden parachutes for sixteen top-ranking

Notice of Offer to Purchase for Cash

Up to 11,900,000 Shares of Common Stock

of

The Bendix Corporation

at

$75.00 Net Per Share

by

United Technologies Corporation

> **The Proration and Withdrawal Deadline is 12:00 Midnight, New York City Time, on Tuesday, September 28, 1982. The Offer Will Expire on Tuesday, October 5, 1982, at 12:00 Midnight, New York City Time, Unless Extended.**

United Technologies Corporation, a Delaware corporation (the "Purchaser"), is offering to purchase up to 11,900,000 Shares of Common Stock, par value $5 per share (the "Shares") of The Bendix Corporation, a Delaware corporation (the "Company"), for . . . . tions set forth in the Offer to

the stockholder list or, if applicable, with . . . . parts in a clearing agency's securi . . . . transmittal to beneficial owners of Shares.

The Offer to Purchase and the Letter of Transmittal contain important information which stockholders are urged to review carefully before making any decision with respect to the Offer.

Requests for copies of the Offer to Purchase and the Letter of Transmittal may be directed to the Information Agent or the Dealer Manager as set forth below, and copies will be furnished promptly at the Purchaser's expense.

Information Agent

Georgeson & Co. Inc.

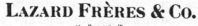

20 North Clark Street	Wall Street Plaza	606 South Olive Street	120 Montgomery Street
Chicago, Illinois 60602	New York, New York 10005	Los Angeles, California 90014	San Francisco, California 94104
(312) 346-7161	(212) 440-9800	(2.3) 489-7000	(415) 781-8860
(Collect)	(Collect)	(Collect)	(Collect)

The Dealer Manager for the Offer is

LAZARD FRÈRES & CO.

One Rockefeller Plaza
New York, New York 10020
(212) 489-6600, Extension (3) 640
(Collect)

September 8, 1982

executives, rejected United's bid as "inadequate" and "unfair" and started searching for relief pitching. Over the weekend its officials ran a competition among investment banks before settling on Bruce Wasserstein and First Boston. Salomon Brothers was unceremoniously shunted aside.

Wasserstein assembled a team of fifteen and outlined a three-pronged approach, handwritten on a four-foot-long sheet of papers pasted together. It looked like a series of spore clusters, listing each day's possible courses of action and the options if each succeeded or failed. First, to talk peace with Martin Marietta; second, to pursue the takeover bid; third, to search for a white knight to rescue Bendix, if need be, from the double clutches of Martin Marietta and United Technologies. Trouble was, he didn't know which course Agee intended to pursue.

While the lawyers battled in the courts of several states, financial observers denounced the debacle first as a "three-ring circus," then as a "seven-ring circus." Other show-business analogies likened it to a soap opera or to the Original Amateur Hour. A scientific analogy likened it to a financial black hole into which billions of dollars would disappear, to no ultimate accomplishment.

The problem was ego. Agee, apparently stung by the barbs about his private life, seemed determined to prove his prowess as a businessman. Pownall was equally determined to preserve the independence of the company he had so carefully nurtured. By this time the battle resembled less a feudal war or a horse race than a potlatch of the Kwakiutl Indians, with each tribal leader apparently willing to throw his most precious possessions into the fire in order to impress his rivals.

If the principals called the shots, the banking professionals had tactical skills to show off—and fees to collect. Victory would mean the difference between hundreds of thousands of dollars and millions.

United Technologies proposed a "friendly" merger with Bendix —upping its cash offer to $85 a share—but Bendix and Martin Marietta continued on their collision course. LTV was sounded out about entering the action—to bid for 5 percent of Martin Marietta, which automatically would have prolonged the tender period another ten days. But the deal fell through.

While Wasserstein, Siegel, and Higgins tried to talk peace, Agee pressed ahead with the acquisition. On Friday September 17 Bendix started buying Martin Marietta shares. By the end of the day it had acquired 53 percent—for a total holding of 57.5 percent—but it could not vote the shares and install its own board until September 30. In the interim Martin Marietta could start buying Bendix. As one banker put it, Agee "pulled the trigger and shot himself in the foot."

With bankers and lawyers in tow, Agee flew to Washington on Tuesday, September 21, to talk peace with Martin Marietta's executives. The bankers and lawyers did not attend the closed-door session, but Mary Cunningham did, and it "infuriated the guys at Marietta," according to one banker. "Just the thought of losing their company to a guy who is being advised or guided by Mary Cunningham was more than they could stand." Instead of passing the peace pipe, Martin Marietta announced that it would begin buying Bendix on schedule—starting at midnight the following day.

Meanwhile Wasserstein had found a white knight—Allied Corp. Allied's entrance added another element of ego to the drama. Edward L. Hennessy Jr., who became Allied's chairman in 1979, previously had been executive vice president of United Technologies —until he and Gray had a falling out. An Allied victory in the four-way contest would be sweet revenge.

Wasserstein and a team of bankers from Lehman Brothers Kuhn Loeb, Allied's investment bank, were racing a deadline. If they could put a deal in place by the close of business on Wednesday— 5:30 P.M.—the tender period for Bendix shares automatically would be extended for another ten days—time enough for Bendix to install its own men on Martin Marietta's board. A tentative agreement was announced at midday, but the details couldn't be hammered out in time.

J. Tomilson Hill III, one of the Lehman bankers working on the deal, was quoted in the *Wall Street Journal* as saying that the crunch "didn't leave us enough time to prepare and file the necessary documents with the Securities and Exchange Commission yesterday. I begged on my hands and knees for some encouragement from Bendix for us to proceed, but they wanted to keep their options open." According to another source, however, Hill's comments, apparently overheard on a speaker phone, were garbled. Even Hill's name was garbled in the *Journal* account.

In fact, though, no one was sure whether Agee intended to stand and fight or to pursue the merger with Allied—perhaps not even Agee himself. He called a special meeting of the Bendix board—at Bendix's New York office in the General Motors Building on Fifth Avenue—and asked for authority, if need be, to proceed with the Allied merger. He pressed for a quick decision, before Allied could change its mind.

Four outside directors resigned in protest: William P. Tavoulareas, president of Mobil, former Defense Secretary Donald Rumsfeld; former HEW Secretary Wilbur J. Cohen; and Hugo E. R. Uyterhoeven, associate dean of the Harvard Business School.

Not until midnight did Agee agree to the Allied rescue operation. By then, Martin Marietta had begun buying Bendix. By the end of the day—Thursday, September 23—it had acquired 46 percent and announced that it intended to purchase the other 5 percent required to achieve control of the company.

Meanwhile, Wasserstein was playing what has been called "the ultimate game of chicken." He upped the ante to Allied from $75 a share to $85. Allied offered $80, but Wasserstein stood firm. For hours the deal teetered precariously. Not until Friday was the final agreement hammered out—the shares already tendered to Martin Marietta were priced at $75, those not tendered—including a large block owned by the Bendix's employees' pension fund—at $85. Total price: $1.9 billion.

A key element in the deal was the so-called crown-jewel option, under which a target company divests or agrees to divest itself of prized assets to make itself less attractive to a raider—in Bendix's case, the aerospace operation that Martin Marietta coveted.

There was no need to exercise the option. Hennessy quickly made peace with Martin Marietta, hammering out an agreement under which the Bendix shares Martin Marietta had bought would be traded—at par—for the Martin Marietta shares Allied acquired through its purchase of Bendix. The swap still left 39 percent of Martin Marietta in Allied's hands.

When the dust settled, few had kind words to say about anyone involved—businessmen, bankers, or lawyers. "After twenty years of encouraging takeovers, investment bankers and lawyers are waking up and wondering what they had created," Ira M. Millstein, antitrust specialist at the Fifth Avenue law firm of Weil, Gotshal & Manges, said at a postmortem symposium sponsored by Oppenheimer & Co. "It's clear that the backlash is going to come."

It was swift in coming. Amid the rising demands for regulatory reform, in February 1983 the SEC appointed a sixteen-member advisory committee on corporate takeovers. Among the matters that the panel was charged to review were the Pac-Man defense, crown-jewel option, golden parachutes, whether stockholders should be required to approve a company's takeover plans and whether borrowing for takeover battles should be restricted. Indeed, the panel's first preliminary recommendation was a requirement for stockholder approval of golden parachutes—a measure drafted by Morgan Stanley's Greenhill and Joseph Flom, takeover specialist at the law firm of Skadden, Arps, Slate, Meagher & Flom.

But how far-reaching the reforms the committee would recommend was questionable, for the panel was loaded with veterans of the Bendix battle, so much so that the *Wall Street Journal* called it a "class reunion."

Nor did it seem likely that the panel would touch on the larger aspects of takeover wars: Are they worth the price? Is it more beneficial for the economy to buy than to build? Couldn't some of the nation's best brains be put to more productive uses than what is, in effect, playing Monopoly with real money?

In the postmortems the Monopoly players were accused of plotting ploys that might have been brilliant in a business school exercise but which proved disastrous in the exercise of business. "The investment-banking community has come out badly," said Lazard's Rohatyn, who escaped relatively unscathed.

Of all the investment banks, Salomon Brothers fared the worst. "This was Salomon's deal, and it exploded," said one banker, "and Salomon went down in the explosion." "The whole thing doesn't make any great point," said another, "except: Don't hire Salomon."

But Salomon had its defenders, among them Kidder Peabody's Martin Siegel, who said that "Salomon is being made the scapegoat." He placed the blame on Agee, whom he likened to New York Yankees owner George Steinbrenner III—"fire the manager."

As for Siegel himself, according to one rival, he "deserves a lot of credit for the tactics and blame for the result."

First Boston's Wasserstein was faulted for his "brinkmanship" that nearly jeopardized the deal with Allied, but he passed it off: "We took the risk, and it paid off." He added, "Normally, that would be considered a brilliant transaction."

If they felt the flak, the investment advisers laughed all the way to the bank. For little more than a week's work, First Boston and Lehman, which brokered the ultimate merger, each received fees estimated at $6 to $8 million. Even though it had been shunted aside in mid-battle, Salomon collected $3 million. Kidder Peabody got $750,000; had Martin Marietta's bid succeeded, the fee would have been in the neighborhood of $3 million. Lazard, which played a relatively minor role in the titanic struggle, got $700,000.

But Salomon had the last laugh in the debacle. I March 1983, Allied, seeking to reduce the debt it incurred in the battle, sold Salomon the 7.2 percent stake in RCA that Bendix had acquired during Agee's aborted bid—5.3 million shares. The $127.5 million transaction was largest ever recorded at the New York Stock Exchange. Salomon immediately resold the shares to some fifty institutional investors, netting approximately $2 million in commissions—for fifteen minutes' work!

What had the bankers wrought for all those shekels? Bendix disappeared. Martin Marietta remained independent—but at a cost of $1.4 billion in debt. By swallowing Bendix and 39 percent of Martin Marietta, Allied wound up with a staggering debt of $2.6 billion. Some suggested that the meal itself was indigestible and that the giant chemical concern was ill equipped to operate a high-tech company.

That's a frequent ailment of white knights. Unlike raiders, who have months in which to plan and survey, white knights must make billion-dollar decisions in a matter of days. In their acquisitive gluttony, they frequently ingest operations ill matched to their customary diet. Indeed, investment banks have developed a lucrative sideline helping corporations divest themselves of unpalatable acquisitions.*

* An esoteric specialty spawned by the merger mania is the leveraged buy-out, under which a company, or one of its divisions, "goes private." In most cases, the managers of the operation borrow against future earnings to finance the deal—in

One unpalatable morsel was William M. Agee. Under the merger agreement Agee became president of Allied. But his tenure there was brief, to say the least. Allied and Bendix formally merged on February 1, 1983. Within a week Agee was out on his ear. But his fall was cushioned by a golden parachute—$825,000 a year for five years.

Martin Lipton could have predicted it:

In rides the White Knight. . . . He vanquishes the Black Knight, repacifies the serfs and rebuilds the Castle. But alas, it is the White Knight's man who now sits at the Council table. The Count either swears fealty to his new overlord or joins his fellow exiles in Palm Beach or La Jolla.

So goeth the takeover wars.

One final quotation:

Unfortunately, too many lawyers seem incapable of stepping back from the papers and thinking in economic terms about a transaction. Does it really make sense? Can it be done a better way?

The author of those words—written four years before the Bendix battle—was First Boston's Bruce Wasserstein. They apply equally to investment bankers.

Presciently, Wasserstein added in his next sentence:

But it is also true that for a lawyer to be effective, an understanding and perceptive client is a must.

---

effect, "buying a company with its own cash flow." Leveraged buy-outs are used not only to divest unpalatable acquisitions, but as the ultimate defense against hostile takeovers—a company that isn't publicly traded can't be raided. The prime practitioner of this esoteric specialty is the "boutique" firm of Kohlberg, Kravis, Roberts & Co., followed closely by Merrill Lynch. In 1983 Kohlberg Kravis, which already had acquired such concerns as Congoleum and Handaille Industries, offered to outbid Chairman David Mahoney—$826.5 million to $738.8 million—on a proposed leveraged buy-out of Norton Simon, Inc., the conglomerate that started with Hunt tomato paste and grew to include Avis Rent A Car, Max Factor cosmetics, Johnnie Walker whiskey, and others. Significantly, Kohlberg Kravis retained an outside bank to handle its bid—Lehman Brothers Kuhn Loeb. Norton Simon wound up being acquired by white knight Esmark—the old Swift & Co., a client of A. G. Becker Paribas.

VIII

"PEOPLE HAVE TO STEAL OR KILL TO GET THIS KIND OF MONEY"

As the merger mania mounted and "hostile" takeovers threatened to supersede professional football as a spectator sport, the possibilities for illegal insider trading proliferated. Takeovers—even "friendly" ones—are labor-intensive, requiring corporations, investment banks, law firms, and public relations offices to mobilize scores of troops, many privy to highly sensitive secret information worth hundreds of thousands of dollars on the market. Said SEC Commissioner Bevis Longstreth: "The temptations have become dazzling."

Speaking of temptations, this seems the proper place to tell the story of two clerks at First Boston who were wheeling a cart filled with $4 million worth of negotiable bonds from one office to another. The younger man was tempted to grab the bonds, make a hasty getaway, and live happily ever after.

"I'm an Irish citizen," he explained. "They can't extradite me."

His companion, still working even though he was a dozen years past retirement age, was dubious.

"You know what will happen to us?" he asked.

"What?"

"We'll never work on Wall Street again."

Insider trading was not as cut-and-dried as a smash-and-grab job, but the setup was simple: Company A plans to bid for Company B.

Company B's stock is selling for $10 a share. Company A plans to offer $15. The insider buys Company B's stock for $10. Company A makes its offer public and Company B's stock soars—perhaps even beyond $15, as arbitrageurs rush in, hoping that Company B's resistance or interest from a white knight will force an even higher offer. The insider sells out at a huge profit. Perfectly simple—and completely illegal.

But in practice it was very difficult to prove, for a shrewd insider could mask his deals through intermediaries. Even though SEC Chairman John S. R. Shad gave top priority to illegal insider-trading cases and the commission brought more of them under the Reagan administration than in all its previous forty-six years, it touched merely the top of the iceberg. (Shad called for stiffer penalties for illegal insider trading, especially a triple-damage clause equivalent to that in antitrust cases.)

"It is very hard to prove insider trading," explained Wall Street lawyer Stephen Volk. "Unless you have a confession or eyewitness testimony, it is difficult to establish. You need a 'smoking gun,' and it's not easy for the SEC, with limited staff and limited resources, to locate such a gun in most cases."

Nevertheless, the SEC netted a varied bag of businessmen, bankers, lawyers, and others. Among them:

In a series of suits, officials and employees of Santa Fe International, their friends, relatives, and business associates were charged with buying the company's stock with inside knowledge of its pending purchase by Kuwait Petroleum. After the announcement the stock jumped 140 percent, while some options to buy soared from $37.50 to $1,925. Most of the defendants disgorged their profits and signed consent decrees—nebulous documents in which they denied doing anything wrong . . . and promised not to do it again.

This policy brought scathing criticism from Federal District Judge William Orrick Jr., who presided over one Santa Fe case in San Francisco: "These are thieves we're talking about. . . . Here these people come down and get a slap on the wrist. That isn't much in the way of deterrence."

In his written opinion, handed down six months later, Judge Orrick rejected the SEC's proposed settlement as "no more than telling a person caught stealing cookies that he must return them to the cookie jar, and agree never to do it again."

Indeed, in the half century that the SEC has been monitoring the markets, only six men have been found guilty of criminal charges of illegal insider trading—and one of those convictions was overturned on appeal. Among them was Carlo R. Florentino, an associate at two prominent New York law firms and later a partner at one. He traded in stock of seven targets of his firms' clients and in little more than three years ran a $50,000 nest egg into $450,000. However, he made no effort to conceal his dealings, and E. F. Hutton finally blew the whistle on him. He was forced to disgorge his profits and received a year's suspended sentence and two years' probation.

SEC scrutiny even extended to a paralegal's love life. The paralegal—never identified—had been dating Frederick Wyman II, a broker at L. F. Rothschild, Unterberg, Towbin, and told him about takeover cases she was working on—unaware that Wyman and his father Frank, a wealthy investor, were using the information for their own profit. Although the target companies were not named in the papers she handled, the younger Wyman had no trouble identifying them. Both Wymans signed consent decrees and returned their $99,000 profit. No action was taken against the paralegal.

The commission's net also snared a proofreader at Bowne of New York Inc., the big financial printer. Anthony Materia combed through the fine print of tender-offer prospectuses and allegedly made $215,000 trading in stock of five companies about to be sold or merged.

And more . . .

But the case that really rocked Wall Street involved two young bankers at two of the bluest of blue-chip investment houses—Morgan Stanley & Co. and Lehman Brothers Kuhn Loeb.

Adrian Antoniu met James Mitchell Newman in the mid-1960s when they were electrical engineering students at NYU, and their friendship continued after graduation when they both went to work at Bell Labs.

"We went to lunch sometimes," Antoniu later recalled. "We played tennis sometimes. I slept over at his apartment in New

Jersey sometimes when I didn't want to drive all the way back to New York. Occasionally we played bridge."

Antoniu was a penniless Romanian refugee who had arrived in the United States at the age of nineteen. Within a month his father died, and he had to go to work to support his mother and put himself through college. Blond and well built, he obviously was a man on the make.

After two years with Ma Bell, both men decided on career changes. Antoniu, who had taken an M.S. in electrical engineering at NYU, took off for Harvard Business School; Newman returned to NYU, also to business school. Upon graduation in 1972, Antoniu went to work as an associate at Morgan Stanley. Soon afterward, he bumped into Newman, who had become a trader in over-the-counter securities at the small brokerage house of Greene & Co., and they renewed their friendship.

Newman filled in Antoniu on the machinations of the market, and the two men soon hatched a get-rich-quick scheme. Antoniu would slip word of takeover targets to Newman, who'd buy the company's stock and wait for a propitious time to sell. Newman would put up his own money, but they'd split the profits fifty-fifty.

Although Antoniu worked in Morgan Stanley's corporate-finance department, which was separated by a "Chinese wall" from mergers and acquisitions—so that trading desks could not deal on the basis of inside information—occasionally he was drafted to work on corporate takeovers. Such calls soon started coming more frequently. Under the leadership of Robert R. Greenhill, Morgan Stanley's mergers-and-acquisitions department—the first at a blue-chip house to plunge into "hostile" takeovers—had more business than it could handle. By the end of the decade it would grow from a handful of persons to a staff of fifty-one. At any given time as many as one hundred different mergers and acquisitions would be in the hopper—$10 billion worth of deals a year.

In their early conversations Antoniu stressed that information about corporate takeover targets was extremely "sensitive" and that he'd surely lose his job if they were discovered. Newman arranged to camouflage the transactions by using his mother's former names—Jennie Glickstein and Jean Feifer—and spreading the trades through several brokers. As an added precaution, nothing was put in writing.

"The whole arrangement was based on trust," Antoniu said.

After he was caught, Antoniu claimed that he'd gotten into the scheme because he needed the money to repay school loans. But others viewed him as a relentless social climber who used the funds to finance a jet set life-style that included a plush Park Avenue apartment, an expensive BMW automobile, and weekends at the fashionable Hamptons on Long Island.

The conspirators' first opportunity came in the spring of 1973 when Antoniu was assigned to work on a "friendly" tender offer by Compagnie de Saint-Gobain-Pont-à-Mousson for CertainTeed, Morgan Stanley's client. Antoniu tipped Newman, who bought 1,000 CertainTeed shares in the name of Jean Feifer at 17¾ on April 30. The tender offer was announced the next day. On May 17 Newman sold out at 19⅛. The first of the conspirators' seventeen illegal insider trades had been completed successfully—at a profit of $1,375, minus brokers' commissions.

In 1973 Newman moved to Miami, where he became vice president in charge of the over-the-counter department at Executive Securities. To disguise his dealings, he did not use either of the firms where he had worked. Instead, he placed the trades through G. H. Sheppard—a now defunct brokerage run by three of his friends—with instructions to spread them as a "courtesy" to several other houses.

The second candidate for their illegal insider training did not come along until nearly a year later, when Morgan Stanley advised Ciba-Geigy on its takeover bid for Funk Seeds. Again, Antoniu tipped Newman, who bought 3,000 Funk shares, held the stock for three weeks, then sold out at a profit of $3 a share.

"The whole arrangement was based on trust," Antoniu had said. But there was no honor even among white-collar thieves. Although Antoniu and Newman had promised each other not to let anyone else in on their scheme, both broke their word—for their own profit.

Newman bought stock in target companies for one of his best customers, a La Jolla, California, businessman named Bruce Steinberg. Impressed with Newman's ability to pick "winners" and unaware that he was acting on inside information, Steinberg proposed that the broker act as his "eyes and ears on Wall Street." Steinberg put up the money, and Newman got 20 percent of the profits on the stocks he selected. Later, because of Newman's unusual string of successes, Steinberg upped the broker's share to one third. Over three years Newman netted $180,000 profit from Steinberg's trades alone. Neither Antoniu nor Steinberg knew of each other's part in the plot and, unbeknownst even to Newman, Steinberg tipped his father David to some of the deals.

Meanwhile Antoniu had begun illegal trading on his own, this time through two old friends—Frank Carniol, a fellow Romanian immigrant whom he'd known since childhood, and Constantine Spyropoulos, a Greek national who also had been an NYU classmate. Antoniu channeled some of his illegal profits from the Newman trades to Carniol, a Europe-based sales engineer for ITT and later for Westinghouse, who reinvested them—along with his own money—in other insider transactions. Carniol made his trades in his wife's name through secret bank accounts in Luxembourg and France. Spyropoulos, a Europe-based sales engineer for Raychem Corp., traded through secret Swiss accounts. In the early stages of the scheme Antoniu also tipped two other friends—Arnold Koetzen and Marc Glassman—to two pending deals.

In mid-1974 Antoniu was assigned to work on North American Philips' bid for Magnavox—a deal that would bring the conspirators their greatest single profit. Again, Antoniu tipped Newman, who over several months amassed 6,000 shares of Magnavox.

In August, Antoniu called Newman: "Jim, would you buy some more of this stock, because it looks like it's going to happen in the next few days."

Accordingly, Newman increased their Magnavox holdings to 17,600 shares.

On August 28 North American Philips made public its bid for Magnavox at $8 a share, but Antoniu advised Newman not to sell. Through his work at Morgan Stanley he knew that North American Philips planned to increase its offer. On September 5 North American Philips upped its bid to $9 a share—and Newman sold out. Both he and Steinberg made more than $50,000 each on the deal.

By this time Antoniu was becoming more concerned about security. During one meeting with Newman he pointed to an article in the *Wall Street Journal* and said, "Look what happened to these people at Sorg"—three employees at Sorg Printing Co. who had been caught trading in the stock of a company that had been the target of a tender offer they'd prepared.

Newman glanced at the article and replied: "Well, you see the worst that could happen in a case like this: they ask you for your money back, and they give you a slap on the hand." Then he added: "People have to steal or kill to get this kind of money, but you don't have to go to jail for it."

Yet there *was* cause to worry. Harold Hodor, one of the three partners of G. H. Sheppard, had asked Newman about his heavy purchases of Magnavox. Without identifying Antoniu, Newman said that he had an inside source working on takeover negotiations for the company. As a result, Hodor bought Magnavox stock for Sheppard's house account and for some of his customers.

After reaping their reward, Hodor and his partner, Norman Gomberg—the "G.H." in G. H. Sheppard stood for "Gomberg" and "Hodor"—arranged a cover story with Newman to explain their heavy trading in Magnavox. In fact, Sheppard was visited by a New York Stock Exchange examiner, but the cover story held.

In October 1974 Antoniu was assigned to another takeover project at Morgan Stanley—Standard Oil of Indiana's bid for Occidental Petroleum. Again, Antoniu tipped Newman, and on Newman's advice, Steinberg bought thousands of Occidental shares. Although the merger never was consummated, Occidental's stock rose, and the conspirators—as well as Steinberg's father—reaped another large profit.

Then disaster threatened to scuttle the scheme: Antoniu was told that his two-and-a-half-year apprenticeship at Morgan Stanley had not worked out and that he should seek employment elsewhere. December 31, 1974, would be his last day.

While he sought other employment, Antoniu looked for a candidate to carry on the conspiracy inside Morgan Stanley. Over a game of chess at the Harvard Club, he sounded out his Harvard Business School classmate, E. Jacques Courtois, Jr. For reasons known only to himself, Courtois accepted.

Unlike Antoniu, Courtois did not need the money. He was the son of a wealthy and prominent Montreal attorney who served on the boards of several banks and corporations and as president of the Montreal Canadiens hockey team. He had attended McGill University and Oxford before taking his M.B.A. at Harvard. At twenty-four, he was two years younger than Antoniu. They had started at Morgan Stanley's corporate-finance department at the same time, but Courtois clearly was on the "fast track." Although some acquaintances considered him "arrogant and socially condescending," he was more the "Morgan Stanley type" than the immigrant upstart Antoniu.

With Courtois aboard, the conspirators' profits had to be split three ways. "I was the middleman in the situation," Antoniu recalled. Obviously Newman knew of the existence of a new source inside Morgan Stanley, but he was not told his identity. Similarly, Newman's identity was not revealed to Courtois. For Antoniu, such secrecy was self-protection: If Courtois and Newman knew each other, they could cut out the middleman.

Even before Antoniu departed Morgan Stanley, Courtois came through with his first tip—Pan Ocean Oil, a Morgan Stanley client that was talking merger with Marathon Oil. From December 1974 through March 1976 Newman bought Pan Ocean shares at 10 to 10 1/2. Finally, on April 2, 1976, Marathon announced its bid, Pan Ocean's stock shot up, and Newman sold at 18 7/8—although some of his shares had been unloaded earlier at lower prices to finance faster-moving deals. The conspirators made a profit of $118,709.

A year earlier, in April 1975, Antoniu had found a new job in the mergers-and-acquisitions department of Kuhn, Loeb & Co. Unfortunately for the conspiracy, Kuhn Loeb was far less active in takeover work than Morgan Stanley—the department consisted only of one partner and one associate—and its targets were far smaller—companies whose stock often traded over the counter, where high-volume transactions were more likely to be noticed. Nevertheless, Antoniu soon started sending a steady stream of takeover tips to Newman in Florida and to Carniol and Spyropoulos in Europe. Courtois was not cut in on the Kuhn Loeb trades.

During this transition period, further security precautions were taken. Antoniu had suggested to Newman that they trade through foreign accounts—as Carniol and Spyropoulos did—but Newman balked, fearing that he'd have to disclose the existence of such accounts on his tax returns. However, after Steinberg explained the tax advantages of offshore trusts, Newman relented. On December 31, 1974, Steinberg set up the First Plimpton Trust, ostensibly for the benefit of Newman's mother, at the Trust Company of the Bahamas. Later, Steinberg set up the Midget Trust and Newman the Jennie Glickstein and Jean Feifer trusts at N. T. Butterfield & Sons in Bermuda.

Newman soon discovered another advantage in the offshore trusts—trades could be made in the banks' names, further preserving the secrecy of the illegal transactions, but Butterfield balked at his suggestion that the trades be spread among several brokers, as G. H. Sheppard had done.

To disguise the paper trail further, the accounts were financed with U.S. Treasury notes. Newman argued that the notes did not identify the bearer and thus could not be traced, apparently unaware that the serial numbers *were* recorded by the banks—a point that eventually contributed to his downfall. As a further precaution, Newman insisted that the notes be redeemed only by their depositors—which meant that he had to take frequent flights to New York, even though Antoniu worked only a block away from the depository.

In another precautionary move, Antoniu and Newman agreed to phone each other only over public phones and WATS lines, so the calls could not be traced—using aliases. Antoniu's was "Barnett," because Newman knew no one else named Barnett.

For nearly a year and a half, however, the scheme was virtually stagnant. The few takeover tips received by the plotters produced paltry profits. From Kuhn Loeb, Antoniu tipped Newman to buy Hudson Pulp & Paper, target of a "friendly" takeover by the Times-Mirror Co. On some days Newman's and Steinberg's purchases accounted for 100 percent of the Hudson trades, but the takeover fell through, and no profits were realized.

Antoniu's next tip proved more successful—Copperweld, target of a "hostile" and ultimately successful bid by Societe Imetal. The Midget Trust made a $13,787 profit on the transactions.

The Romanian immigrant's third tip from Kuhn Loeb was Hygrade Foods, target of a three-stage takeover bid by Hanson Trust. Again, on some days Newman's and Steinberg's purchases accounted for 100 percent of the trades in Hygrade. But Newman sold out before the second stage so he could use the money to buy more Pan Ocean stock. Again, no profit was realized.

In February 1976 Courtois tipped Antoniu to Société Nationale

Elf Aquitaine's bid for Ventron Corp. However, Ventron was a thinly traded stock, and Newman could amass only 700 shares. Although the stock rose nearly two points in three weeks, the conspirators' profit was only $1,094.

Meanwhile, Antoniu was working on Chemischewerke Huls' bid for Robintech. Newman bought several large blocks of stock in the target company, but midway through the preparations Huls changed its mind and decided not to undertake the acquisition. Robintech's stock fell, and the conspirators took a $100,000 bath.

"I was wrong, and we lost a great deal of money in the stock," Antoniu admitted.

It was the only large loss the schemers suffered.

During the doldrums Newman sold jewelry and made plans to build paddleball courts in Florida. He and Antoniu also gambled on stocks without inside information—and without any great success. But by the late summer of 1976 the scheme started to take off —largely as a result of Courtois' tips from Morgan Stanley.

In August Courtois started working on Sandoz Limited's bid for Northrop King & Co. He called Antoniu at his weekend retreat in Maine and told him, with "a sense of urgency," that a foreign buyer would be bidding for Northrop King.

Antoniu immediately called Newman: "Jim, will you buy a position in Northrop King as soon as possible."

Newman bought 10,000 shares at 9 to 9½. On September 17 Sandoz sent a secret "bear hug" letter to Northrop King's management—an offer to buy at a premium in a "friendly" takeover. Again, Courtois tipped Antoniu, Antoniu called Newman, and Newman purchased another 2,500 shares at 11⅜ to 11⅞.

The public announcement of the proposed acquisition was made four days later. Northrop King's stock shot up, but antitrust problems—widely recognized in the financial community—threatened to block consummation of the deal. The conspirators started to sell, unloading 300 shares at 16 to 16½.

Then Courtois tipped Antoniu that the antitrust problems had been resolved. Again, Antoniu told Newman, who bought another 10,000 shares at 16½. After resolution of the antitrust problems was announced, Northrop King's stock shot up again. On November 1 Newman sold 20,500 shares at 19 1/2. The Midget Trust alone netted $144,503.

Later that month Courtois tipped Antoniu that Monroe Auto Equipment was the target of a takeover by Tenneco. Antoniu passed on the tip to Newman, who instructed Steinberg to buy Monroe Auto for the Midget Trust. He did—14,500 shares at 8 3/8 to 10.

On November 30 Courtois passed on another tip to Antoniu—Warner-Lambert's bid for Deseret Pharmaceuticals. He told Antoniu that he had to act "very fast": "Buy immediately." Antoniu, in turn, called Newman, who instructed Steinberg to buy 6,000 shares for the Midget Trust—16 percent of the day's volume in Deseret—at 27 5/8 to 29 1/2. The stock shot up so quickly that the New York Stock Exchange suspended trading in Deseret.

Disturbed by this turn of events, Steinberg called Newman and asked what was happening. For the first time the broker let the cat out of the bag. He said that Warner-Lambert was about to make a "run" on Deseret. Steinberg asked how he knew.

"Morgan Stanley," Newman replied.

The revelation made Steinberg even more disturbed. A few days later he called Newman again and asked about the purchases of Monroe Auto. Newman told him that Tenneco was about to bid for the company and, without identifying his source, again said that the information came from Morgan Stanley.

After the public announcement of Tenneco's bid, Steinberg called Newman a third time and "questioned the legality or illegality" of trading in Monroe Auto. He urged Newman to sell the stock immediately. Newman did—netting the Midget Trust alone another $21,734 profit.

When Antoniu passed on a tip from Kuhn Loeb that Revere Copper & Brass was the target of secret takeover negotiations by Arasco, he and Newman decided to seize the opportunity to transfer some of their profits out of the trust accounts. They realized $130,000 in trades of Revere stock and options and, through a series of complex transactions, transferred the funds to the Banque de Paris, where the money was mingled with Carniol's account and eventually funneled back to the stateside conspirators.

They tried the same thing with Bancal Tri-State—another tip from Courtois—but the takeover was aborted, and there was no profit to transfer. In fact, the Midget Trust lost $8,369 in Bancal Tri-State transactions. This time, Newman did not tell Steinberg that his information came from Morgan Stanley. Instead he lied, saying that he'd heard that a large stockholder was planning to unload his Bancal Tri-State stock.

In the interim Steinberg had consulted counsel—a New York attorney named Neil Baron. In a letter to the La Jolla businessman, Baron warned that "the SEC has taken a very clear position against trading on nonpublic, material market information." He advised Steinberg to cease such trading and said that, if he persisted, he would resign as Steinberg's counsel.

Accordingly, in March 1977 when Newman asked Steinberg to buy Gerber Products—target of a takeover bid by Anderson Clayton—for the Midget Trust and admitted that his information came from Morgan Stanley, the Californian refused to execute the order. That effectively ended the participation of Steinberg and the role of the Midget Trust in the illegal scheme.

Undaunted, Newman bought 4,000 Gerber shares for the Glickstein Trust at 31 to 31 1/8. Although Anderson Clayton's bid ultimately failed, Gerber's stock rose. Newman sold at 38 7/8 to 39, reaping a profit of $28,798.

Within a month Antoniu was visited by SEC investigator Thomas Valery and questioned about his dealings with Newman. Antoniu lied, saying that Newman had sought to act as *his* investment adviser and that his purchases of suspect stocks had been made on Newman's recommendations.

As soon as Valery left, Antoniu called Newman, and they agreed to "cover for each other." They also agreed that further trading on the basis of inside information from either Morgan Stanley or Kuhn Loeb was too risky, but to avoid suspicion by closing their accounts, they continued to trade in other stocks.

There was one final act of bad faith. Unbeknownst to Newman, Antoniu placed two more orders based on inside information from Kuhn Loeb through Carniol and Spyropoulos.

With that, the conspirators' illegal insider trading ceased.

It took the authorities nearly four years to unravel the tangled threads of the conspiracy.

The investigation began at the New York Stock Exchange when

market surveillance experts noted flurries of activity in shares of companies soon to become takeover targets. The NYSE went to the SEC with its findings, and after several months of combing through trading records, the SEC's enforcement investigators concluded that the market corner wasn't the work of some lucky investment guru, but of an organized conspiracy. The SEC, in turn, took its findings to the U.S. attorney's office and assigned an investigator, Lance Clifton, full-time to assist the prosecutors.

"It was a very difficult case to break," said Lee S. Richards, the assistant U.S. attorney in charge of the investigation and prosecution. "We took baby steps. Sometimes we stepped in the right direction and sometimes we stepped in the wrong direction."

Because so many of the transactions were made through offshore and European banks that guaranteed their clients' anonymity, it was next to impossible to identify all the participants in the scheme. But one common thread wound through all the suspect transactions—either Morgan Stanley or Kuhn Loeb had been involved, representing either a raider or a target. And that led the investigators to Adrian Antoniu, who had worked at both houses.

"Usually you start from the bottom up," said one investigator. "This time it just happened that you started with the top and had to work your way down."

By then, Antoniu had become engaged to Francesca Stanfill, a former reporter for *Women's Wear Daily* and a fashion writer for the New York *Times Magazine.* More important, she was the daughter of Dennis Stanfill, chairman of Twentieth Century-Fox. The marriage would be the capstone to Antoniu's career of social climbing.

During the spring of 1978 Antoniu was called in for questioning by the U.S. attorney's office. Again, he lied, telling the prosecutors that his purchases of suspect stock had been made on Newman's recommendations, not his or Courtois' inside information. He didn't report the incident to his superiors at the firm—which, by then had become Lehman Brothers Kuhn Loeb—but he immediately called Newman.

Meeting clandestinely on a street corner near Central Park, the two decided to continue with their cover story, but they feared that a mutual friend named Mike Negoescu might reveal the true nature of their relationship if he were questioned by the authorities.

Antoniu said he'd tell Negoescu "to take a trip abroad"—and accordingly Negoescu left the country.

By June federal investigators had descended on both Morgan Stanley and Lehman Brothers Kuhn Loeb. Morgan Stanley was asked to supply the home telephone numbers of all its employees. Then the corresponding records, as well as Morgan Stanley's, were combed for any calls to area code 305—Miami's.

The investigators merely told Morgan Stanley that the government was conducting an industrywide inquiry into insider trading, but Lehman Brothers Kuhn Loeb was informed that the investigation focused directly on Adrian Antoniu. Eric Gleacher, head of the mergers-and-acquisitions department, was aghast and called Antoniu on the carpet for failing to advise the firm that he was under investigation. He also asked Antoniu if he'd informed his prospective father-in-law. Not only was Twentieth Century-Fox a longtime Lehman client, Stanfill himself was a Lehman alumnus.*

"Adrian told me there was nothing to the federal charges and indicated he didn't want to bother the Stanfills by informing them," Gleacher said.

Gleacher then told Antoniu: "If there is nothing to the charges and you want to have the Stanfills stand by you in defending against them, you really ought to tell them."

Instead, Antoniu took off for Europe. On June 28 he and Francesca Stanfill were married at a civil ceremony in Venice.

"Eric exploded when he heard they had gone through the civil ceremony without telling the Stanfills," said a former Lehman banker who had heard Gleacher's end of the transatlantic telephone conversation the next day. "He finally told him flatly that 'unless you tell Mr. Stanfill before the church wedding, I will!'"

Apparently Antoniu told Stanfill—whose reaction is not recorded —and the lavish church wedding was held on Saturday, July 1, in the Basilica di San Pietro di Castello. (The bride's mother had been active in raising money for the Venice preservation project.) Among the congratulatory messages was one from Venice's Albino Cardinal Luciani, soon to become Pope John Paul I.

At the wedding reception afterward Antoniu toasted his bride: "Here's to the longest run Twentieth Century-Fox will ever have."

---

* Although he was considered a protégé of Lehman's new chairman, Lewis Glucksman, in November 1983 Gleacher jumped ship to join Morgan Stanley.

The crusty Stanfill confined himself to a simple: "To the bride and groom."

Over the weekend Antoniu's office at Lehman Brothers Kuhn Loeb was cleaned out. Within the month his marriage was annulled.

Having lost both job and wife, a distraught Antoniu returned to New York. He told some friends that he was considering suicide. Instead, according to the government, he "fled to Europe" and landed a job with Egon Zehnder International, executive "head-hunters" in Milan.

Still, no stigma or suspicion attached to Jacques Courtois. In 1977 he had been promoted to a vice presidency at Morgan Stanley and transferred to the mergers-and-acquisitions department, the house's "hot shop." But early in 1979, apparently sensing that the net was closing on him, he resigned, saying he planned to enter the computer softwear business. Instead he went into import-export—in Bogota, Colombia.

Unlike Antoniu, Courtois didn't leave under a cloud. "Morgan Stanley was rocked at the time," said a former colleague in mergers and acquisitions. "They had lost three people, including Jacques, in something like three weeks. They had a series of meetings to make sure they were hanging on to the rest of us."

It took another two years for the authorities to close the net—and by then many of the fish had escaped.

Antoniu, his ill-gotten gains squandered on high living and legal fees, returned to the United States and worked out a plea bargain with the government. On November 15, 1980, he pleaded guilty to a two-count information charging him with violating the securities laws. Both the information and the plea were kept secret while Antoniu, mastermind of the illegal insider-trading scheme, informed on his fellow conspirators.

On February 13, 1981, a twenty-six-count indictment, charging conspiracy, securities fraud, and mail fraud was filed against Courtois, Newman, Carniol, and Spyropoulos. The investigation had taken so long that the statute of limitations had lapsed on most of the illegal transactions. The substantive counts included only the trades made in 1976, 1977, and 1978—Pan Ocean Oil, Ventron, Northrop King, Monroe Auto Equipment, Deseret, Gerber, and Bancal Tri-State.

Only Newman showed up for the arraignment. Courtois was believed to have been in Colombia and Carniol in Belgium, while Spyropoulos simply disappeared.

News of the indictment sent tremors through the financial community. It was the sort of thing one expected of sleazy operators in back room "bucket shops," but not of bankers of the stature of those at Morgan Stanley and Lehman Brothers Kuhn Loeb.

"I've always thought of Morgan Stanley as the crème de la crème," said Benedict T. Haber, dean of Fordham University's Graduate School of Business. "It's like an icon has been knocked down."

Morgan Stanley, which had tried in vain to induce the government to announce that it had cooperated in the investigation, did so itself and contacted clients to reassure them and say that the firm was an innocent victim. "If you've got a clever crook in your midst, there is not much you can do about it," explained John G. Evens, one of the firm's managing directors.

The wheels of justice ground slowly. Judge Charles Haight threw out the indictment of Newman on grounds that his conduct constituted neither securities nor mail fraud. The government appealed, and the court of appeals reinstated the indictment. Then the indictment was dismissed again, on a technicality—a special assistant U.S. attorney who had presented some of the evidence to the grand jury had not been properly appointed. So the four defendants had to be indicted again.

Meanwhile—on December 8, 1981—Steven Nussbaum, a Long Island dentist, pleaded guilty to a single conspiracy count for trading on tips supplied originally by Antoniu and Courtois. In his brief courtroom apperance Dr. Nussbaum said that he had paid Bruce Paul, a broker friend of Gomberg's, for the information. Paul, in turn, was indicted for perjury and obstruction of justice in the SEC inquiry. The Nussbaum and Paul cases indicated that the illegal insider-trading scheme had even wider and still unexplained ramifications.

A year later Dr. Nussbaum still had not been sentenced—an indication that he, too, was cooperating with the authorities. Prosecutor Richards would say only that the investigation was "continuing," though by the end of 1982 the statute of limitations had lapsed on nearly all of Antoniu's and Courtois' trades.

Newman was finally brought to trial on April 19, 1982. Both Antoniu and Steinberg testified for the government. (Steinberg asked for—and received—immunity from prosecution, even though the government said it was not "presently possessed of information that [he] has committed a crime.") Newman did not take the stand in his own defense. After a monthlong trial and a day of deliberations the jury found Newman guilty on all counts. On July 16 Judge Haight fined him $10,000 and sentenced him to a year and a day in prison and three years' probation, during which he had to perform unpaid public service. But he remained free on bail pending appeal.

Spyropoulos, who had been living in Athens, returned to the United States in February 1983, pleaded guilty to a single count of conspiracy, and was released pending sentence. The government finally obtained an order to extradite Courtois from Colombia, but by then he too had disappeared. He was tracked down in Montreal in September, after two and a half years as a fugitive. He was returned to New York and released on bail pending trial. A petition for Carniol's extradition from Belgium remained pending.

On August 11, 1982, Judge Charles Stewart fined Antoniu $5,000 and sentenced him to three months in jail and three years' probation, but he, too, remained free while his attorney argued for a reduction of sentence.

The scheme's mastermind may have admitted his guilt, but he was far from contrite. "This case is not something unique," he told the New York *Times* in a telephone interview from Milan. "I'm not saying I'm not guilty, because I've pleaded guilty. . . . But anyone familiar with the securities markets knows these circumstances are not uncommon."

Which might give Wall Street pause to ponder.

There was another cause for concern: A decade after the illegal insider-trading scheme was hatched, a half-dozen years after the investigation was launched, months after three men pleaded guilty and another was convicted, after the expenditure of hundreds of thousands of dollars of the taxpayers' money, not one of the admitted or alleged conspirators had spent one second behind bars or been forced to disgorge one penny of profit.

IX

"THE BRITISH ARE COMING!"

As old-line investment houses expanded to become full-service securities firms—adding retail, trading, venture-capital, international, and other departments—they required massive infusions of capital. In the past, investment banks raised money by assessing partners or taking in new ones. Under incorporation, this no longer was possible, even if the vast amounts required had been within the means of managing directors.

Some firms solved the problem by going public—others, by going international.

The fifty-year-old strictures of Glass-Steagall made it impossible for investment houses to turn to commercial banks. But the act was designed to protect American depositors, who, presumably, did not maintain accounts overseas. As a result, foreign banks were not precluded from investing in American underwritings—or American underwriters. When Wall Street's investment houses needed capital, they could turn to Barings but not to Bankers Trust, to Crédit Suisse but not to Citibank.

Thus, European banks wound up with significant holdings in several major Wall Street investment houses—Credit Suisse in First Boston, Banco Commerciale Italiana in Lehman Brothers Kuhn Loeb, Banque Bruxelles Lambert in Drexel Burnham Lambert, and Skandinaviska Enskilda Banken in Dillon Read.

"The real change goes back to who provides the capital," explained Drexel Burnham Lambert Chairman Robert E. Linton. "This has traditionally been an industry of mortals. In the old days you invited a partner to come in, and he put up some capital. That doesn't happen anymore. Incorporation led to the institutionalization of capital."

Before long, European banking houses began to eye Wall Street not only as an investment, but as a natural extension of their own economic empires. They started gobbling up American securities firms, in whole or in part, so much so that a modern-day Paul Revere might gallop through the canyons of Manhattan's financial district sounding the alarm: "The British are coming! The British are coming!"

And the French . . . and the Belgians . . . and the Swiss . . . and the Italians . . . and the Arabs . . . and more. Not since the days of the Robber Barons had there been such a flood of foreign capital into the United States. Except in the 1980s they didn't buy the underwritings—they bought the underwriters.

Phibro's acquisition of Salomon Brothers fits another part of the pattern—the sale of a privately held investment house for the partners' profit. Strictly speaking, the sale is not an example of foreign investment; Phibro, after all, is chartered in Delaware and headquartered in New York. But it is a truly international institution, with branches and subsidiaries around the globe, while its largest shareholder—with 27 percent—is Harry F. Oppenheimer, the South African minerals magnate whose interests include Anglo American Corporation and De Beers, the diamond-marketing monopoly.

One year later a similar scenario was enacted at the medium-sized house of Oppenheimer & Co. Founded in 1950 by Max Oppenheimer,* the firm got its start trading in postwar German marks. Although it participates in syndications, Oppenheimer eschews managing underwritings as too tame. "We don't want those fairly doltish three-piece-suiters," one employee explained. But Oppenheimer became a major merger maker and venture-capital concern, plunging in millions to rejuvenate such bankrupt enterprises as the

---

* No kin to the South African family.

St. Louis railroad terminal and the Chicago Milwaukee Corp. It also raised $40 million to finance John Z. DeLorean's ill-fated sports car venture.

In recent years the firm was headed by the "Odd Couple" combination of Jack Nash and Leon Levy. They are a study in contrasts. Nash is breezy and informal, insisting on being addressed as Jack. "Mr. Nash is my father," he explains. Levy, on the other hand, is the epitome of an absent-minded professor. The tale is a Wall Street legend: Levy ushered a woman into a taxi, then walked around the cab to the opposite door and, on opening it, exclaimed: "I'm sorry, I didn't know this cab was taken." Nash concentrated on administration of the firm, Levy on investment ideas becoming, as *Institutional Investor* put it, "the partner in charge of interplanetary affairs."

In the mid-1970s Oppenheimer, too, received an infusion of foreign capital—a 10 percent investment by Britain's Electra Investment Trust. Then in 1982 the twenty-six Oppenheimer partners decided to take the money and run, selling their firm for $162.5 million to an Electra subsidiary, Mercantile House Holdings, P.L.C. The price tag was nine times Oppenheimer's earnings and treble its book value.

Although Nash went onto Mercantile's board and Levy onto Electra's both men gradually withdrew from Oppenheimer's day-to-day management to devote themselves to other ventures. (Among other things, they formed Odyssey Partners and acquired a 5.2 percent interest in Trans World Corp., parent company of TWA, Hilton International hotels, Century 21 real estate, and two food and restaurant chains. However, they failed in their effort to achieve a sort of reverse synergy—to break the conglomerate into separate parts that individually might have been worth more than the whole.*) With the withdrawal of Nash and Levy, Stephen Robert, who succeeded Levy as chairman in 1983, became the prime mover at Oppenheimer.

Like Phibro at Salomon, the hand of Mercantile scarcely made itself felt at Oppenheimer. As one banker there put it, "As far as walking in the door, it makes no difference at all."

* After rebuffing Odyssey, Trans World itself spun off the ailing airline. Odyssey teamed with other investors to buy New American Library, the paperback publisher, from the Times-Mirror Co.

This was not the case at two other European-controlled investment houses.

In 1854 Baron Alphonse de Rothschild sent a letter from the New World to the Old, suggesting that Europe's richest family—which owned banks in London, Paris, Frankfurt, Vienna, and Naples—set up shop in America. Nothing came of it. "They were too rich and too fat," explained a present-day scion, Nathaniel de Rothschild.

More than a century passed before the Rothschilds set up an American branch—New Court Securities Corp., named for the London address of N. M. Rothschild & Sons. For fourteen years, under the presidency of John F. Birkelund, New Court operated as an independent arm of the Rothschilds' far-flung financial empire. The British and French Rothschilds owned 60 percent of the enterprise; New Court's American management the remainder. It seemed a profitable arrangement for both sides; between 1977 and 1980 New Court earned an annual average of 35 percent of capital.

American independence came to an abrupt end on the Fourth of July 1981, when the Rothschilds bought out the minority ownership and bounced Birkelund, who wound up as president of Dillion Read. Baron Guy de Rothschild, grandson of Alphonse and head of the French branch of the family, and Evelyn Rothschild, chairman of N. M. Rothschild, installed themselves as cochairmen, while Gilbert de Botton, who headed the Rothschild Bank AG of Zurich, was named interim president. To symbolize the change, the firm was renamed simply Rothschild Inc.

The ostensible reason for the Rothschilds' action was their desire to integrate the American operation into the family empire. But the immediate cause, undoubtedly, was Birkelund's independent course. He had proposed increasing management's ownership share to 51 percent and, when that was rejected by the Rothschilds, talked openly about forming his own firm, taking with him a cadre of key New Court employees.

"We did what had to be done," Baron Guy said succinctly.

Nine months after New Court's non-Independence Day, the Rothschilds completed the transition by naming a new president of their American subsidiary—Robert S. Pirie, the forty-seven-year-old protégé of Joseph Flom, "King of the Takeovers," at the midtown law firm of Skadden, Arps, Slate, Meagher & Flom. At "Skarp," Pirie, the Boston-based scion of the Chicago department-store family, had been in charge of the New Court account.

"I'd been practicing law for twenty years," Pirie recalled. "The last ten at Skadden Arps had been marvelous. I never really thought of leaving. My initial reaction was to say no."

Then he reconsidered. He was reaching an age in life when few opportunities for career change are left—"except perhaps to become ambassador to Denmark.

"If I was going to move, the only area I was going to go to was investment banking," Pirie continued. "The opportunities here are just terrific. So it all added up to, 'Why not?' "

Pirie started his new career on June 1, 1982. Unlike Birkelund, he showed proper deference to his Rothschild masters: "Now it's going to be part of the Rothschild operations worldwide. We think there's a tremendous opportunity to use the relationship the family has for American and foreign clients." But his actions paralleled many of those Birkelund was making at Dillon Read.

Rothschild was a small house—only eight managing directors, a total staff of about seventy. "Small, but very profitable," Pirie noted. Its strengths were money management and venture capital. It had a small—and very new—real estate section, but it did very little trading and very little in the way of underwriting or syndication. Most important, "this place had been run totally independent of the rest of the [Rothschild] group," Pirie noted. "There was no interchange."

Pirie soon started putting his stamp on the operation. Within two weeks he recruited Madelon DeVoe Talley, director of investments and cash management for New York State's $16 billion pension funds. At Rothschild her accounts would be far less—some $500 million, down from $900 million since Birkelund was bounced.

"We lost a lot of that business because of the turmoil," Pirie said. "But that's building back up. You'll see that department grow very handsomely."

Next he lured Gerald Goldsmith from E. F. Hutton, where he had built up the firm's trading and arbitrage, to head a new department, Rothschild Trading.

"The new trading operation with Gerry Goldsmith—that's the most dramatic change," Pirie said. "We're getting into classic arbitrage—not risk arbitrage. We're going to trade in gold bullion. We'll be open twenty-two hours a day trading gold around the world."

Creation of Rothschild Trading meant tripling the firm's capital and increasing the staff to ninety in 1982 and to a projected 130 in 1983. "It was luck that half a floor [in the old General Dynamics Building in Rockefeller Center] became available," Pirie noted.

Under Pirie, Rothschild became more active in underwritings and syndications, managing issues for Monolithic Memories and Horn & Hardart, placing many of the shares overseas. Pirie has no expectation that the House of Rothschild's American branch will rival Morgan Stanley or Goldman Sachs, "but we hope to carve out niches so we can place stocks in Europe."

Pirie also beefed up the real estate and venture-capital operations, but "it's very unlikely that we'll be active in hostile take-overs," said the lawyer-turned-banker who once specialized in them. "Four or five firms are clearly identified as experts," he explained. "No matter how good you are, you're going to be everybody's last choice."

To head Rothschild's new venture-capital operation, Pirie snared a prize catch—Archie J. McGill, the onetime whiz kid at IBM who had been chosen by AT&T to launch its Baby Bell operation. But McGill's freewheeling ways soon clashed with those of Ma Bell's bureaucratic bosses, and he was left on hold. Disgusted, he soon quit.

At Rothschild, McGill had about $225 million in venture capital to play with—principally for investment in small high-tech companies. Like Mrs. Talley's transfer, however, McGill's arrival at Rothschild was something of a comedown. At "Baby Bell" he had commanded a work force of 18,000; at Rothschild he headed a staff of eight.

Pirie's surgery was not painless. "Several people I let go," he noted, while others departed before the ax could fall. Pirie runs the day-to-day operations, but major decisions remain the province of the Rothschilds—"the shareholders," as Pirie calls them.

"The key thing is to create the impression that the shareholders have a commitment to do innovative and imaginative things," Pirie said of the changes he's wrought. "The theme that goes behind all these developments is to integrate with the rest of the group. A lot of stuff is going back and forth between us on a scale that has never happened before. That's what the group ought to be doing."

The Rothschild process was repeated one year later at Warburg Paribas Becker–A. G. Becker.

In 1974 S. G. Warburg & Co., the London merchant bank founded in 1946 by the late Sir Siegmund George Warburg, a scion of the Hamburg banking family who had fled Nazi Germany,* and Compagnie Financière de Paris et de Pays-Bas—Paribas, in short— each bought a 20 percent interest in A. G. Becker & Co., a Chicago-based brokerage founded in 1893. With the infusion of $25 million of foreign capital, A. G. Becker acquired a new name and branched out from brokerage into investment banking.

On July 1, 1982, after Warburg Paribas Becker announced that it had lost $2 million over the previous eight months—actually, a loss of $9 million, except for an accounting adjustment—the two European banks exercised options and increased their total stake to 51 percent. Ira Wender, the New York lawyer who had headed the company since 1978, was bounced.

In Wender's stead, Warburg and Paribas installed two cochairmen of the house's executive committee—Daniel Good, an eighteen-year veteran in Becker's Chicago office who had risen to become the firm's senior vice chairman, and John G. Heimann, who had spent eight years as a senior vice president of E. M. Warburg, Pincus & Co.† before becoming New York State's superintendent of banks and Jimmy Carter's comptroller of the currency. Heimann had become a partner in Warburg Paribas Becker's growing New York office only a year before. Most of the firm's employees were relieved that outsiders had not been brought in.

After its European owners assumed control, Warburg Paribas Becker accelerated the shift of operations from Chicago to New York. "That had been going on for a long time," Heimann explained. "New York is, after all, the financial center not just of this country but of the world. This is the investment-banking center,

---

* Sir Siegmund, who became Britain's premier merger maker, was a first cousin once removed of Kuhn Loeb's Felix and Paul Warburg.
† Founded in the 1930s by Eric M. Warburg, a second cousin of Sir Siegmund and nephew of Paul and Felix, who reestablished the Hamburg house after World War II.

and if you're going to be an investment bank, you damn well better be here."

The tripartite partnership lasted less than a year. In March 1983 Paribas bought out Warburg's interest in the firm—ending up with slightly more than 50 percent—and the company was renamed A. G. Becker Paribas. Within a month, and without fanfare or official announcement, Paribas brought in its own man to head the firm as chairman and chief executive officer—Hervé M. Pinet, the fifty-seven-year-old president of Compagnie Financière de Paris, Paribas' holding company. Heimann was named deputy chairman and chairman of the policy committee; Good, president and chief operating officer.

"We were already the three top people of the firm," Pinet said, "so it's not a change in people. But what is different is the way we are organized. The previous structure was confusing. I was chairman, and Mr. Heimann and Mr. Good were cochairmen of the management committee. We needed a structure to make it clear to everybody who was doing what."

"I have a very strong idea of what the future looks like," Heimann said. "The firm is not going to be a broad-based distributive firm. The firm has to evolve into an international banking firm. The debt markets are becoming international, so the intermediaries must have global reach. That's the way investment banking has to go."

Although there were widespread rumors that the firm was in financial trouble when Warburg and Paribas bought into it, by 1983 Pinet was insisting, "Things are well. The firm is in good shape and making money."

Rothschild's move into the American market was prompted in part by socialist president François Mitterrand's nationalization of the French banks—including de Rothschild Frères. "A Jew under Pétain, an outcast under Mitterrand—for me it is enough," Baron Guy said in an angry letter to *Le Monde*. "I am forced into retirement." But he didn't retire; denied investment opportunities at home, he came to America and started afresh.

It was a different story at Becker. By the time the European banks assumed control of the American operation, Paribas had been nationalized. "People here thought there'd be a gendarme sitting at our table," Heimann quipped, "but they're as competitive as any capitalist bank."

So socialists as well as capitalists found the New World a fertile field. "I think that foreign capital still finds American investment the best investment of any because of our political stability," said American Stock Exchange President Arthur Levitt.

But he saw a potential area of conflict: "The history and work ethic of foreign capital may be at variance with the companies that they're investing in. Securities firms are collegial entities, and they may be coming into conflict with the systematized levels of European investors."

In any event, the trend toward internationalization showed no sign of abating. Later in 1982 Britain's RIT and Northern P.L.C. paid $30 million for a 25 percent stake in L. F. Rothschild, Unterberg, Towbin, another medium-sized house. The American firm had been founded in 1899 by Louis F. Rothschild, a bond dealer, and merged in 1977 with the young investment-banking house of C. H. Unterberg, Towbin & Co. Headed in recent years by Thomas I. Unterberg, it—along with San Francisco-based Hambrecht & Quist—became a prime mover in taking high-tech companies public.

Louis Rothschild was not related to the European banking family, but the RIT and Northern investment brought the "real" Rothschilds into the affairs of the firm he'd founded, for RIT came into being in 1980 after Jacob Rothschild broke with his cousin Evelyn and left N. M. Rothschild & Sons. The initials "RIT" stand for Rothschild Investment Trust.

As with the Oppenheimer takeover, the RIT and Northern investment boded no immediate change in L. F. Rothschild's management or operations.

In August 1983 RIT and Northern put up another $33.6 million to acquire a 50 percent interest in the American firm. Vice Chairman A. Robert Towbin said that RIT's increased holdings would not affect L. F. Rothschild's operations: "They're making an investment. We're going to run the business." That remained to be seen: He who pays the pipers usually calls the tune—or at least appoints the conductor.*

* In November 1983, after a merger with Charterhouse Group P.L.C., the parent company was renamed Charterhouse J. Rothschild, which retained a 50 percent

In a sense, there was nothing new in such foreign investments. After all, Rothschilds and Warburgs had been dealing with American bankers for more than a century. A more ominous part of the trend of foreign investment is the infusion of Arab oil money into the American securities industry.

It started in the mid-1970s when a group of Saudi investors bought a slice of Reynolds Securities Inc., but they soon lost it when the firm was merged into Dean Witter Reynolds and then conglomerated by Sears. Then Competrol BVI Ltd., owned by Khaled ibn Abdullah ibn Abdul Rahman al-Saud, a member of the Saudi royal family, and Suliman S. Olayan, a Saudi businessman, acquired a 15.9 percent interest in Donaldson, Lufkin & Jenrette. In 1982 it increased its stake, first to 19.1 percent, then to 24.

In July 1982—on the same day that Warburg and Paribas completed their takeover of A. G. Becker—the Al-Saghan Fund, a consortium of Saudi, Kuwaiti, and Baharani individuals and corporations, paid $40 million to acquire 25 percent of SBHU Holdings Inc., parent company of Smith Barney, Harris Upham & Co., the nation's fifteenth-largest brokerage and a growing force in underwriting. Smith Barney continued to "make money the old-fashioned way" for its new Arab shareholders.

Arab investment in American securities firms seems certain to increase, simply because so many targets are vulnerable and the Arabs have petrodollars to burn. So far, the oil sheikhs have stayed out of sight, content to count their profits, rather than try to exercise control and dictate investment decisions. Both Competrol and Al-Saghan denied any interest in increasing their holdings beyond one fourth.

David Toufic Mizrahi, editor of the influential newsletter *MidEast Report*—he broke the Smith Barney story four months before it was announced—doubted that sheikhs clad in kaffiyehs and burnooses would soon be sitting in the boardrooms of Morgan Stanley and Goldman Sachs: "It's mostly investment. What they are trying to do is get a vehicle in the U.S., a company that they own and take out

---

stake in L. F. Rothschild. In the "City," Charterhouse was quickly dubbed "Jacob's Ladder," an indication that Jacob Rothschild was showing the same empire-building enterprise as his great-great-great-grandfather Nathan.

part of the profits. If they wanted to control, they would have gone into Merrill Lynch, Hutton or Bache."

Compared with the flow of European money into Wall Street, Arab investment is a mere trickle. That of the Far East is a drop in the bucket—only Fung's stake in Merrill Lynch is of any significance.* But that, too, seems certain to increase—not only by Hong King businessmen who fear that the crown colony will revert to China, but by investments of Japanese yen and possibly even Singapore dollars.

---

* The Japanese, on their own, already had made some startling inroads into North American markets. Many American and Canadian businesses and municipalities bypassed New York and Montreal to arrange financings—in yen—through syndicates of Japanese banks. On the Street, such issues were known as "samurai bonds."

X

GOOD-BYE TO GLASS-STEAGALL?

In January 1981 Citibank/Citicorp Chairman Walter B. Wriston boldly invaded the lair of the opposition—the annual luncheon of the Securities Industry Association. His address was titled, "You Can't Tell the Players *with* a Scorecard." He noted:

Company F is in the financial services business. It "provides a full line of banking and investment banking services." In its annual report, Company F states that it is the country's "leading corporate investment banker." In October of 1979, they "handled 67 percent of U.S. corporate financings." And they're not resting on their laurels either: "We expect that our company," their annual report states, "will be even more innovative and reach new heights in the financial services industry in the 1980s." . . .

Company F is Merrill Lynch. The heights they've already reached so impressed the New York *Times* that it headlined a story, "Merrill Lynch and Company, Bankers." The lead sentence nailed down the point precisely: "It sponsors a major credit card, holds billions of dollars in accounts subject to demand checking, and generates two-thirds of its profits from interest."

In the 1960s, Merrill Lynch didn't even sell mutual funds. Now, less than 30 percent of their income derives from commissions on listed stocks. The rest of their revenue comes from such diverse sources as option trading, investment banking, insurance sales, money-market funds, government bond trading, interest income and real estate sales—sales made by Merrill Lynch's own force of 4,000 realtors —and still growing—who operate throughout the country.

As some of you may remember, I have frequently applauded Merrill Lynch for offering the public, right now, the financial services of the bank of the future. Merrill Lynch accurately reflects the financial world as it really is, and offers a package of services that no U.S. bank can match.

Merrill Lynch, of course, was the first of the "financial supermarkets." It attained the heights by pulling itself up by its own bootstraps—"big bootstraps," noted Sandy Weill of Shearson/American Express. The others got there by conglomeration—all in the months following Wriston's speech. Prudential acquired Bache Group; American Express acquired Shearson Loeb Rhoades; Sears acquired Dean Witter Reynolds.

Wriston obviously aspired to join this select group. "He sees Citibank as one of a handful of financial supermarkets—including the likes of Prudential-Bache and Merrill Lynch—that will be able to handle virtually any transaction," noted banking writer Robert A. Bennett. "These giants, communicating with customers by means of computer terminals in the home, will sell stocks and bonds and insurance and even permit a customer to shop for food and clothing without moving from his chair."

Unlike industrial conglomerates, the financial supermarkets sought true synergy, with each unit feeding and reinforcing the others. Just as department stores design their layouts so that customers who come for furniture or appliances are tempted to tarry and buy socks or bandannas, the financial supermarkets structured themselves so that those buying stocks and bonds could be interested in insurance or money market accounts. Soon Sears made the term "financial supermarket" more than a mere figure of speech by installing Dean Witter offices in its stores—right alongside Allstate's insurance counters and its own displays of power tools and auto parts.

The financial supermarkets provided a range of services that the banks could not match. According to a compilation by Citibank, of eighteen different financial and commercial services, American Express offered sixteen; Prudential and Sears, fourteen each; Merrill Lynch, twelve, commercial banks, only five:*

* Citibank's compilation apparently was made before Sears's acquisition of Dean Witter or introduction of its own money market fund.

	Commercial banks	American Express	Merrill Lynch	Prudential	Sears
Take money-pay interest	x	x	x	x	x
Check writing	x	x	x	x	x
Loans	x	x	x	x	x
Mortgages	x	x	x	x	x
Credit card	x	x	x	x	x
Interstate branches		x	x	x	x
Money market fund		x	x	x	x
Securities		x	x	x	
Life insurance		x	x	x	x
Property insurance	x		x		x
Casualty insurance	x		x		x
Mortgage insurance		x	x	x	
Buy/rent real estate	x	x	x		
Cash management account	x	x	x		
Travel agency	x			x	
Car rental				x	
Data processing	x				
Telecommunications	x				

Integrating freewheeling financial firms into more staid and structured organizations wasn't always easy. The difficulties were particularly acute with Prudential and Bache Group. Founded in 1892 by Jules Semon Bache, Bache Group expanded from a far-flung brokerage into a full-service securities firm with its acquisition of Halsey, Stuart & Co., the maverick investment bank, in the 1970s.

By the end of the decade, however, the 191-branch firm was in deep trouble. It had backed the Hunt brothers of Texas in their frenzied silver speculations, not only suffering large losses, but getting scathed by the SEC and hit with the largest fine in the history of the New York Stock Exchange—$400,000. Worse, it had become the target of a takeover raid by Canada's Belzberg family.

At this point, in rode Prudential Insurance Company of America —Bache's white knight. The *Wall Street Journal* likened it to Daddy Warbucks' rescue of Little Orphan Annie. "But leaping lizards!" the paper continued. "One year after the Prudential-Bache merger, Annie still looks a bit like a battered orphan, and Daddy Warbucks appears to have seen better days, too."

As a result of their acquisition by a new non-Canadian firm, Bache's eight Canadian offices, which previously had been "grandfathered," were suspended by the Toronto Stock Exchange, while the giant insurance company did nothing to streamline Bache's fragmented management or modernize its overstaffed operation. Bache brokers generated fewer profits than those of any major house. In the first half of 1982 Bache lost $49.4 million.

The message got through to Prudential Chairman Robert Beck. Two days after the *Journal* article appeared, July 19, 1982, he relieved Bache Chairman Harry A. Jacobs of his duties—if not his title—and stunned Wall Street by luring George L. Ball from E. F. Hutton, where he had been president and No. 2 man, to become Bache's chief executive officer.

Ball,* an avid tennis player who runs two miles a day to keep in shape, came on like gangbusters. Although the forty-four-year-old financier suffered a slipped disk playing squash and had to spend several weeks working while flat on his back, he made so many changes so quickly the Prudential executives started referring to his "First Hundred Days." In their own way, they were as dramatic as those of F.D.R.'s New Deal.

Ten of Bache's twenty-nine securities analysts were purged, department heads were bounced, and the firm's general counsel was replaced by a Hutton alumnus. Worse, Ball lured away the top three researchers from E. F. Hutton—an action that left his old boss, Robert Foman, fuming. "Outrage" was one of the milder terms he used.

"Bob Beck at Prudential must wish he never heard of Bache," Foman said. "They've got unprofessional account executives and

---

* No relation to the George *W*. Ball at Lehman Brothers Kuhn Loeb, the former U.N. ambassador.

have never known how to make money. Everybody considered Bache the lousiest firm on the street, and that's not just me talking, but George Ball. George ridiculed Bache the most."

As one Prudential official put it, Ball "effectively de-Bached Bache." He bounced the firm's advertising agency and introduced a "partnership bonus plan" to reward Bache's top performers. His reach even extended to putting plants—instead of warning signs—in the office lobby at 100 Gold Street and linen towels in the executive washrooms.*

In effect, he made Bache "a piece of the Rock." To emphasize that the combination of Prudential and Bache was a true "supermarket" offering a full range of financial services, he eliminated the old names "Bache Group" and "Bache Halsey Stuart Shields" in favor of the simple Prudential-Bache Securities—at a cost of $4 million for new stationery, forms, and flyers.

Before long, Prudential's insurance salesmen started sending form letters to their customers:

> As you know, one of Prudential's subsidiaries is Prudential-Bache Securities, a major Stock Brokerage firm. Their investment expertise and advice is now available to all our clients.

Among the services offered were advice on investment portfolios, tax shelters, and Keogh plans—previously the province of brokers and banks. It was typical of the synergy of the financial supermarkets.

Fortunately, Ball's arrival at Bache coincided with the stock market boom touched off by the prognostications of Salomon's Henry Kaufman. The brokerage business rebounded and Prudential-Bache recorded a $40 million profit in the second half of 1982.

Beck and Ball soon set out to fight the banks on their own turf. "We're not talking about a little S&L, either," Ball said. "We plan to get into banking in a big way."

However, its first acquisition was anything but "big." In April 1983 Prudential announced plans to buy the Capital City Bank of Harperville, Georgia, assets $25 million—as opposed to Prudential's $60 *billion*.

---

* In November 1983 Prudential-Bache signed a ten-year, $100 million lease for a new headquarters in New York's historic South Street Seaport.

Merrill Lynch quickly followed suit by buying the Raritan Valley Savings & Loan Association in East Brunswick, New Jersey, for $5 million, and Shearson/American Express also announced interest in acquiring a bank. Sears, through its California-based Allstate Savings & Loan Association, already was involved in banking, but it, too, eyed the acquisition of thrifts in other states. The E. F. Hutton Bank opened in Delaware.

Other securities firms got in on the action. Dreyfus Corp., parent of the giant mutual fund, acquired the small Lincoln National Bank in East Orange, New Jersey, then in February 1983 received permission from the comptroller of the currency to establish a national bank in New York. Thomson McKinnon, a New York brokerage, planned to acquire a small Madison, Connecticut, thrift—First Federal Savings & Loan Association. But J. & W. Seligman, relic of the Our Crowd house a century before and which continued to run a mutual fund, ran afoul of conflicting federal regulators on its plan to establish a national bank. It got the go-ahead from the comptroller of the currency, but the Federal Reserve Board threatened it with fines of $1,000 a day if it branched into banking.

Finally Treasury Secretary Donald Regan called for a moratorium on mergers of banks and nonbanks, pending possible congressional revision of the banking laws.

To many observers, financial supermarkets are the wave of the future.

"I guess, over the rest of the decade, major consolidations are still to come," said Shearson's Sandy Weill. "If legislation moves away from regulation, investment banks will become part of, or by acquiring become, broader financial institutions. I think the competition will be good for the marketplace. It will force better service and better products for the customers, be they individuals or corporations."

Privately held houses like Morgan Stanley and Goldman Sachs, with vast financial reserves and solid bases of clients and customers, seemed immune from this orgy of conglomeration. "We at Morgan Stanley have determined that we wish to remain an independent, privately owned banking house controlled by a group of hands-on, active managing directors and principals," said Chairman Robert H. B. Baldwin.

So, too, were those in which foreign banks already held a substantial interest—like First Boston, Drexel Burnham Lambert, and what is now A. G. Becker Paribas. Smaller privately held houses could be conglomerated only if the partners agreed—as happened at Salomon and Oppenheimer.

The most likely candidates for conglomeration into financial supermarkets were publicly held houses with wide-reaching brokerage and distribution systems. The names most frequently bandied on Wall Street were E. F. Hutton and Paine Webber.

Weill's old partner, Arthur Levitt Jr., now president of the American Stock Exchange, saw the rise of financial supermarkets (or "department stores," as he preferred to call them) producing a counter trend—the growth of "boutiques."

The chic boutiques of Greenwich Village and Madison Avenue don't attempt to compete across-the-board with Macy's and Gimbel's. They offer only a few specialty lines and attract customers by offering personalized service, higher quality, and—often—lower prices. So, too, the financial boutiques don't attempt to compete across-the-board with Morgan Stanley and Goldman Sachs, much less with Merrill Lynch or Shearson/American Express.

"What some of the boutiques can do is give clients a service that can't be replicated by the department stores," Levitt explained. "As fast as you get department stores, you get boutiques which get clients who just want to have their hands held.

"For years firms talked about creating financial department stores, but they've become financial smorgasbords with no clear identity. This is an age of specialization and sophistication. Under the umbrella of one firm, you have specialists, but their entrepreneurial spirit is stifled.

"You're going to see constant breakaways of people," he continued. "I don't think we'll have a diminishing number of firms. If anything, there'll be an increasing number of firms."

Similar sentiments were expressed by Prudential-Bache's Ball.

"Middle size isn't a good size," he told a conference at New York's New School for Social Research early in 1983. "And many of the so-called middle-sized firms will probably find it desirable and/or expedient to affiliate elsewhere.

"I think, unless you're up between $1 billion and $2 billion in revenues with, let's say, a 5 percent or 6 percent profit margin, your opportunities to compete in those big marketplaces, those broad niches, are going to be very difficult."

Like Levitt, he saw the boutiques surviving and prospering: "By being very small, very concentrated, and very specialized, some of the minnows will do even better than the whales. They will have the agility, the maneuverability, the knowledge of the specific market.

"But I think that the middle-sized fish are just going to be bait," he continued. "They won't have the muscle to lead, nor the adroitness to dodge. They are, in my estimation, an endangered species."

While financial supermarkets poached on some of the preserves of commercial banking, the banks, in turn, started trespassing into the traditional territory of other industries—interstate banking, insurance, securities. As they scaled the solid wall of Glass-Steagall that had separated commercial from investment banking for a half century, some of the bricks began to topple.

Drexel Burnham Lambert's Robert E. Linton, chairman of the Securities Industry Association and self-acknowledged "point man" in the campaign to preserve Glass-Steagall, likened developments not to the crumbling of a wall, but "peeling the onion, a layer at a time."

"I believe that will continue to happen," he added.

He saw the immediate threat not so much to old-line investment houses like Morgan Stanley and Goldman Sachs, but to the financial supermarkets and firms with substantial retail brokerage operations.

The first incursions came far from Wall Street. On November 25, 1981, San Francisco's BankAmerica Corp., parent of Bank of America, the nation's largest bank, announced its intention to acquire, for $53 million, Charles Schwab & Co., the nation's largest discount broker. With fifty-two offices around the nation, Schwab offered not only twenty-four-hour-a-day securities service, but money market and cash management type accounts, as well as IRAs —individual retirement accounts. BankAmerica argued that since Schwab did not engage in underwriting, its acquisition did not violate the strictures of Glass-Steagall. The following day Los Angeles' Security Pacific National Bank also announced its intention of setting up a securities subsidiary for discount brokerage.

Who rules on bank acquisitions depends on the legal fiction of who makes them. Because BankAmerica structured its acquisition by the parent bank holding company, its application went to the Federal Reserve Board. Security Pacific's bid, made by the subsidiary bank itself, went to the comptroller of the currency. The comptroller acted first, granting approval in August 1982. Security Pacific entered into an agreement with Boston's Fidelity Brokerage Service to create Security Pacific Discount Brokerage Services, becoming the first commercial bank in forty-eight years to buy and sell stocks and bonds for its customers. The SIA immediately denounced the decision as a "piecemeal erosion" of Glass-Steagall and filed suit in the District of Columbia Circuit Court of Appeals to reverse the comptroller's action.

After sitting on BankAmerica's application for more than a year, the Federal Reserve Board gave its approval to the acquisition of Schwab in January 1983. BankAmerica and Schwab soon advertised that they would "bring America's investors an outstanding variety of financial services and strengths." Again, asserting that the board displayed "its probank bias," the SIA—unsuccessfully—challenged the action in the Circuit Court of Appeals.*

What started as isolated pieces of poaching soon became a full-scale incursion, as banks around the country scurried to set up discount-brokerage operations: Citibank with Quick & Reilly ("Quick and Dirty," to many on Wall Street); Chemical with Pershing & Co., a division of Donaldson, Lufkin & Jenrette; San Francisco's Crocker National Bank with Bradford Broker Settlement. Chase Manhattan laid plans to acquire Chicago's Rose & Co. As its ad proclaimed, "The Chase is on."

The chase gained momentum in May 1982 when the Federal Home Loan Bank Board allowed savings banks to operate brokerages. In September the Federal Deposit Insurance Corporation ruled that the strictures of Glass-Steagall applied only to the approximately 6,000 banks in the Federal Reserve System. Banks outside the system were free to set up securities subsidiaries.

By September 1983 approximately six hundred commercial and savings banks had set up links with discount brokerages.

* In October 1983, the SEC proposed that banks with securities subsidiaries be brought under its purview—a suggestion that was promptly blasted by the American Bankers Association. It also threatened to create a crazy quilt of conflicting bank regulations by the Fed, the Comptroller, and the SEC.

The bricks continued to fall. In a case in which the SIA and A. G. Becker had challenged Bankers Trust—the District of Columbia court of appeals, splitting 2 to 1, ruled that commercial paper was not a security under Glass-Steagall and that banks could trade—and even underwrite—the notes. The issue was destined for final determination by the Supreme Court.

For the banks, which lacked experience and expertise in the securities industry, acquiring or teaming with established discount brokers enabled them to reach the marketplace without start-up costs. Although a few looked upon brokerage as a source of profits, most saw it simply as an additional service to keep customers—or lure them back from the financial supermarkets.

"I don't think banks themselves will be any major threat to an efficiently run discount-brokerage firm," said Charles Schwab. "Banks won't be aggressive merchandisers. They will offer this service as one more item on their menu. It will be like offering traveler's checks."

Even less would bank brokerage be a threat to full-service investment banks. But the banks kept up the pressure on other fronts.

Citibank escalated the incursion by offering an Asset Management Account akin to Merrill Lynch's highly successful Cash Management Account. "Now all the 'management accounts' from ordinary brokerage firms are outdated," the bank stated in its brochure. However, the Asset Management Account relied on the securities industry—Quick & Reilly for discount brokerage, Lehman Brothers Kuhn Loeb for margin transactions.

At year's end interest rate restrictions were lifted, allowing commercial and savings banks to compete directly with the money market funds of the financial supermarkets. The only restriction was a $2,500 minimum balance. Three weeks later another rule change further blurred the distinction between savings and checking accounts. Under the new plan—soon dubbed "super-NOW"—a $2,500 minimum balance also was required, but interest rates were unrestricted, and checking was unlimited.

The banks, which had seen $230 billion flow into money market funds, decided that government insurance was their chief attraction in trying to lure some of it back. "What does Emigrant's Money Market Account have that money market funds don't?" one ad asked. "$100,000 FDIC insurance, for openers." Or another:

"Now you can sign up for a high interest money market account at Citibank that's FDIC insured."

If deregulation allowed commercial and savings banks to compete with financial supermarkets, it also pitted them against one another. At the outset, at least, most money market managers were content to sit back and watch the carnage. As one put it, "Let the banks and the thrifts beat each other to death for now."

Few could predict how far the onion would be peeled—or how much the wall eroded.

In investment banking, the commercial banks' main thrust was directed at gaining the right to underwrite revenue bonds—state and municipal securities repaid out of user fees, like road and bridge tolls, rather than taxes. Decrying the "Alice-in-Wonderland world of Glass-Steagall," Citicorp's Wriston told the Securities Industry Association:

> Revenue bonds . . . barely existed in the 1930s; in fact, the Glass-Steagall Act never mentioned them. Today, however, they account for more than 70 percent of all long-term funds raised by state and local governments. General obligation bonds, which banks are permitted to underwrite, typically carry lower yields than revenue bonds, and the reason is obvious—more people are scrambling for the same business. When banks are kept out of the revenue bond market, the public is hurt since borrowing costs for local government are higher. And those who aspire to keep them out are hurting the entire investment community by joining the enemies of free enterprise.*

There were few in the Reagan administration willing to be linked with—much less join—"the enemies of free enterprise." SEC Chairman John S. R. Shad—himself an alumnus of E. F. Hutton—argued that Glass-Steagall and other Depression era legislation was "no longer responsive to the major problems and opportunities of the 1980s":

> Under these laws, securities, banking, savings and loan and insurance

---

* Wriston neglected to note that the main reason that general obligation bonds carry lower yields is because they are backed by the "full faith and credit" of the state—a first claim against tax yields. Revenue bonds carry higher rates because they're chancier. If no one drives across the toll bridge, the bonds that built it won't be repaid. Or if the nuclear power plants never come on line . . . (see Epilogue).

companies are regulated according to *historical industry classifications,* by different groups of state and federal agencies. However, as a result of changing economic conditions, new financial products and major mergers have bridged the gaps between these industries.

Also, major securities firms have merged into larger financial service corporations; depository institutions are entering the securities industry, and securities firms have acquired insurance companies and other financial service concerns. The list is long and growing.

Shad called for "regulation by functional activities rather than by outmoded industry classifications," as well as "simplification and rationalization of excessive and conflicting regulations."

Some members of the Reagan administration, as well as some Republicans in Congress, called for outright repeal of Glass-Steagall and deregulation of both banking and securities. The 98th Congress, which convened in January 1983, was slated to take up the issue. Because of the GOP's tilt away from Wall Street toward the Sunbelt in recent years, it seemed likely that the eventual legislation would favor commercial banks. After all, Morgan Stanley and Goldman Sachs carry little clout in Albuquerque and Amarillo; the local banks do.

Chase Manhattan saw the handwriting on the crumbling wall. It set up an investment-banking subsidiary, Chase Manhattan Capital Markets Holdings Inc., so it would be ready to move, if and when the strictures of Glass-Steagall were lifted. Citibank, Chemical, and Morgan quickly followed suit. Chemical's Alan H. Fishman confidently predicted that repeal "will come."

To Drexel Burnham Lambert's Linton such moves conjured up "the specter of a handful of giant financial conglomerates dominating the scene." As he said in his inaugural address as chairman of the Securities Industry Association:

> Put yourself in the place of a business owner in the heartland of the country where only one or maybe two banks dominate the local economy. His inventory is often financed by this bank, his receivables and perhaps even his payroll are met with support from the same source. Now it comes time for an external financing—can he turn elsewhere if this same source is allowed by regulation to handle all his needs?

Indeed, according to the *Wall Street Journal,* this was exactly what had been happening with municipal bonds. The banks used letters of credit to "leverage" the municipal bond business of local governments:

> Banks that grant the letters of credit also are demanding other business, such as managing the bond underwriting that the letters of credit guarantee. The bankers have muscled some securities firms out of the municipal underwriting business entirely and forced others to take smaller underwriting profits. This has created fears among securities dealers and investment bankers generally that the commercial banks will deepen their inroads in the investment business and eventually control it.

Some investment houses decided that they'd rather switch than fight. They teamed with commercial banks to secure municipal underwritings. Kidder Peabody joined with Citibank in popularizing "put bonds"—in which the bank's letter of credit guaranteed that the bonds could be "put," or sold back, at face value after a period of time, usually five years.

Thomas Becker, who devised put bonds, was named Kidder Peabody's Man of the Year for 1981. At the same time, Kidder Peabody president Ralph D. DeNunzio was serving as Linton's predecessor as chairman of the SIA, supposedly leading the fight against the commercial banks' intrusion into the securities markets. The *Journal* noted that "executives of smaller securities firms that have lost underwriting business didn't lose the irony."

Yet the future was not wholly bleak.

"The principle on which Glass-Steagall is founded will remain intact," Linton predicted. "I don't believe that in this decade we're going to have a situation in which government will say all rules are off and anybody can do anything. Banks may win the right to underwrite revenue bonds, which they've been after for years." But he doubted, for the foreseeable future, that they'd be allowed to underwrite equity offerings.

In any event, investment banks would weather the storm. "I don't think the banks and insurance companies will be effective competitors," he explained. "We're brought up on risk, they're brought up on protection. Our compensation systems are different. They'll nibble away at certain ends of our business, just as we have nibbled away at some of theirs. This investment-banking industry, at the least, will hold its own."

Epilogue

WHOOPS !

The big bull market began in August 1982, and ten months later still showed no sign of turning bearish. The investment banks basked in the sunshine of unprecedented prosperity.

But an ominous cloud loomed in the Pacific Northwest, an economic eruption equivalent to the geologic explosions of Mount St. Helens that sent a smog of financial dust from Washington State to Wall Street, threatening to undermine investor confidence in the nation's municipal bond markets and make it all but impossible for many state and local governments to sell their securities.

The cloud was called Whoops—a not quite accurate acronym for Washington Public Power Supply System. Just as a housewife inadvertently gasps, "Whoops!" when a cherished chafing dish goes crashing to the floor, securities dealers screamed, "Whoops!" when one of their favorite investment instruments started to topple. Although nowhere near as lethal as Three Mile Island, Whoops boded to become the nation's costliest blunder in nuclear power.

Seeds of the impending tragedy were sewn in the 1930s when the New Deal built the giant Bonneville Dam across the Cascade Rapids on the Columbia River. At the time, an exultant Woody Guthrie sang:

Roll on, Columbia, roll on,
Your power is turning our darkness to dawn. . . .

With Bonneville's annual output of 518,400 kilowatts, plus the production of Grand Coulee and twenty-eight other dams on the Columbia, it seemed that hydroelectric projects could supply the power needs of the Pacific Northwest for generations to come.

Because of the ready supply of excess electricity, the plant that produced the plutonium for the first atomic bombs was built at Hanford, Washington. Another—producing uranium 235—was constructed at Oak Ridge, Tennessee, where there was excess power from the Tennessee Valley Authority.

After World War II, however, population growth, the development of aluminum smelters, giant shipyards, and aircraft factories along Puget Sound and the Willamette River, as well as consumer demand for such appliances as electric ranges and microwave ovens, hair dryers and vacuum cleaners, soon rendered the area's hydroelectric power system inadequate to meet the demand. By 1983 the Columbia dams could supply only half the power needs of the Pacific Northwest.

The same thing happened in the Tennessee Valley, but the cradle of country music rocks above some of the nation's richest coal fields. Consequently, the TVA soon became the nation's largest producer of steam-generated electricity.

But coal is scarce in the Pacific Northwest. So, spurred by the Bonneville Power Authority, which operates most of the area's dams—and scared by the rise of OPEC and dire predictions of an "energy crisis"—Whoops launched what has been described as "the most ambitious nuclear power plant construction program in the nation's history." At the time, Bonneville's administrator was Donald P. Hodel, now Ronald Reagan's Secretary of Energy.

Originally, three plants—unimaginatively named Nos. 1, 2, and 3—were to be built by the Bonneville Power Authority. Later, after Congress barred Bonneville from constructing future nuclear power projects, Whoops arranged for a consortium of eighty-eight utilities—private, public, and cooperative—in Washington, Oregon, Idaho, Montana, Nevada, and Wyoming to raise the funds to finance plants Nos. 4 and 5.

Construction of the five plants started in 1977, with the total budget initially targeted at about $4 billion.

Then disaster—or, rather, a whole series of disasters—struck.

Whoops proved totally incapable of coping with construction projects of such magnitude. There were labor disputes and regulatory red tape. Deadlines lapsed—then lapsed again, until there were backups all along the line. Construction schedules fell, first months, then years behind, while construction costs escalated astronomically—to $23.8 billion by 1982, more than five times the original estimate.

The utilities challenged the validity of their "take or pay" (or, variously, "hell or high water") contracts, obligating them to subsidize the construction of plants Nos. 4 and 5, "whether or not the projects are ever completed, operable or operating." As construction costs soared, so did Whoops's demands on the utilities. Some were hit with increases of as much as 1,000 percent!

The costs, of course, were passed on to the consumers. Kaiser Aluminum's electric bill went from 3 mils per kilowatt in 1979 to 25.9 mils in 1983—an increase of $68.7 million.

One utility—Orcas Power & Light Co.—filed for bankruptcy rather than pay its $14.3 million debt to Whoops. Only two of the utilities continued their payments to the projects—$9,435 out of $19 million owed—and ratepayers revolted against inflated bills. As one local politician put it: "Why feed oats to a dead horse?"

Courts in Idaho and Oregon barred utilities in their states from paying their share of the $2.25 billion required to construct plants Nos. 4 and 5, while similar suits pended in Wyoming and, most importantly, in Washington itself.

Worse, as inflation took its toll, the recession restricted production, and unemployment rose, the demand for electric power subsided. Even the weatherman failed to cooperate with Whoops: the winter of 1981–82 was unusually mild, again decreasing the demand for electric power. By the early 1980s it became questionable whether nuclear power plants were needed at all.

So, with construction only 24 percent complete on plant No. 4 and 16 percent on plant No. 5, Whoops decided to "mothball" the projects. But, as the Washington State Supreme Court noted, under the "take or pay" contracts the eighty-eight utilities were obligated to "pay approximately $7 billion for nuclear plants which will never generate any electricity," and "ultimately the rate paying customers . . . would pay for the nonexistent electricity."

In addition, it cost Whoops a whopping $900,000 a month in legal fees and administrative expenses merely to "operate" the two mothballed plants, so the agency was forced to return to the well repeatedly for new financing. By 1982 Whoops had $8.2 billion in bonds outstanding, making it the nation's largest municipal borrower.

By contrast, when New York City was forced to the wall in 1975, its long-term debt was $7.766 billion. But there was an even more important difference. New York City was an ongoing institution, raising revenue and levying taxes. Straphangers still dropped 75-cent tokens in subway turnstiles, drivers continued to toss quarters into the toll booths of the Big Apple's bridges and tunnels, and pennies from virtually every dollar spent on goods and services went as taxes into city coffers.

"New York was an operating, viable city with a constituent base," said Jan Bardway Courlas, a Seafirst—Seattle First National Bank—vice president. "Here, you've got five white elephants that are doing nothing but soaking up money."

After seven years and the expenditure of $8.3 billion, Whoops had yet to produce one kilowatt of electricity. A farmer with a handmade windmill would have done better.

With construction costs mounting, power demand declining, and revenue nonexistent, in May 1983 Whoops decided to "mothball" plant No. 3, laying off some 1,900 workers. Meanwhile the agency still owed $58 million to contractors—two of whom were subsequently indicted for bid rigging—and suppliers on plants Nos. 4 and 5.

By then only one of Whoops's original five proposed plants, No. 2, was scheduled for completion in the foreseeable future—in February 1984, seven years behind schedule and $2 billion over budget. The future of plant No. 1 remained in doubt.

As Whoops's woes mounted, it faced the prospect of the largest municipal default or bankruptcy in the nation's history.

"A WPPSS default would set off a chain reaction across the country," the *Wall Street Journal* reported. "Analysts say the resultant loss of investor confidence in the municipal-bond market would make it virtually impossible for dozens of state and local governments to borrow money."

Sterling Munro, a former Bonneville administrator who had become national director for public power at John Nuveen & Co., a Chicago-based firm that is one of the nation's largest dealers in municipal bonds, used a homelier analogy:

"It's the old story: Once the cat has been burned, it won't sit on the hot stove again. And it won't sit on a cold stove, either."

Others felt the ill effects of Whoops's economic fallout. Some local governments in Washington State were forced to pay a "point" or two more for borrowed money than their counterparts in other sections of the country.

"The situation is destroying the public's confidence in municipal bonds here," said a Seattle bond dealer. "It makes every issuer of debt suspect."

In 1982 the Snohomish County Public Utility District, largest in the area to be served by plants Nos. 4 and 5, found it impossible to refinance $215 million in short-term borrowing.

In May 1983 Standard & Poor's, which had already lowered Whoops's bonds from triple-A to double-A, suspended its rating entirely. Moody's Investor Services followed suit a month later. But the actions came too late to prevent the bond-rating services from being hit with a spate of class action lawsuits filed by irate bondholders in the federal courts of New York, Seattle, Portland, and San Francisco, while a "byzantine labyrinth" of Whoops cases cluttered the calendars of the Washington State courts.

Other legal targets included Whoops's chief underwriters—Merrill Lynch, Salomon Brothers, Smith Barney, Harris Upham & Co., and Prudential-Bache. But virtually every major investment bank and brokerage house had put its prestige behind Whoops's bonds and, as a result, became potentially liable.

Wood & Dawson, the underwriters' Wall Street bond counsel which had called the "take-or-pay" contracts a "valid and binding agreement," also was sued, as was Whoops's Seattle law firm, Houghton, Cluck, Coughlin & Reilly.

The slew of suits promised to keep scores of lawyers busy for years. One Wall Street attorney, searching for a local representative in one Whoops action, complained: "There isn't a lawyer in the whole Pacific Northwest who hasn't already got a piece of this case."

One citizens' group calling itself Don't Bankrupt Washington even took a case directly to the U.S. Supreme Court, but the justices declined to hear it.

If, between the time the prospectus is printed and the security is issued, a lawsuit is filed or there has been a significant change in the issuer's financial status, the underwriter or its counsel is required to paste a "sticker" on the cover of the prospectus, noting the change and asserting that it will not affect the value of the security.

"On Whoops issues," said the Wall Street lawyer, "there were stickers on stickers. The prospectuses looked like Phileas Fogg's steamer trunk."

Basically the lawsuits pitted the bondholders against the ratepayers as to who, ultimately, would cough up the cash to pay for Whoops's fiasco. Among the largest bondholders was American Express, with approximately $180 million in Whoops securities. The nation's fifteen largest insurance companies accounted for about 10 percent of the total investment, with State Farm leading the list with $257 million. As much as 7 percent of the trust funds managed by Merrill Lynch, Prudential-Bache, E. F. Hutton, Smith Barney, and Nuveen were invested in Whoops.

But many of the bondholders were "mom and pop" investors, who had counted on clipping coupons as financial security in their old age. Now they faced an uncertain future.

"Bondholders must brace themselves for a long period of chaos, discomfort, and personal financial loss," warned one securities analyst.

"There is no way bondholders are going to come out whole," said another.

As a result, the SEC quietly launched an investigation into possible fraud in the sale of Whoops bonds, and the House Energy and Commerce Committee threatened a congressional investigation.

There was no shortage of schemes to save Whoops—only of money.

American Express, retained by Whoops's member utilities to launch a rescue mission, came up with a plan for a federal bailout, while Whoops itself proposed a Municipal Refinancing Authority, akin to New York City's Big MAC.

George V. Hansen, the Idaho Republican congressman who had played a quixotic role in the Iranian hostage crisis by flying to Teheran and trying to mollify the mullahs, introduced legislation for a federal bailout, but few Washington insiders gave the measure any chance of success. After all, Whoops wasn't a vital defense industry like Chrysler or Lockheed. The Reagan administration, for reasons both budgetary and philosophical, was averse to the idea. And lawmakers were loath to aid a power system that, despite its economic woes, still offered lower rates than most and threatened to lure industry away from their own districts.

"The prospects for a federal bailout are incredibly bleak," a congressional aide reported.

A more viable scheme called for the utilities to put their scheduled payments to Whoops in escrow, until the courts could decide how the money—inadequate in any event—should be allocated.

One solution that no one seemed to suggest was more borrowing. And yet . . .

As the June deadline for mothballing plant No. 3 approached, rumors surfaced that James D. Perko, Whoops's chief financial officer, was trying to arrange private financing for the $35 million a month required to complete construction of the project. Banks and insurance companies were cited as the most likely sources for the funds.

"Getting the financing is going to be a tough job," Perko admitted. "We have worked hard in an effort to find conventional funds and finally determined we couldn't find any."

A few days later Perko announced that Whoops would seek a three-year, $960 million loan from a consortium of commercial banks, repayment to be guaranteed by the Bonneville Power Authority—a condition at which the agency's administrators balked.

"We haven't discussed it at all with any of the major banks," Perko said. "We would intend to undertake that shortly. Our first goal was to develop a proposal."

Meanwhile, Whoops bonds went begging. "The market is so thin that it's very hard to tell you what these bonds are worth," said one Wall Street dealer. "The gap between the bid and offered sides is so

wide you could drive a truck through it." Many investors sold out
—at losses of as much as 13 percent of face value.

The crisis deepened.

On May 31 Whoops failed to make a $15.6 million monthly
debt-service payment to New York's Chemical Bank, trustee for the
bonds. Despite Chemical's urging, a Seattle judge, H. Joseph Cole-
man of the state's superior court, issued a curious ruling, unsup-
ported by a written opinion, that Whoops wasn't in "default"—
pending a definitive decision on the validity of the "take-or-pay"
contracts.

And that, according to *Newsweek*, "gave Wall Street the jitters."

"Who is going to lend money for thirty years if you don't know
if the contract is binding?" asked James Glynn, executive vice president of Prudential-Bache, a major underwriter of Whoops issues.
"If [this] case comes out negative and the bondholders and the
people who underwrote the bonds are left holding the bag, it will
permanently end that type of financing."

On June 15 Wall Street's nightmare became a reality: By a 7 to 2
decision Washington State's supreme court declared that the utilities "lacked substantive authority" to sign such "take-or-pay" contracts. The utilities wouldn't have to pay Whoops, while Whoops
would wind up without funds to pay its bills—or pay off the bonds
on plants Nos. 4 and 5.

"It came down to a financial tug-of-war between Pacific Northwest ratepayers and Wall Street," gloated a local lawyer. "Wednesday, the Washington Supreme Court sided with the ratepayers."

The reactions were immediate—and varied.

Chemical announced that it was considering an appeal to the U.S.
Supreme Court, but Justice Robert F. Brachtenbach had carefully
crafted his forty-page decision to interpret state statutes and consti-
tutional provisions—matters on which the federal courts rarely in-
tervene, and then usually only when a fundamental civil right or
liberty is involved. Even Whoops doubted that the high court
would consider the case.

The Clark County Public Utility District immediately demanded
the return of the $4.1 million it had paid into the escrow account.
The state's other utilities seemed certain to follow suit.

The North Carolina Municipal Power Agency No. 1 postponed
its $350 million bond offering, originally scheduled for June 16 or

17. "We aren't going to be the first one out in the deep water," explained James T. Bobo, assistant secretary-treasurer of the agency. "There isn't any sense even in considering coming to market in these conditions."

For Whoops bonds, the bottom fell out. On the market, they dropped by as much as $20 per $1,000 on Wednesday and by another $20 on Thursday—and even then there were few takers—while speculators offered to buy for as little as 15 cents on the dollar, face value.

"If I were an investor, I would not buy the bonds," said analyst Howard P. Colhoun. "If I owned bonds that are behind plants 1, 2, and 3, I would hold on to them on the hope that the government guarantee would be good. On plants 4 and 5 I would sell even at those distressed prices. What you had here in Whoops is a financial meltdown, and I don't see any bang for your buck."

Bear Stearns & Co. took the opposite view:

> Is there a liquidity crisis for Washington Public Power Supply System Securities?
> No!
> Bear Stearns & Co. is continuing to make bids for obligations of the Washington Public Power Supply System.
> Recent developments have not altered our commitment to provide liquidity for investors in these obligations.*

Not all bondholders stood to lose, for $23.7 million worth of Whoops bonds on plants Nos. 4 and 5 were insured by American Municipal Bond Assurance Corp. In case of default, it was obligated to make principal and interest payments of $76.4 million

---

* In recent years Bear Stearns has become an aggressive bidder in the market for municipal issues, jumping from manager or comanager of 91 in 1981 to 192 in 1982. It also lavished largess upon politicians with power to place them, operating the fourth-largest PAC (political action committee) in the country, larger even than those of such defense contractor giants as Grumman and General Dynamics. Of its $439,153 in 1982 contributions, only $19,000 went to candidates for federal office. Nearly 10 percent—$39,000—went to New York Governor Hugh L. Carey, who wasn't running for anything, but who soon became a limited partner in Bear Stearns. Bear Stearns also contributed to the campaign chests of all three candidates vying to succeed Carey. "We're ecumenical because we're trying to support good government," explained the firm's chief executive, Alan Greenburg. "Good government" apparently meant Bear Stearns's management or comanagement of $13.11 billion in New York State bond issues.

over thirty-five years. American Municipal was a subsidiary of the already troubled Baldwin-United Corp., the piano maker that had overextended itself into a host of financial enterprises.*

Ironically, the day of the decision saw a stampede on the New York Stock Exchange. The Dow Jones industrial average soared 10.02 points to hit an all-time high of 1237.58. The following day it jumped another 11.02 points to another record—1248.30. As Ma Bell's analysts had noted, the bond and equity markets don't always move in tandem. The Big Board was never more bullish.

But most observers saw dire days ahead for the bond business in general—and Whoops in particular. "Nothing the size of the potential WPPSS default has ever happened before," the *Wall Street Journal* observed, adding another superlative to an account already overflowing with them.

"Default is now pretty much assured," a Washington State legislator predicted, "and bankruptcy is much more likely."

For a more ominous deadline loomed. Only July 1 Whoops was scheduled to make a $94 million semiannual interest payment to its bondholders. It could raise the money and fulfill its obligation only by tapping the $102 million it had on deposit with Chemical. But that would only postpone the inevitable, for then there would be no funds on hand when the next payment came due on January 1, 1984. Whoops would have to default—or file for bankruptcy.

And that could trigger the collapse of the whole municipal bond market.

---

* Baldwin-United, the piano maker that recklessly expanded into a financial conglomerate, soon filed for bankruptcy, further fueling Wall Street's woes. While six Baldwin-United insurance subsidiaries (not including American Municipal Bond Assurance) were placed under court trusteeship, irate purchasers of the company's special premium deferred annuities (SPDAs) filed class actions against the houses that had sold them—including Drexel Burnham Lambert, E. F. Hutton, Merrill Lynch, Paine Webber, Prudential-Bache, and Thomson McKinnon. Although a Baldwin brochure distributed by Merrill Lynch rhapsodized, "Our SPDAs are virtually risk-free," and Kidder Peabody had compared them to federally insured CDs, the suits charged that the dealers knew—or should have known—of Baldwin-United's shaky financial footing. In an unprecedented stettlement, Hutton, Merrill Lynch, Prudential-Bache and Shearson/American Express agreed to refund some $30 million to New York residents who had bought Baldwin-United annuities not registered in the state, while negotiations with Kidder Peabody, Paine Webber, and Smith Barney continued. So did investigations in other states.

The expected happened—sooner than anyone expected. On July 27 Whoops defaulted on the $2.25 billion it had borrowed to build plants Nos. 4 and 5.

"We didn't have the money to pay the interest, let alone the principal," a Whoops official explained.

Even though the amount was far less than the total of $8.3 billion owed by the entire system, it still was the largest municipal default in American history, and it boded to burgeon, for the fate of the bonds for plants Nos. 1, 2 and 3 remained uncertain.

The State of Washington—tainted by name and geography, if not direct political and financial association with Whoops—had difficulty selling its "full faith and credit" bonds, even though they had been given the highest A rating by Moody's. Governor John Spellman used both the carrot and the stick to woo institutional investors, many of them already burned by the Whoops default.

"What is to prevent the population from walking away from this obligation?" one portfolio manager asked at a New York sales luncheon thrown by Spellman.

When Oppenheimer & Co. advised its customers not to buy Washington bonds, Spellman threatened to sue the investment house and to withdraw state funds from its management. Even so, Washington wound up paying 10½ percent interest for $149.9 million in tax-free borrowed money, at least a half point more than other states. And there were those who predicted that, after Whoops, the nation's municipal bond markets would never be the same again.

A month after Whoops defaulted, Standard & Poor's finally got around to reducing the rating for bonds on plants Nos. 4 and 5 from CC to D, lowest rung on the ladder. Even so, there were a few folk foolhardy enough to buy them. To cover its flanks, Shearson/American Express sent letters to purchasers asking them to sign forms stating that the decision to invest in Whoops had been made on their own, not as the result of high-pressure salesmanship.

In a case that threatened to drag through the courts for years, Chemical Bank, on behalf of the bondholders, sued Whoops, Bonneville, the 88 utilities, 23 Washington municipalities, more than 500 individuals and "John Does No. 1–100"—as yet unnamed individuals—for fraud and negligence in the bond sales, but, strangely, neither the underwriters nor their counsel were charged. Some saw it as another example of the old case of Wall Street protecting its own. In any event, those who stood to profit from the lengthy lawsuit surely were not the beleaguered bond-holders, but the legions of lawyers involved in the case.

Chemical also scheduled simultaneous bondholder meetings at Manhattan's Madison Square Garden, Chicago's Regency Hyatt O'Hare hotel and Seattle's Center Coliseum, though there seemed little the bondholders could do at such gatherings except vent their anger and frustration. Indeed, as Chemical said in its notice: "It is not contemplated that the Bondholders will be asked to take any formal action at the Meeting. Therefore, no voting procedures have been set forth in this Notice and no proxies are being solicited thereby."*

Meanwhile the Senate, by 57 to 40, rejected a $1 billion federal bailout of plants Nos. 2 and 3—those closest to completion—and Whoops started selling the physical assets of plants Nos. 4 and 5 for scrap. It expected to receive only $30 million to $50 million—for equipment that originally cost $500 million.

Whoops!

---

* As it turned out, Whoops's bondholders were given little opportunity to vent . . . anything. Uniformed guards searched bags and briefcases for cameras and tape re-corders, which were barred from all three meetings. The bondholders were not allowed to speak, only to submit written questions. Chemical officials further pre-cluded any possibility of confrontation by not even showing up at the Garden gath-ering, only a few blocks from the bank's New York headquarters. Instead, two bankers and three lawyers spoke via closed-circuit television from a Manhattan stu-dio, while brokers in Florida, Texas, and California "tapped" the satellite transmis-sion to Chicago and Seattle for showing to their customers. So did the "enemy"— Whoops's officialdom in Richland, Washington.

One of the most frequently asked questions concerned Chemical's failure to sue the underwriters who had sold the bonds. "The focus of Chemical's action has been against those primarily responsible for putting the projects together and those who promised to pay the bonds when due," explained Vice President William H. Biels.

But the banker offered little encouragement to the bondholders. "Where events will lead from this point is uncertain," he said. "There is no cash distribution that is going to be made in the foreseeable future."

Although organization of a bondholders' committee was on the agenda, the trustee's future communications with its wards promised to be equally antiseptic— via tape-recorded telephone messages (800-233-2113 or, in New York State, 212-930-5007). The first message advised callers about "progress" in court cases in Washington ("A hearing on the motion to dismiss is set for December 2") and Idaho.

Acknowledgments
And Notes

Many persons contributed to *The Dealmakers,* too many to list here. Most of the information was gleaned in oral interviews. Many bankers gave generously of their time and knowledge, for both background and attribution, while their houses provided annual reports, promotional brochures, and other materials. Several persons reviewed portions of the text and made suggestions of substance and style.

Among those who provided documents, clippings, and other materials were Robert H. Bing, Harriet Brown, Peter M. Collins, Raymond L. Dirks, Loretta Geffinger, John Gold, Robert E. Linton, David A. McCabe, David T. Mizrahi, Donald Moffitt, George Penty, Peter G. Peterson, D. Philipps, Lee S. Richards, P. B. Roche, Thomas A. Saunders III, Deborah Sugrue, and Bruce Wasserstein. Thanks also to Joy Gilmont for her patience and perseverance.

Finally a word of appreciation to Dolores Cannata for mounting the illustrations.

In the notes that follow I have not attempted to cite sources for every quotation and statistic. To have done so would have made the notes longer than the text. Newspaper sources especially are too numerous to cite; ditto data from annual reports and promotional brochures.

The following abbreviations are used:
    NYT—New York *Times*
    WSJ—*Wall Street Journal*

INTRODUCTION: THE CATALYSTS OF CAPITALISM
D'Amato's remark is from Tom Goldstein, "D'Amato: At Home in the Senate," *NYT Magazine,* Feb. 13, 1983. David Rockefeller's successor as chairman of Chase Manhattan is Willard C. Butcher.

I   INVESTMENT BANKING FROM A TO A$_1$
The standard history of the industry is Vincent P. Carosso, *Investment Banking in America* (1970). Twain's quote is from his and Charles Dudley Warner's *The Gilded Age* (1873).
    The tombstone ad appeared in *NYT*, Mar. 11, 1983.
    For the ambiance of the eras they cover, see Matthew Josephson, *The Robber Barons* (1934), Frederick Lewis Allen, *Only Yesterday* (1931), and *Since Yesterday* (1940). Kennedy's comment is from his *I'm For Roosevelt* (1936). Schlesinger's comment is from his *The Coming of the New Deal* (1959). The C&O board meeting is described in Josephson's *The Money Lords* (1972).
    U.S. v. *Morgan,* 118 F.Supp. 621 (1973).
    For events since midcentury, see John Brooks, *The Go-Go Years* (1973) and Michael C. Jensen, *The Financiers* (1976). Lipton's comment is from *NYT,* Mar. 11, 1982.

II   THE TOP TEN
Figures for underwritings were supplied by Securities Data Co.
    Judge Medina's decision contains short histories of many of the firms. Stephen Birmingham's *Our Crowd* (1967) provides a colorful history of the German-Jewish banking families.
    The privately printed *Morgan Stanley & Co.: A Summary of Financings: 1935–1965* (1966) is less a history than a catalog of issues the firm managed. Baldwin was profiled by Richard L. Stern, "A Street-Fighting Man," *New York,* Nov. 12, 1979. See also John Brooks, "The Adventure of Morgan Stanley & Co.," in *The Games Players* (1980) and *NYT,* Mar. 21, 1982.
    For Salomon Brothers, see *WSJ,* June 5, 1981. Also, "Behind the Salomon Brothers Buyout" and "The Morning After at Phibro-Salomon," *Fortune,* Sept. 7, 1981, and Jan. 10, 1983.

For Goldman Sachs, see *WSJ*, Dec. 3, 1982. E. J. Kahn profiled Weinberg in *The New Yorker*, Sept. 8 and 15, 1956.

Lee Smith, "The High Rollers of First Boston," *Fortune*, Sept. 6, 1982.

For Lehman Brothers Kuhn Loeb, see the privately printed histories, *A Centennial: Lehman Brothers 1850–1950* (1950) and *Investment Banking Through Four Generations* (1955). Also Allan Nevins, *Herbert H. Lehman and His Era* (1963). Sachs's role in "selling" the atomic bomb to F.D.R. is described in James MacGregor Burns, *Roosevelt: The Soldier of Freedom* (1970). "Back from the Brink Comes Lehman," *Business Week*, Nov. 10, 1975.

Carosso draws so heavily on data from Kidder Peabody that it could be considered a semiofficial history of the firm.

Blyth Eastman's ad appeared in *WSJ*, Oct. 7, 1982.

The Dillon genealogy is from E. Digby Baltzell, *The Protestant Establishment* (1964). The Dodge deal is described in *The Money Lords*. See also *WSJ*, June 23, 1982.

III SIX DECADES IN INVESTMENT BANKING

Buttenwieser's biography is derived primarily from three sources: a personal interview, his five-volume memoir for Columbia University's Oral History Project (the author repuncutated and reparagraphed the text to his own style and corrected obvious errors of transcription), and an eightieth-birthday interview in *NYT*, Oct. 1, 1980.

IV A BEVY OF BANKERS

A rare profile of the Allens appeared in *Fortune*, Feb. 22, 1982. See also Lucien K. Truscott IV, "Hollywood's Wall Street Connection," *NYT Magazine*, Feb. 26, 1978, and the news story and correction on May 16 and 21. Allen's role in the Begelman case is detailed in David McClintick's *Indecent Exposure* (1982). See also *WSJ*, July 22, 1982.

Irwin Ross, "How Henry Kaufman Gets It Right," *Fortune*, May 18, 1981. See also *NYT*, Aug. 18, 1982.

Perella and Wasserstein were profiled in *WSJ*, April 21, 1982. See also Bob Tamarkin, "A Crazy Kid from Newark," *Forbes*, Sept. 29, 1980, and Stephen Adler, "First Boston's M&A Prodigy," *American Lawyer*, Jan. 1983. Wasserstein's contributions to

Nader's Raiders are Mark J. Green and Wasserstein [ed.], *With Justice for Some* (1970) and Green et al., *The Closed Enterprise System* (1972).

Peterson was profiled in *Fortune,* Jan. 16, 1978. Safire's comment is from his *Before the Fall* (1975), White's from his *Breach of Faith* (1975). The Bi-Partisan Budget Appeal appeared in *WSJ,* Jan. 23, 1983, and *NYT,* Feb. 24, 1983. For his departure, see *NYT,* July 31, 1983.

Rohatyn was profiled by Peter Hellman, "The Wizard of Lazard," *NYT Magazine,* Mar. 21, 1976, and Jeremy Bernstein, "Allocating Sacrifice," *The New Yorker,* Jan. 24, 1983. See also Anthony Samson, *The Sovereign State of ITT* (1973), Fred Ferretti, *The Year the Big Apple Went Bust* (1976), and this author's *Lions of the Eighties* (1982). The falling out with Koch was described by Andy Logan in *The New Yorker,* Apr. 20, 1979.

Weill was profiled in *Fortune,* May 18, 1981, and *Business Week,* Nov. 9, 1981.

V MA BELL DONS A GREEN SHOE

Unfortunately, the mechanics of divestiture—severing AT&T's twenty-two operating companies and reassembling them into seven new corporations; the competition among investment houses to represent them; preparing, printing and filing prospectuses for each of the new companies as well as the restructured AT&T itself, and printing 600 million stock certificates and distributing them to nearly all of AT&T's 3.2 million shareholders (enough paper, according to one account, to carpet all of Manhattan), creating "Humpty Dumpty accounts" which, on paper at least, put AT&T back together again, eliminating bookkeeping chores for small shareholders and creating a new source of profit for investment houses; the surge in trading as seven of the most widely held issues in America (after only AT&T itself) hit the market at once—all these occurred too late to permit discussion in this chapter. In size, scope, and complexity, they would merit—and require—a volume in themselves.

Rule 415 is reported at *Delayed or Continuous Offering and Sale of Securities,* 26 SEC Docket 3, 6 (1982). Lehman and Morgan Stanley provided copies of their submissions to the commission. For shelf registration's effects, see *NYT,* Mar. 11, 1982, *WSJ,* June 21, 1982,

A. F. Ehrbar, "Upheaval in Investment Banking," *Fortune*, Aug. 23, 1982, and Richard L. Stern, "Lions Want Lion's Share," *Forbes*, Nov. 22, 1982.

Saunders provided the AT&T prospectuses and other documents pertaining to the offering. The Moody's table was adapted from *NYT*, Mar. 11, 1983.

VI THE RISE AND FALL OF A HOT HOUSE

Dirks was profiled in *WSJ*, Aug. 11, 1972, and *NYT*, Jan. 2, 1982. His remarks on gambling are from his *Heads You Win, Tails You Lose* (1979)

Dirks and Leonard Gross told the story of Equity Funding in *The Great Wall Street Scandal* (1975). *Matter of Dirks*, 21 SEC Docket 1411, 1413 (1981). *Dirks* v. *S.E.C.*, 675 F.2d 1339 (1982); 681 F.2d 824 (1982),—U.S.—(1983).

The listing of Muir issues is adapted from an exhibit in the trial of *S.E.C.* v. *Cayman Re.* The June figures are from *Forbes*, July 4, 1983.

Mailer's description of Rubin is from *The Armies of the Night* (1968).

For the fall of Muir, see *WSJ*, Nov. 6, 1981, and *Forbes*, Oct. 25, 1982. *S.E.C.* v. *Cayman Re*, 26 SEC Docket 483 (1982). *Matter of Dirks and Sullivan*, 26 SEC Docket 483 (1982).

VII PAC-MAN, CROWN JEWELS, AND GOLDEN PARACHUTES

Lipton's allusion is from his and Erica H. Steinberger's *Takeovers and Freezeouts* (1978). Auchincloss' comment is from his *Narcissa and Other Stories* (1983).

Fortune's listing of deals appeared on Jan. 24, 1983. Fehrenbach's and Cheney's comments are from a symposium in the *Wall Street Transcript*, Nov. 2, 1981. Boesky was profiled in *Time*, Aug. 23, 1982.

Two books about the Bendix battle—Hope Lampert's *Till Death Do Us Part* and Allan Sloan's *Three Plus One Equals Billions*—were published after this chapter was written. The fullest contemporary accounts are in *WSJ*, Sept. 24, 1982, and *NYT*, Sept. 25. The Bendix ad appeared in *WSJ*, Aug. 26, 1982, Martin Marietta's, Aug. 31, United Technologies', Sept. 9. Siegel's comment is from *WSJ*, Mar. 18, 1983. Millstein's comment is from a symposium at Oppenheimer & Co., reprinted in *NYT*, Oct. 10, 1982. Figures for fees are from *NYT*, Oct. 4, 1982.

Wasserstein's final comment is from his *Corporate Finance Law* (1978). In the previous sentence, he quotes the author.

VIII "PEOPLE HAVE TO STEAL OR KILL TO GET THIS KIND OF MONEY"

Most of the information for this chapter was gleaned from the testimony, exhibits, and briefs in Newman's trial. *U.S.* v. *Newman*, 664 F.2d 12 (1981);—F.2d—(1983). See also, *WSJ*, Feb. 13, 1981, and *NYT*, Feb. 14, 1981.

Volk's comment is from the *Wall Street Transcript* symposium.

IX "THE BRITISH ARE COMING!"

For the foreign invasion, see *NYT*, July 11, 1982.

Frederick Morton's *The Rothschilds* (1961) and David Farrer's *The Warburgs* (1975) record the histories of these far-flung banking families. See also, Murray J. Rossant, "Baron Guy de Rothschild—Starting Over in America," *NYT Magazine*, Dec. 5, 1982.

X GOOD-BYE TO GLASS-STEAGALL?

Wriston's address was published as a pamphlet by Citicorp/Citibank (1981). The chart was adapted from the bank's curious brochure, "Old Bank Robbers' Guide to Where the New Money Is" (undated). Bennett's comment is from his "Inside Citibank," *NYT Magazine*, May 29, 1983.

For a general discussion of financial supermarkets, see *NYT*, Mar. 7, 1982. Thomas Moore, "Ball Takes Bache and Runs With It," *Fortune*, Jan. 24, 1983. Ball's comments on "whales" and "minnows" were reported in *WSJ*, Jan. 31, 1983.

For the banks' invasion of the brokerage business, see *NYT*, Dec. 28, 1982, *Securities Industry Association* v. *Board of Governors of the Federal Reserve System*, 716 F.2d 92 (1983). *A. G. Becker* v. *Board of Governors of the Federal Reserve System,* 502 F.Supp. 378 (1980); 693 F.2d 136 (1982). *A. G. Becker* v. *Board of Governors of the Federal Reserve System*, 519 F.Supp. 602 (1981); 694 F.2d 280 (1982);—U.S.—(1983).

Shad's comments are from *NYT*, Nov. 24, 1982. Linton provided a copy of his inaugural address and elaborated upon it. The *WSJ* article appeared Feb. 11, 1982.

EPILOGUE: WHOOPS!

For Whoops's woes, see *Business Week,* Feb. 7, 1983, *U.S. News & World Report,* Apr. 4, 1983, *WSJ,* Mar. 4, 1983, passim; *NYT,* June 5, 1983, *Time* and *Newsweek,* June 13, 1983. For Hansen's views, see his letter to *NYT,* June 11, 1983. Colhoun's comment is from *Wall Street Week,* "Higher and Higher," 1249, June 3, 1983. The Bear Stearns ad appeared in *WSJ,* June 29, 1981. *Chemical Bank* v. *Washington Public Power Supply System,*—P.2d—(1983). Notice of the bondholders' meeting appeared in *WSJ,* Aug. 23, 1983. Data on Bear Stearns's PAC is from *WSJ,* Oct. 18, 1983.

Index

In recent years, the merger mania struck Wall Street with the fury of Hurricane Dora and the names of many time-honored banks and brokerages changed as rapidly as housewives trying on dresses in Filene's basement. The names of some houses became merely the last listing in a long litany; others disappeared entirely; and at least one went through three name-changes in a single year. To list them all would require an index as lengthy as a telephone book—and as useful as one that referred callers with all-digit dials to "Butterfield" and "Longacre."

Ergo, a rule of thumb: If the initial name of a house remained unchanged, it is indexed only under its most-recent incarnation. Thus, "Shearson/American Express," but not "Shearson, Hammill & Co.," "Shearson Hayden Stone" or "Shearson Loeb Rhoades," but "Halsey, Stewart & Co." *and* "Bache Halsey Stuart Shields" and "Prudential-Bache Securities." Similarly, subsidiaries with identical initial names are indexed under the parent: "Merrill Lynch & Co.," but not "Merrill Lynch, Pierce, Fenner & Smith," "Merrill Lynch White Weld Capital Markets Group" or "Merrill Lynch Capital Markets."